W9-CHA-975

BLOC BY BLOC

BLOC BY BLOC

HOW TO BUILD A GLOBAL ENTERPRISE FOR THE NEW REGIONAL ORDER

STEVEN WEBER

Harvard University Press

Cambridge, Massachusetts, London, England

2019

LIBRARY OF CONGRESS CATALOGING-IN-PUBLICATION DATA
Names: Weber, Steve, 1961– author.
Title: Bloc by bloc : how to build a global enterprise for the new regional
 order / Steven Weber.
Description: Cambridge, Massachusetts : Harvard University Press, 2019. |
 Includes bibliographical references and index.
Identifiers: LCCN 2019010209 | ISBN 9780674979499
 (hardcover : alk. paper)
Subjects: LCSH: Trade blocs. | Economic geography. | International
 economic relations. | Globalization.
Classification: LCC HF1418.7 .W43 2019 | DDC 658/.049—dc23
 LC record available at https://lccn.loc.gov/2019010209

CONTENTS

PREFACE

I MUST HAVE STARTED THINKING about this book around thirty-five years ago when I moved to the San Francisco Bay Area and had my first personal encounter with economic geography. Or at least with economic geography that really mattered but was not about New York. I was lucky to be living in Palo Alto and watch the digital revolution kick into high gear. I realized I had a front-row seat to the modern experience of Silicon Valley, when in 1984 one of my friends whispered in my ear about this new machine that her company, Apple Computer, was about to release. It was called "Macintosh." I was doing clinical rotations in medical school at the time and the absolute last thing I needed was a personal computer at home. I definitely couldn't afford one. Naturally, I bought it anyway.

More than a decade later I became fascinated with open-source software communities and the experiments with intellectual property and governance that they were engaged in. I was lucky enough to have a job at UC Berkeley that allowed me to follow my instincts toward a new substantive area of thinking and research, and to do it in some nontraditional ways for an academic.

I have worked with some extraordinarily generous and talented people over the years. They granted me phenomenal opportunities, and I was able to combine my academic research and teaching with corporate and government advisory work in ways that made the whole greater and definitely more fun than the sum of the parts. I have always cared about theory but equally about practice, and I learned in the consulting business that it takes more than coherent arguments and falsifiable hypotheses to change the world. You really don't understand your own arguments fully unless and until you can see and articulate clearly what should be done with them and why. I've come to believe that the most valuable social science is urgent social science, the kind that has direct implications for the things that human beings care about the most.

It's that sense of urgency that inspired me to write this book. New information technologies are changing radically the political economy of nations and of the world as a whole. The spatial dimensions of that change—economic geography—are going to be the most important determinant of what life is like for individuals and societies going forward. How people understand that geography and act on those understandings now will shape what the strong do to press their advantages and their vision, and what the weak do to compensate, respond, arbitrage, and sometimes play spoiler. The purpose of this book is to inform those understandings so that people can act to make the outcomes better on the whole. As obvious as that sounds, it takes clear-headed thinking and conviction to make it true. I hope the arguments in this book will contribute to both.

Human agency is a big part of the reason I chose to write this book in a somewhat less formal style and to lace in a personal anecdote here and there. I want to highlight the point that while economic geography does have within it big structural elements that form the basis of my argument, how those elements manifest in the world is in practice a story about *people making decisions*. And so how people make those decisions, at the time and with the knowledge and models they have when they make them, is a very important part of the story of the past as well as of the future.

I had an enormous amount of help and support from friends, colleagues, and institutions as I worked through these ideas. It really would take another chapter to list them all and describe their contributions, so I hope you will all accept my thanks in this simpler way. I am particularly grateful to my colleagues and students at UC Berkeley in the School of Information, the Department of Political Science, and the Center for Long Term Cybersecurity; to my collaborators across the United States in the Bridging the Gap project; to my colleagues from

Global Business Network in the 1990s and the Monitor Group after that. Digital life for me would be unbearable without my snarky texting buddies (and occasional coauthors) Nils Gilman and Jesse Goldhammer. And I need to thank deeply my advisory clients in the private and public sectors, and in particular the strategy group at IBM in the early 2000s, where I was lucky enough to help a group of courageous thinkers grapple with the logic of the globally integrated enterprise. That logic grounds this book, even though I now believe and argue here that the world has moved past it. How and why that happened, and what comes next, is the problem this book is meant to solve.

I had financial support for this work from the Carnegie Corporation of New York and the William and Flora Hewlett Foundation. Portions of Chapter 6 were first published as "Data, Development, and Growth," *Business and Politics* 19, no. 3 (2017): 397–423, copyright © 2017 by V. K. Aggarwal, and are reprinted here with permission of Cambridge University Press.

I dedicate this book to Regina, who is the perfect best friend, a co-survivor of New York Giants fandom, and everything else a person could imagine in a partner. She reminds me also to thank our feline children, Napoleon and Mrs. Peel, who occasionally made unauthorized edits while sleeping on the keyboard. The cats are certain they made this a better book.

BLOC BY BLOC

1

TO REACH THE WORLD

ANYBODY CAN BE ANYWHERE, but everybody has to be somewhere.

That's one half of a core reality that human beings face in the contemporary internet era. The popular image of life in a networked economy and society says that where you are in a physical sense matters much less right now than it has for all of human history, as long as you have a decent amount of bandwidth at your disposal. But people are still embodied in physical form, and groups of people take up even more space. So you, as an individual or as part of a company or family or country or anything else, still have to *be* somewhere.

The other half of internet reality is that nearly everybody wants to *reach* the world from wherever they happen to be. This is true far beyond the recognizable multinational company with high-rise offices in London, New York, Beijing, and Delhi. Small firms, and even micro-entrepreneurs, are told they can and should seek to export their products and services to global markets. A Korean teenager puts a dance video on YouTube and becomes a global media star. Most individuals may not think about reaching the world in precisely the same way, but perhaps they should, because the world is certainly reaching out to impact their lives in the most profound ways.

This is a work of economic geography that explains how these vectors intersect to shape the global landscape of political economy. The book focuses on the triangular relationship between contemporary technologies, the policies of governments, and the big ideas about organization that make sense for a particular era. The core question is how should an aspiring global enterprise organize itself to reach the world in the coming decade? The answer centers on a new concept of regionalization, which is superseding a set of ideas about globalization, globally integrated enterprises, and the enabling notion that there will eventually be one global regime governing the movement of products, ideas, and most importantly data.

Foreign policy specialists still use the term "global account" to describe a set of issues that span the world and that they are supposed to take charge of—climate change, nuclear stability, and so on. The term barely makes sense anymore, as the global account has now reached down into the local day-to-day lives of just about everyone on the planet. Your job and my job are now part of the global account, as is our ability to read a newspaper, receive an antibiotic, watch a movie, or sip a cup of coffee. We are becoming increasingly aware of how the world is reaching us, but we are not often as conscious of how we reach out toward the world in response.

So how should we organize to reach the world in the coming decade? This book puts forward a new answer to that question. My main focus is on the "we" that is an aspiring global enterprise, by which I mean the firm or nongovernmental organization that seeks to operate on a global stage, serve global markets, influence the global account, or make a positive difference in human lives on a global scale. The analysis and argument, of course, then holds relevant lessons for other global actors—governments, super-empowered individuals, international organizations—but not only them. It's also a story about roughly seven billion people. Because the most important determinant of what life is going to be like for those seven billion is how we organize ourselves to reach the world going forward.

If that sounds obvious or tautological, it isn't. Consider one more aphorism from popular culture. If you've worked in a Silicon Valley firm over the last twenty years, you've probably heard someone use the phrase "no one is as smart as all of us." If you've worked in knowledge management or professional services, you've almost certainly heard a leader lament: "If this group of people only knew what we actually know."[1] Open-source software communities cite as one of their core constitutional principles the Eric Raymond axiom that "with enough eyeballs, all bugs are shallow."[2]

These aphorisms share a common foundation: the notion that knowledge, intelligence, and other capabilities are broadly distributed among human beings. How we organize ourselves to find and extract the relevant pieces of knowledge, and put them together to solve a problem, determines whether we have a chance of solving problems of any complexity at all.

It's certainly true that no one is as smart as all of us. It's equally true that no one is as dumb as all of us. Anyone who has been part of a work team, or a football team, or a family for that matter, knows both of those things through experience. The whole can be much greater than the sum of the parts, if we organize well. The whole can be much less than the sum of the parts if we get the organizing principles and practices wrong. That is why NFL teams and large firms fire their head coaches and CEOs on a regular basis, companies restructure their divisions and lines of business, and countries amend and rewrite their constitutions (on a somewhat less regular basis).

How to organize people and technology in space to make the whole greater than the sum of parts is the most critical strategic question facing the leadership of firms and organizations right now. Getting the formula right will determine how quickly the global economy can move past the long hangover from the 2008 financial crisis and create sustained robust growth of output and jobs. It will determine whether the Long Peace (the historian John Lewis Gaddis's way of describing the absence of major-power war in the period after 1945) can be maintained for another decade or more. It will determine whether future generations look back on the internet as one of the greatest and most transformative inventions of humankind, or something much more insidious than that.

The good news is, how to organize is a variable that human beings have firmly within their control. It's not a matter of nature or laws of physics. Another thing that you hear in large enterprises is people saying "that's not in our DNA" when they want to resist a particular change that someone else thinks is needed. Bluntly, it's a ridiculous statement. Culture (the way we do things around here) and organization (the way we set ourselves up to get things done) are not written in genetic code.[3] Culture and organization might be hard to change, but only because people choose and act to make it so. Is it lack of courage? Partly. Emotional resistance and fear? That too. But it's also—and most fundamentally—because people arguing for change often lack a truly compelling theory of the case. What's needed is a clear set of propositions about how best to organize going forward, that push through the resistance that humans offer by explaining why a difficult and sometimes gut-wrenching set of changes really does need to be made, and why things will actually be better on the other side.

It's important to keep in mind that "how to organize" is not an abstract question of purely theoretical interest to academics or philosophers. It is a real question that resolves immediately into concrete and consequential decisions about where to locate production, how to distribute and connect people, what technologies to buy or make and from whom, as well as how aspiring global organizations work with governments and governance institutions. And it's important to recognize right now that the discourse around globalization of the last twenty years or so hasn't come to closure on any of this.

If a leader today asks a deceptively simple question about where to store her firm's data, where to seek a legal foundation for its intellectual property, where its people should live and work, and where its robots should do the same, there is no coherent conceptual framework to guide her.

This book sets out that new conceptual framework for the next decade. Starting from fundamental insights of economic geography, I will put forward an argument that explains how successful global organization is a strategic response to the political-economic landscape of an era, emphasizing developments in *technology* and in *the state* (the state is a political science term that refers to government and formal governance institutions, distinct from "the society" that coexists with it). I will pay particular attention to the most recent changes in that landscape, and how the globally integrated enterprise (GIE), which was developed as an organizing principle and put into practice during the first decade of the 2000s, became the successor to the "multinational" of the 1970s and the "transnational" of the 1990s.

Each organizing principle was a response to interpretations of contemporary economic geography, and the GIE (as I explain in Chapter 3) was the most well-developed and coherent concept for global reach in the modern era. The GIE model had very clear implications for those deceptively simple questions, like where to locate people and intellectual property, and how to structure flows of money, ideas, and goods across political and other boundaries.

But the GIE logic was incomplete and is now obsolete. An important proposition that grounds the book is that the technical and political landscape that enabled the globally integrated enterprise is gone. The world has shifted into a new era and that shift is accelerating, on the back of three specific driving forces: economic nationalism, the new political economy of data, and the decline of the post–World War II standardization regimes dominated by the United States. As a result, the 2020s is too late for becoming a globally integrated enterprise. That was the "right" organizational form for a time that has come to an end. What to do instead?

The answer lies in seeing and responding to a new model of modern economic geography. I argue that the global political economy is decomposing into regional systems that are densely linked internally, and much more loosely linked to each other. Why that is happening and what to do about it makes up the bulk of the case. For the moment, it's important to note one proposition that is crucially different from previous regionalism perspectives. It is that the emerging regional systems are not principally defined by physical geographic features—mountains, oceans, and other natural boundaries. The new geography is defined by politically determined boundaries, which are put in place by governments and manifested by technology rules and standards. These are largely independent of physical geography and will become more so as time progresses. Increasingly, the most important delimiters that constitute a region are the rules and standards that oversee the flow and use of data. What information technology refers to as "logical" rules are replacing in significance the physical boundaries that conventional geographers and cartographers have long emphasized.

That is a major twist on the conventional notion of a region, and it will be tricky for maps to represent and for decision makers to fully understand. This book will help with that process by explaining the logic for a new template of global organization. To be a global organization on this playing field will mean developing three or possibly four copies that operate substantially on their own. The new organization will be less centralized in a formal sense, while cultural fit and government relations within regions will matter more than it has for decades. No longer will Apple design its products in California, build them in China, and ship them around the globe. Apple 2025 will have at least three such systems, each of which will be relatively self-contained—with design, production, and distribution largely internal to each region. The role of "global" Apple will be to synthesize the knowledge flow of this "scale-free network" and translate what is learned back into the individual regional systems.

That's a very different snapshot of economic geography than most expect. Is it going to be a better world than we live in today? The good news is that the model will foster greater diversity on a global scale—and we won't have to worry so much about cultural and other kinds of homogenization as some globalization skeptics did during the 2000s in particular. But it is also going to be a more dangerous world, because the high levels of interdependence between major powers and the regions defined around them, which partly constrained conflict for the last several decades, will gradually but visibly decline. New flash points will develop where the old geography of physical boundaries and the new geography of politico-technological boundaries create friction with each other—for example, in a place like Japan that is in East Asia's physical space but locates schematically in America's technological region.

Because the decomposition of a global economic system into several regional copies offers greater diversification of risk and opportunities for experimentation and innovation, economies will grow more quickly than our now-subdued expectations in the post–global financial crisis era. But in another twist to conventional wisdom, faster growth will increase rather than reduce the risks of economic and military conflict between major powers that anchor each region.

There's quite a lot to unpack, explain, and defend in those last several paragraphs, and that is the purpose of this book. This chapter sets the stage with two interconnected arguments. The first argument is an explanation of and justification for using the lens of economic and political geography—why is the spatial dimension so important in a digital era? The second argument introduces several looming disequilibria—or, in plain English, problems we've accumulated over the last several decades that no one has yet figured out how to solve on that landscape. The ongoing search for economic growth and political stabilization is running up against those disequilibria and demands a new organizing principle, which will define the next phase of modern globalization. The chapter ends with a set of provocations, in a bit of a foreshadowing look at some of the surprising consequences and ramifications of this new way to reach the world.

GEOGRAPHY

What if you have been asked to design a new village from scratch? Imagine that this village is going to locate in a part of the world that has just recently become accessible and habitable. Perhaps a new road has been built to reach a previously frozen tundra that has warmed up sufficiently to make it livable. How will you organize the village? It's not surprising if the first images that come into your mind are physical spaces like buildings, sidewalks, and roads. There's probably a "main street" (or "high street") that is a focus for stores and offices, and possibly "official" buildings like a post office or a city hall. The template likely includes a clinic or a hospital not far from the center of town, and a facility for dealing with garbage and recycling farther from the center. There might be a police station and even a small jail somewhere. And then we might start to think about the flows that tie these things together and make a village into a living ecosystem. We'll need water pipes, electricity, and other utilities. Perhaps the first and most important pipe should be a fiber-optic cable carrying bits, not molecules—but how big (bandwidth-wise) should that pipe be? And should the roads be optimized for bicycles, cars that people drive, or cars that computers drive?

The job of a city planner or an architect is to pose these complicated, interconnected questions in a tractable fashion so that decisions can be made and implemented. If you step back and think about that job, it's phenomenally complex because it encompasses so many dimensions at once. Possibly the most complicated issue lies at the intersection of space and time. What you plan today will be built over a number of years and then used in the course of many tomorrows—perhaps for decades. And you simply can't know what that future will need. Maybe there won't be garbage anymore. Maybe data won't travel through fiber-optic cables at all but only through radio waves. Maybe jails will be unnecessary because crime will become impossible in a fully surveilled society. Your mental model of organized space has to accommodate the fact that it is going to be in motion through the dimension of time.

Stewart Brand once captured this challenge in a beautiful statement that "all buildings are predictions, and all predictions are wrong."[4] The difference between a good design and a bad one is probably best thought of not as a function of how well it fits today's needs, but rather how easily it can adapt to the unpredictable changing needs that will confront it over time. In Brand's words, "how buildings learn" and what happens after they are built is what really matters about organizing principles for the use of space. Survival of the fittest isn't a good principle for human designers to employ; survival of the most adaptable is much better.

If you now step back and ask what makes a good foundation for that kind of adaptability, the answer breaks down into two sets of propositions that you must establish a point of view on to go forward. How you organize for now and the future depends on these.

The first is a model of the landscape on which you are organizing. What are its most important and relevant characteristics? How fast are those characteristics changing and in what directions? Are there immovable constraints that have the force of nature, like a mountain that is too dense to tunnel through? Is anyone else present in the landscape and, if so, are they trying to help you or hurt you; or are they just doing their own thing without regard to what you do?

The second set of propositions makes up a theory of human interaction. How do people interact with each other and with the artifacts in the environment, including the ones that they themselves create? Do these interactions tend toward positive-sum, where everyone can be better off at least in principle? Or perhaps toward zero-sum, where a gain for one party reflects a loss for someone else? The nature-nurture question, albeit oversimplified, is often an important subtext here. These patterns of human interaction might be inherent to the people playing the game, or to the landscape on which they are playing. Or you might work

Figure 1.1: The Earth Seen from Space. Credit: NASA

from the proposition that organizing principles can change the way these interactions are experienced and lived, from zero-sum to positive-sum (if that's your goal) or perhaps the other way around.

Economic geography at the highest level is a way of thinking about all of those questions, even as it privileges the first one (about landscapes). Sometimes these models and theories can be captured in a summary phrase or image, like zero-sum or positive-sum. When it comes to landscapes and what they tell us about organizing principles, images can matter quite a lot.

Consider the way in which the "blue marble" picture of Earth taken by the crew of Apollo 17 was received and interpreted in 1972. It wasn't, of course, anything like the first image of Earth taken from space, but it became one of the most widely distributed photographs in existence (Figure 1.1).[5] It captured a moment that the environmental movement articulated as the geography of "spaceship earth," a small and fragile but elegant sphere in the vast expanse of empty space. We were all supposed to see this and come to think of ourselves as fellow travelers on Spaceship Earth, where caring for its health would have to become a predominant goal of societies and economies.

The blue marble image didn't prescribe a precise organizing principle for doing that, but it certainly motivated discussion of organizing principles that were revolutionary in many respects: at a minimum, pretty far off from the conventional wisdom of only a few years earlier. The timing isn't coincidental—the principle "think global, act local" became popular as a phrase in the mid- to late 1970s; and "small is beautiful" was the title of a book published in 1973.[6]

Fast-forward to the present. Is there an equivalent image that captures the modern zeitgeist? Probably not so vividly and uniformly as the blue marble, but I think it's fair to say that today's closest analogy would be what shows up when you google "image of the internet" (Figure 1.2). It looks and feels like a vastly complex network, where the background, as with the blue marble, is black—because if you're off the marble or not in the network, you don't really exist in a meaningful way. What's equally important is that the universe of connections dominates your attention and in doing so overshadows the importance of the nodes (those things that are in fact connected to each other).

This is a twist on the way most people tend to think about networks and nodes. Which comes first in an ontological primitive sense? Put simply, is the world made up fundamentally of nodes, which are then connected together—or is it made up of connections, and with the nodes we see really just a distillation of places where lots of connections come together? The network image tilts most people toward the latter interpretation, even though it's not uniform in the sense that all the connections are equally "strong," and there are indeed a few nodes that are very sparsely connected.

Whatever your ontological reaction might be, the image does speak loudly to broad organizing principles that have become some of the

Figure 1.2: The Internet Visualized as Connections and Nodes. Credit: The Opte Project Map of the Internet, Barrett Lyon, 2003, licensed under CC BY-NC-ND 4.0, https://creativecommons.org/licenses/by-nc-nd/4.0/legalcode

common idioms of our time. Consider "the network is the computer," a tagline from Sun Microsystems (one of the most important internet firms of the 1990s). Sun's vision was not about a bunch of separate computers that would be connected together by the internet to make something bigger (which is how history actually unfolded). Sun's ontological claim was the other way around, about a bunch of connections that have become "the computer." The network, in other words, gave birth to the nodes. Less dramatic but still consistent phrases that might come to mind are "the net interprets censorship as damage and routes around it."[7]

Or "the Internet of Everything," a phrase that Cisco coined in the early 2010s to describe "the intelligent connection of people, process, data and things"—that is, just about everything.[8]

These idioms share an obvious common theme around connectivity— connectivity that is dense, robust, resilient, and generative. And this connectivity is generally assumed to be good for humanity overall. If there's any one single shared belief that unites the people, communities, and companies that make up an informal internet society, it's something like "making the world a more connected place."[9]

It was a heady mix in the late 1990s and well into the 2000s for anyone who has ever been frustrated by the dysfunctions of the "nodes"—a bureaucracy, a company, or any other kind of hierarchical organization. There simply had to be a way to use the internet to make these things more efficient. In this context, Ronald Coase became an unlikely hero of the times.

Coase's formative 1960 paper "The Problem of Social Cost" and the Coase theorem were mined for a particular argument about the relationship between transaction costs, organizations, and markets.[10] In the simplest terms, the Coase theorem (which will come up in greater detail in Chapter 2 and later) was interpreted to say that if we could get the transaction costs involved with an exchange down toward zero, then we could efficiently move that exchange outside of a formal organization and into a market, and that this would make the world a better place. The dysfunctions of the nodes would fade as the network came to the fore.

There are restricted conditions under which this argument makes sense, and a fair amount of conceptual economics (more discussion later) about why, how, and to what extent the Coase theorem works in the real world. But leaving all that aside for the moment, the point is to recognize the excitement that emerged when the new image of connectivity found its conceptual muse in Coase. The internet appeared to be really good at reducing transaction costs. Markets (which naturally want to expand through barriers and borders) would supplant the constraints and deadweight losses of organizations and bureaucracies. Resources would find their way to the places where they could be used most effectively, rather than being locked up in countries or companies that couldn't make the most of them. People would be able to "organize without organizations."[11] The directionality seemed inevitable. "Connected" as the master organizing principle would come to mean rich, free, efficient, and perhaps even happy.

But discrepant signals about that narrative have been piling up, and particularly since the global financial crisis (GFC) in 2008–2009. Consider one simple headline statistic about the reversal of momentum for international trade (about which I will have much more to say in Chapters 5 and 6). For most of the two decades prior to the GFC, transborder flows of goods, services, and finance together were growing around twice as quickly as the world economy itself grew. An aggregate measure, imperfect but indicative, puts those flows in 2007 at 53 percent of GDP, a historic high. In 2009 that measure fell to 31 percent. The recovery was tepid at best, hitting 37 percent in 2013 and 39 percent in 2014.[12] If connectivity is partly about international trade, the vectors have been pointing in a less-connected direction.

In June 2016 Great Britain voted to leave the European Union in what has become known as Brexit. European integration is no longer a one-way bet. If connectivity is partly about the political transcending of national borders, the vectors are pointing in a less-connected direction.

A few months later the United States elected as president Donald J. Trump, an avowed economic nationalist who in his January 2017 inauguration speech said, "We assembled here today are issuing a new decree to be heard in every city, in every foreign capital and in every hall of power. From this day forward, a new vision will govern our land. From this day forward, it's going to be only America first—America first. . . . Every decision on trade, on taxes, on immigration, on foreign affairs will be made to benefit American workers and American families." It's possible to imagine a synthetic formulation in which an America-first argument is made consistent with the connectivity and globalization memes of the pre-GFC world. Imagine what Trump could have said— something like, "Our goal is to connect the world and do so in a manner that benefits first and foremost the United States." That is the kind of thing his rival candidate Hillary Clinton would have likely said had the inauguration speech been hers to give. But that is not what President Trump said. And it is certainly not the mood of the times.

The point is that connectivity is now at risk of going out of fashion. More precisely, the burden of proof lies with the champions of connectivity to demonstrate that their view of economic geography and their favored principles of organizing the world are worth the downside risks that are now, almost suddenly, acknowledged to be profound.

For decades it was an article of faith—more than just trade theory from David Ricardo forward—that global trade would create sufficient surplus to compensate the losers and at the same time leave plenty of aggregate benefits and wealth to distribute and make the world better off overall. The technical phrase for that is pareto-improving and it means that it is possible to improve the position of some without making anyone worse off as connectivity expands. The basics of trade theory are perfectly stable, but pareto-improvement is no longer an article of faith in a practical sense, even among experts.

For at least a decade it was an article of faith that improved connectivity would promote a greater diversity of voice in public discourse. And that this democratization and proliferation of media channels would on the whole accelerate or improve the social processes through which people try to converge on beliefs about what is true, what is false, and what it is that they simply cannot agree about. The theory counterpart that underlies this vision of discourse, like Ricardo did for trade, might be John Stuart Mill, who believed that open argumentation between strongly competing views would gradually but ineluctably move societies toward the discovery of truths. That's no longer an article of faith either, as the "fake news" debate around the 2016 US presidential election showed so vividly.

This reversal in the burden of proof signals a change that will have ripple effects for a long time to come. The sense of inevitability that crept into discussions about connectivity and globalization has been undermined. That's a good thing, because it was never a fact of nature but only a product of human ideas and decisions, neither of which benefit from complacency about very long-term historical trends. Ideas about walls and barriers are more prevalent now, whether those are set to be built in physical space (for example, at national borders) or in digital space (for example, through data localization laws, which require companies to store data associated with a country's citizens in machines that are located on that same country's soil). National currencies run by central banks have proven robust and resistant to invasion by distributed ledger systems (blockchain) that underlie currencies like Bitcoin. For most people even in rich and technologically advanced countries, the once-exciting visions of a connected home with Internet of Things devices everywhere have dimmed considerably in the face of cybersecurity threats—which (at least in 2019) are a lot more worrying than are the upside advantages of a smart refrigerator or a WiFi-connected front-door lock.

The death of distance, the end of geography, the connection of everything to everything else were powerful memes that shaped public discourse and politics, corporate strategy, and many individual people's mind-sets about the world through much of the 1990s and 2000s. The "antiglobalization" label back then was mostly a pejorative attached to traditionalists and reactionaries who didn't "get it." These backward-looking people just couldn't tear themselves away from anachronistic attachments to old boundaries. They were stuck on the power of large companies to manage value chains, of governments to manage flows across borders, and of the *New York Times* and a few other authoritative media channels to manage truth. For everyone else, the shift away from classic geography all seemed manageable and exciting (if more than a little unsettling at times)—until the world economy hit a massive speed bump with the GFC of 2008–2009.

Just about a decade past that shock, the center of gravity for thinking about connectivity has moved dramatically toward its discontents. And they do have a real point.

DISEQUILIBRIA

From the perspective of the connectivity narrative, the world is entering the 2020s in a very troubled place. I steer clear of the word "crisis" partly because it is overused but more so because the word itself implies the immediacy and necessity of a "fix"—a crisis can't go on indefinitely, can it? Instead I think it is more accurate to talk about looming disequilibria, conditions that are out of balance and that create dynamic tensions and frictions that won't remain in the state in which they are without significant compensatory counterforce. The difference is more than semantic. Disequilibria can go on for a long time and they can get worse—that is, move farther away rather than closer to an equilibrium state—as long as a constant infusion of energy to keep centrifugal forces in check is being applied by someone, somewhere. Disequilibria don't necessarily signal an imminent break of some kind, but they do represent a build-up of entropy and sometimes destructive energy beneath the surface.

You don't have to look very far beneath the surface to name some of the looming disequilibria that confront the connected global system right now. My list would start with unconventional monetary policy, as a highly visible example of continued government intervention in the world's most important financial markets. Second would be mounting anxiety about the loss of jobs to robots and, more immediately, to machine learning or artificial intelligence systems.[13] And third would be what we know about the deteriorating status of the United States' nuclear arsenal, at once the most dangerous weapon invented by humans and the most important and likely final deterrent to major-power war.[14]

And consider the proliferation of jurisdictionally ambiguous spaces— or frankly ungoverned areas—on a world map of physical territory. Large swathes of Iraq, Libya, Yemen, and Syria (to name only a few prominent examples) lie outside the control of formal government authorities and are managed by terrorist groups, criminal gangs, pirates, and warlords. And though it might seem a bit dramatic to include in this category, 2016 saw 762 murders within the city of Chicago, a major US city that is seemingly on the verge of losing control over violence.[15] The world has never been neatly divided up into sovereign states that have a de facto monopoly on the legitimate use of violence within their cleanly defined borders, as Max Weber would have had it. But it is still notable, and a bit terrifying, to realize just how much of the world's population today lives in spaces where power actually does flow directly from the barrel of a gun (as Mao would have had it) rather than through the conduit of formal governance institutions.

Disequilibrium by itself isn't always a bad thing. It can be a boon for invention and innovation. It can break up encrusted stalemates and drive people and organizations to experiment outside of comfortable but sub-optimal (or worse) conditions that are the Devil We Know. Few of us would want to live for long in a world that was satisfied and enduring in its current status quo. Stability is almost always a word that the wealthy and powerful find captivating; the less advantaged find it repressive or even repulsive. But at a certain level of entropy, you have to make a judgment call about what are the acceptable risks. And that in turn means making a judgment about where the future is heading if we don't find a way to re-equilibrate from all the entropic energy that is building up. Charles Dickens said the same thing much more simply and memorably: the creative and destructive tensions of these disequilibria at once mean it is in fact the best of times and the worst of times.

The economic landscape of the present moment reflects this tension through the thinking of Joseph Schumpeter, who understood the contrasting possibilities inherent in market power, concentration, and monopoly profits.[16] There is no question that in the US economy market concentration has been increasing for some time now, in no small part because of the extremely rapid growth of a small number of very large internet-era firms. In 1994 the 100 largest US companies generated about a third of nominal GDP; in 2013 it was about 46 percent. The revenues of the Fortune 500 in 2013 were 73 percent of GDP.[17] Despite the hyped reporting and the buzz in cafés around Silicon Valley, startup rates and IPOs have actually been declining now for about a decade.

The best big companies are really big, really profitable, and really productive; and then there's just about everybody else. There are many arguments about the driving forces behind this trend and whether it will naturally reverse itself or possibly even accelerate. I'll take up many of those arguments later in the book. But, for now, the question that engages a dialogue with Schumpeter is simply this: is the trend itself a good thing or a bad thing for economy and society? Are these disequilibria in their current state something to be celebrated or feared?

To believe that it's a good thing, focus on Schumpeter's hopeful view of what the best companies would do with excess rents or monopoly-style profits. They might experiment with high-risk, high-reward moon-shot investments—things that when proposed would sound completely audacious (like building a self-driving car did just a decade ago). They might remake entire industries that no "sane" person would have had the impudence to take on (the gasoline-powered car industry? the aerospace industry? the entire retail sector?). They might channel some of those profits into absurdly ambitious philanthropic ventures (like curing all disease by the end of the century).[18] And they might keep all that going by winning some of these bets and reigniting the animal spirits of capitalism in entirely new sectors and geographies. You can't do any of that stuff if you're stuck in a truly competitive market with your profits whittled down toward an asymptote of zero.

But Schumpeter also illustrates some of the ways in which concentration and monopoly profits can be a bad thing. Big players have the power to squash competition in all manner of ways. They can get lazy, complacent, bureaucratic, and defensive not just as a matter of strategy but as a matter of mind-set (the enfeeblement of animal spirits). They can entrench themselves by capturing regulators, financiers, and politicians. In today's world, they seem to have a distinctive capability to avoid paying much tax. And there is always an explanation at the ready about why all of these things are actually good for society in general.[19]

In the end we don't really know which of these directions will dominate the current cycle of power consolidation and concentration. What we do know is that the most powerful firms have not really put on the table plausible solutions to the disequilibria that I spoke of earlier, or for a number of others. And the economic landscape is sure to reflect that fact. Firms can't wait for unqualified signals of how disequilibria will be resolved to make decisions about where to locate factories, laboratories, and design centers. Individuals have to decide where they want to live and work, which might include buying a very large fixed asset tied tightly to geography (a house). Pension funds need to decide where to invest for the long term. Governments may have to decide what physical territories are worth taking meaningful risks to defend.

There is one very important summary point about how the consequences of all those decisions come together. The world needs economic growth, and badly. This is more than just a capitalist imperative but also a human and moral one.[20] "Small is beautiful" was a great slogan for the 1970s, but it isn't a viable future for a world in which more than one out of ten people likely still live on less than $2.00 a day.[21] Contemporary obsession with the word "innovation" reflects this awareness. We obviously can't make the world rich by burning more petroleum or doing other things that will kill off humans through pollution, poison, or climate change. But we still have to find a way to make the world wealthier.

Call it what you will—sustainable growth, smart growth, human-centered growth—but the common thread is growth. Angus Deaton popularized a chart estimating economic growth through the course of human history, and this acts as a powerful reminder of why growth matters. For most of human history economies barely grew at all, and there was very little measurable improvement in the human condition as a consequence. That changed dramatically in 1900. For the next hundred years, human beings overall became better educated, healthier, less likely to die at a young age, and more likely to experience some of the possibilities of life, which is surely a moral good.

Growth fluctuates as a matter of economic cycles.[22] Recessions are followed by bounce-backs and recoveries and later by another recession and so on. The GFC wasn't an unprecedented downside shock, though it was certainly a very large one. But on the other side of the acute phase of what is sometimes called the Great Recession, the world has not experienced the expected recovery bounce that is typical of sharp downturns. There was a bit of a bounce in 2010 when global economic growth jumped to about 4.3 percent growth. But that didn't continue. Global growth was 3.2 percent in 2011, 2.4 percent in 2012, and 2.6 percent in 2013.[23]

What does this mean in aggregate? One way to see that is through an estimate of lost output—the difference between the output we have seen from growth that was actually achieved, and the output that would have been seen if growth had averaged in the last decade roughly what it did for the decade prior. (The same result could have also been arrived at through a vigorous bounce-back after the GFC, where the economy acts a little bit like a spring that extends itself faster after being compressed by a sharp recessionary shock.)[24] Calculating the counterfactual is methodologically tricky, but a reasonable estimate of lost output along these lines for the United States during the period between 2008 and 2013 is $6–14 trillion. That number represents 40 to 90 percent of one year's output. If it is anywhere near correct, it's fair to say that the United States and of course the world are *much* poorer places than they would have been.[25]

In early 2017 the International Monetary Fund (IMF) issued updated global growth forecasts for the next few years, predicting a jump from 3.1 percent in 2016 to 3.4 percent in 2017 and 3.6 percent in 2018. These forecasts also should be taken with a huge grain of salt and will likely be fully obsolete by the time you read this book—but they say something important about what people expect from the vantage point of a particular moment. The numbers are improving, but from the perspective of long-term growth they really should be seen as "less disappointing" rather than "good." The average global growth rate for 1990–2007 was 3.7 percent. Global growth hasn't reached that number (except for the short-lived recovery burst in 2010) and wasn't projected to do so before 2019 at the latest—more than a decade after the GFC. That projection was over-optimistic. The year 2016 was the weakest for growth since the acute phase of the crisis. What these data points and many others show is that the world is still struggling to grow as fast as it had been able to before the GFC.

Growth can be influenced by fiscal and monetary policies, by regulation and culture, by technology and politics. But all of this embeds within the deeper question of organization. Growth ultimately depends on getting the organizing principles right. That means dealing with the disequilibria, not ignoring them. We're not going to achieve the growth we need anymore (nor should we want to) by increasing the throughput of physical resources and human effort in factories. We're not going to grow by burning more carbon-intensive fuels for power. We're not going to grow in the long run by currency inflation or, for that matter, by adopting a gold standard or its modern equivalent. We can only grow if we get the organizing principles aligned so that we can take advantage of the most promising intersections among people, technology, and markets. That sounds obvious in the abstract, but it is indeed complicated in the particulars.

The particulars, as I have said, depend on a point of view about how technology and the state together shape the landscape for aspiring global enterprise. And so the rest of this book takes that on, in a synthetic argument about the present era's global economic geography, and a set of principles that follow from that about how we need to organize to reach that world.

Chapter 2 grounds the argument in a very short history. It tells the story of how a series of comparable arguments about organizational principles developed over the course of generations, to underpin an evolving set of models for global enterprise from the East India Trading Company of the seventeenth century to the multinational and transnational firm of the late twentieth century. Each model made sense for a particular era—but in a kind of historical dialectic each also helped call into being forces of dis-equilibration that would eventually undermine its own technological and political foundations.

Chapter 3 extends this story to the GIE of the early twenty-first century. The GIE concept was extraordinarily ambitious and at the same time highly unstable against the backdrop of its own co-evolving technological and political foundations. It was an electrifying and revolutionary idea in the best sense of that term, but the world for which it made sense didn't last very long.

Chapter 4 asks and answers the question, "what went wrong?" The GIE vision didn't suffer a single point of failure, and it wasn't an exogenous shock or historical accident that led to its passing. The GIE lost out because of a "systems failure" at the intersection of three big forces that it unleashed: competition, intellectual property, and employment dynamics. The most important argument in this chapter is that system failure was endogenous to the GIE model. In other words, failure was built-in. Slower and more gradual change might have reduced the immediate demands on people and institutions to adapt; more enlightened political and corporate leadership around the world might have softened some of the hard edges. But it wouldn't have mattered much to the outcome. The GIE model was not sustainable.

Chapter 5 connects the crumbling of the GIE model to the most important features of modern economic geography at the end of the 2010s and start of the 2020s. Slow growth, a changing innovation environment, and the rise of information and data platform firm economics and business models shape the narrative. Economic, political, and techno-nationalisms rise in concert with each other and compose a new economic geography within which today's and tomorrow's organizations will need to reach the world.

Chapter 6 considers the most important technological facet of this new geography, which lies in the distinctive political economy characteristics of data and machine learning. The key argument in this chapter— probably the most important argument in the book—*is that each component of the new economic geography exhibits positive network effects.* In other words, this is a world in which key trends, once started and past a threshold, tend to reinforce themselves and accelerate. Economic nationalism breeds more economic nationalism (rather than a countervailing force of reintegration). The standardization regimes of the twentieth century, once they start to crack, become increasingly unstable (rather than self-repairing).

It is also a world in which leaders tend to gain speed and advantage over laggards. The new political economy of data, driven by machine learning technologies, brings greater benefits, progress, and profits to those who are already in the lead, accelerating their advantage over followers. We won't see a lot of regression to the mean or competitive rebalancing, at least not anytime soon. It is true that no positive feedback loop can sustain itself forever. But this one is just getting started, and it has a long way to run.

Chapter 7 puts forward a model of how to organize for this new era. I show how regional systems are better suited to managing the problems and opportunities of the emerging landscape. But tomorrow's economic regions won't be entirely familiar because the boundaries between them aren't principally written in the mountains and oceans of physical geography that we are used to. They are written in technology standards, which are themselves embedded in politics. The new global enterprise will have to take account of all this by setting up several copies of itself, each copy able to get closer to markets and organize production with relative autonomy in its own region. The role of the global enterprise will be to create a set of mechanisms whereby the regionals can interface in ways that maintain some of the benefits of global scale. Branding and government relations play surprisingly important roles in that model.

So what will this new world look and feel like for the people that live in it? Chapter 7 also offers a perspective that has both good and bad, familiar and unfamiliar aspects. This world will be wealthier and much smarter in some respects than many now expect. It will be less unequal and more diverse than the globally integrated enterprises of the 2000s would have made it. But it will also be more dangerous from a political and security perspective. And it will have embedded within its own logic, as always, specific forces of disequilibria that will eventually undermine its foundations. The book ends with some disciplined speculation about how and when these forces will come to fore, and what the early indicators look like so we have a chance of being less surprised when the landscape changes this time than we were last time.

There's a quip that says the one thing economists should never try to predict is the future, and I would say that applies to just about everyone. To explicate the logic of a newly emerging economic geography shouldn't be taken as a point prediction. The real goal is to articulate and defend some hypotheses about its most important characteristics. And I use hypotheses derived from theory throughout this book in the spirit of Karl Popper's "searchlight" metaphor, which means highlighting some aspects of reality and backgrounding others. I believe this is best done by taking theory seriously but not so seriously that it becomes an obsession. That in turn means being willing to make some bold arguments that emphasize what is different and possibly surprising about the economic geography we are entering and how various actors will respond, rather than focusing on what is stable and expected.

In that spirit, here are some provocations that will emerge along the way in a foreshadowing of what you may find intriguing or surprising.

- Vertical integration of business is coming back into fashion. The long-standing trend of disaggregating value chains is reversing, in large part so that enterprises can reassert control over where data is generated, collected, and processed.
- Machine learning is helping people to get much better at efficiently distinguishing between good ideas (which are few) and bad ideas (which are many). In 2016 nightmarish visions surfaced around filter bubbles and fake news, which suggests the opposite in terms of social discourse. In economic growth terms, the "truth-detection"

systems that generate productivity increases are going to work surprisingly well.

- Intellectual property will continue to be a meaningful currency of power and wealth, but will become less important over time as data becomes more important and more generative of insight and value. Many organizations will give up intellectual property rights when doing so enhances their access to data.

- The United States will become even more influential as a rule setter in transborder flows than it already is—but only in some parts of the world. Competing great powers (including, of course, China) will find their rule-setting influence growing in their regions. The "liberal international order," which has been the loosely defined principle of global order that US power was supposed to help preserve as the post–Cold War era unfolded, will finally be recognized for what it is: a rhetorical mirage.[26] And that ironically will be a good thing for some elements of global liberalism because people will recognize that liberal outcomes actually have to be built, rather than imaginarily "defended."

- The manufacturing obsession (what I call a fetish) that has continued to plague the mind-sets of national capitals in both developing and developed economies will finally start to fade. Making physical things in factories still has a remarkable hold on many people's imaginations, but it will become less of an obsession as we recognize a simple but profound difference between physical products and data products. Physical products undergo corrosion and decay when they are used, a kind of inevitable impermanence of "compound things" that has been apparent to human beings since the time of the Buddha. Data products can do the opposite—if built correctly, they can get better and smarter the more they are used. Not forever, but the positive feedback dynamic can go on for a long time. In many sectors and for surprisingly long periods, the "smartness" of the data component will be able to overcome the inevitable deterioration of physical components. Things will get better the more you use them.

Economic geography and organizing principles that accompany it are theoretical abstractions, but they matter a great deal to the practicalities of how people live. I argued in this chapter that geography is in the midst of a quasi-revolution brought about by shifts in technology and the state. I offered hints of a new organizing principle for global enterprise that could function effectively on this new landscape, and adapt with it over time. And I foreshadowed some of the unexpected consequences for firms, states, and people. We can find ways to make the most of this new world, but first we have to really understand why it is so different.

2

THE LOGIC OF GLOBALIZATION
FOR GLOBAL ENTERPRISE

THE MODERN ERA HAS SEEN a variety of organizational forms for firms that reach beyond borders and around the globe. Today's debates about the success of these ambitions and the concentration of power in global corporate behemoths are not new, of course, and by some measures they are actually rather tame in historical context. Consider just a few examples from the not-so-distant past.

The British East India Company at the height of its power controlled around half of global trade. It had an army and a navy, near-monopolies on trade in several important commodities, its own college and military academy for training clerks and soldiers, and even a private psychiatric hospital (such as these were in the 1800s) where employees who suffered from insanity were treated.[1] If not a de facto sovereign power in India, it was nearly as close to that threshold as any firm has achieved in the modern era.

The Dutch East India Company is still considered by business historians to be one of the greatest and most influential corporations in modern times. Created in response to the British East India charter in 1602, the Dutch East India Company's charter granted it not only a monopoly over the country's Asian trade but also the explicit power to maintain an army and sign treaties with governments. Later it would coin money and establish colonies. It was the first multinational enterprise to issue shares of stock to the public and to be listed on an official stock exchange, and the first to operate officially on several continents. It had its own early human resources strategy in the "battle for talent," as it employed a multinational workforce not only from the Netherlands but also from other countries in northern Europe. In large part because of these organizational innovations, the Dutch East India Company is generally seen to have been a major force behind the unusual economic and political power of the Dutch Republic, particularly in the seventeenth century, when it punched well above its weight in European and global politics.[2]

Fast-forward to several hundred years later, when ITT became an iconic example of the 1960s and 1970s global corporate conglomerate. A force in the telecommunications industry since the 1920s, the firm eventually ran into antitrust issues when it sought to buy a major television network in 1963. The CEO, Harold Geneen, then took the firm in a different direction, diversifying instead into hotels, baking, car rentals, auto parts, cosmetics, and beyond. Along the way ITT became an active player in the Cold War, indirectly in the case of the 1964 Brazil coup against President Goulart and more directly in the case of the 1973 Chile coup against President Allende.[3]

These firms lived in times unimaginably different from each other when it came to politics, technology, and, of course, the daily experience of human life. But at a high level of economic logic, the rationale behind their efforts to reach the world was remarkably consistent. Whether trading spices or textiles, constructing phone networks or buildings, the most basic driving force behind their organizational model was straightforward: seek out large, standardized markets that the firm could control and even dominate by exploiting economies of scale. Put simply, the bigger and the more similar the markets, the better for the aspiring global firm.

To make that work over time, each of these firms had to stay close to the frontiers of technology. As or even more important, they had to stabilize (or in some cases create almost from scratch) the political economy foundations for their market presence and dominance in unfamiliar and dissimilar parts of the world. Sometimes this made them seem heroic and, other times, villainous.

So were they heroes or villains? That's also a very contemporary question with deep historical roots. The answer has always been "a bit of both," with the summary judgment dependent on timing. The multinational firm as a concept does go in and out of fashion on a regular basis, and the cycle appears to have sped up in the last half-century. It's not a perfect periodization but consider the most recent turn of the wheel to see the pattern. In the economic doldrums of the mid to late 1970s it was popular to label the multinational (and not just the oil majors) as a too powerful, near-monopolistic predator on societies, states, and the environment. In the 1980s the perception flipped: it was then just as popular to label them as clumsy conglomerates lacking focus that were too big, broad, and ungainly to innovate or compete effectively in the long term. The 1980s multinational problem was not that the companies were too powerful, it was that they were too dysfunctional. In the 1990s the story flipped again, to portray the multinational as a mostly positive force that spread capital, technology, and management skills across the globe and in particular to emerging economies, helping them climb the ladder of development.

In the early 2000s the multinational was back to villain status in many eyes, seen as too dangerous in its power and reach from economics to politics and even culture. The roots of some of the second half of the 2010s critique can be seen in this period. The allegations at that time centered around the idea that the largest firms had become so extraordinarily competitive, successful, and fast-growing that they could not be compatible with the broader interests of societies. They had lost any meaningful connection or "loyalty" to their home nations and were arbitraging every possible regulatory and tax gradient to maximize overall profits at the expense of everyone else, especially labor. They jumped willingly into bed with repressive political regimes in host countries when necessary to protect investments. They were, at the limit of the villainous narrative, the principal agents of "bad globalization," the kind that was said to be decimating jobs, driving a race to the bottom in labor and environmental standards, emasculating the welfare state, and homogenizing rich national cultures.

This reaction isn't solely tied to the profit motive. Some of the negative reputation effects spilled over onto critiques of the large non-governmental organizations (NGOs) that also had a global presence, charitable institutions like Médecins Sans Frontières (MSF) and megaphilanthropies like the Gates Foundation. These organizations were criticized not for their profitability but rather for power, arrogance, opacity, and lack of accountability that sometimes accompanies a mission-driven mind-set and culture. "Who elected the NGOs?" was more than just a cynical refrain. It was a legitimate expression of concern that an NGO's board of directors would simply not exert the same kind of oversight that voters would of governments, or shareholders would of publicly traded firms.[4]

Where is the cycle at the end of the 2010s? The global financial crisis of 2008–2009 and its aftermath have left global organizations with a powerfully ambivalent reputation. On the one hand, a small number of highly successful and stunningly innovative global firms are spreading an information and data technology (IDT) revolution to people and countries around the world. Suspicions about issues like privacy notwithstanding, Google and Facebook are some of the most respected and admired organizations on the planet. On the other hand, the global money center banks and investment firms remain in the crosshairs of blame for the Great Recession and the halting recovery that has taken up more than a decade. Many global organizations (including, of course, the most prominent IDT firms) are under the microscope for their supposed role as agents of labor-market disruption, which is a complicated way of saying that they get blamed for the destruction of "old" jobs almost as frequently as they get credited for creating amazing technology and "new" jobs. And it would be unwise to downplay some of the deeper structural anxieties that are beginning to attach themselves to the leading IDT firms, the bases for which I will explain in more detail in Chapter 6. The love-hate ambivalence relationship may still be tilted overall toward the love side, but not by much.[5]

This chapter tries to make relatively quick sense of some key parts of history—both the reality of how global organizations are structured and the perceptions of their role in political economy, in a way that accounts for the ambivalence of the present and points toward the future. The central theme is that successful principles of global organization emerge as evolving strategic responses to the political-economic landscape, made up of developments in technology and in the state. An era is delineated by an ideal-type organization, which embodies an internal logic to maximize global reach for that era. Concretely, the 1990s multinational made sense for the 1990s in the same way that the British East India Company made sense for the 1700s.

Understanding in more specific terms how principles of organization are connected to the political-economic landscape of the era sets up two important arguments for later in the book: why the ideal-type global organization of the early 2000s had a surprisingly short life-span, and what is coming next.

THE BRITISH EAST INDIA COMPANY

The British East India Company, which was also known as the English East India Company, the Honorable Company, or simply "the Company," began its life with a much more complicated name. The Royal Charter of December 31, 1600, refers to "The Company of Merchants of London trading into the East Indies."[6] It's an evocatively descriptive title. After the defeat of the Spanish Armada in 1588, British merchants saw an opening to spread their trading activities much more boldly overseas and "into" the riches of far-off places like the so-called East Indies.

As the Company's ships set out from Britain in search of new trading routes they carried with them a letter of introduction from Queen Elizabeth. The letter outlined a rationale for an early version of global reach that sounds remarkably modern. It stated that "out of the abundance of fruit which some regions enjoy, the necessity or want of others should be supplied." This is, of course, an argument for comparative advantage and open trade. It extended also to a core argument of commercial liberalism, proposing that through "interchange of commodities . . . far and remote countries" would become more friendly. And there was even a rationale for multilateral trade, in notable contrast to the exclusive trade rights that the Spanish and Portuguese merchants were promoting. The Queen declared that to grant exclusive trading rights was essentially a sacrifice of sovereignty to the European power, and thus could not in the long run benefit the partner to trade.[7]

This wasn't an abstract argument about the aggregate benefits of multilateralism. A multilateral trading system was pragmatically what the

British economy and state needed at the time. The British sought new export markets for their iconic woolen cloth; but the demand for woolens was (not surprisingly) rather more robust in cold places like Russia and the Baltics than in the tropics, where the spices that the Company wished to import back to Britain were grown. For mercantilists obsessed with the accumulation of gold, it was not an attractive proposition to send a Company ship out to the spice islands loaded with gold bullion (to say nothing of the substantial technology risk, that the ship and its gold would be lost at sea before it even had the chance to exchange bullion for spices). The ideal trade was triangular—load the ship with woolen cloth; sail to Japan and exchange cloth for Japanese silver; sail to Java and exchange silver for spices; and return to England with the valuable cargo of spices to sell at home.

Today we might talk about this triangular trade as the conceptual equivalent of a remarkable technology, a machine that could perform a kind of alchemy transforming woolen cloth into pepper, with a profit coming out at the end. But given the actual technology of the time it wasn't a very efficient machine. Maps were inaccurate and ships unreliable. The heroic voyage of Sir Francis Drake in the late 1570s was the exception and not the rule, as ships were commonly brought down by weather, by mutiny, by disease both infectious and noninfectious (such as scurvy), by conflict, and by simple inadequacy to manage the rigors of the ocean. Trade might be an enriching activity in theory, but in practice what we would today call transaction costs were extraordinarily high. And when profits did emerge, they were always subject to the political and economic contingencies of the British monarchy and its constant need to raise funds. As early as 1603, for example, the Crown declared that none of the Company's imported pepper could be sold until the Crown had sold its own stores of pepper, and at higher prices than the market would have borne.[8]

The Company's golden age really arrived in the first half of the 1700s, when a culture of swashbuckling adventurers who had struggled with "interlopers, pirates, the rival Company, and the Mogul emperor" more or less gave way to the serious business of making money. Around 1710 the Company ran ten to fifteen trading ships at around 300 tons each on an annual basis. By 1740 the numbers were up to twenty ships a year

at almost 500 tons each. The significant improvements in shipping capacity along with a somewhat more stable political environment transformed Company stock into a favored security, paying a regular 8 percent
dividend to shareholders for much of this period.[9]

By modern standards it's almost impossible to imagine the dominant
presence of the Company in British national accounts and politics. In
1720, for example, around 15 percent of British imports were coming from
India and almost all of that moved through the Company. It had a dominant position in the trade of cotton, silk, indigo, tea, and saltpeter—
nearly essential commodities at the time. These dominant positions had
to be defended with force on a regular basis. The Company's own
troops—not British Crown troops per se—fought French company
forces, sometimes directly and sometimes though local proxy Indian
groups on and off from 1744 onward for at least fifteen years. By the end
of the 1770s the Company had around 67,000 troops and a navy made
up of both armed merchant vessels and straight-out warships, making
it easily the most powerful military force on the Indian subcontinent.[10]

The melding of commercial and political-military behaviors was almost complete in this regard, and Company officials at the time would
have seen this as entirely expected and normal. Firms were fighting wars
on their own behalf with state interests essentially in the background,
almost the exact opposite of what we might expect to see in the contemporary world.

But not for long. The competition between British and French business interests was not in the final analysis decided on commercial or economic terms. It was decided by political-military maneuvering driven
by the respective governments. Many histories of the Company during
this period are dominated by stories about politics and military battles,
not money-making, and the shift is borne out in one compelling signal:
the Company increasingly found itself having to hold onto loss-making
positions for the sake of British state strategic interests. A good example
of this was the company outpost at St. Helena, which was losing money
(and showed no signs of doing otherwise), yet the Company held on for
fear that if it did withdraw, the French or Dutch would step into the
breach. Another signal: in the mid-1750s the French and British companies came close to a nonaggression pact that would have been auspicious

for business and trade. It was the British Cabinet that shut down the idea, on the principle that while the Company did have de facto sovereign prerogatives to negotiate such deals with Indian authorities, it did not have the same prerogatives when the negotiations involved another European state. In practice, the company was compelled progressively to subjugate its commercial interests to the interests of the British state.

This eventually became a structural feature of the state-company relationship. In 1773 the British Parliament passed a Regulating Act that established the government's de jure power over the Company. Specifically with regard to India, Parliament created a governing council in Calcutta with five members, three of whom were nominated by Parliament and only two by the Company. The East India Company Act of 1784 further differentiated commercial from political activities and reinforced the principle that in political matters, the British government had precedence over the Company.[11] The development of a formal British government bureaucratic administration in India followed. Though it naturally wasn't always possible to cleanly distinguish between political and commercial activities in practice (as it wouldn't be in any colonial setting), the structural principle was now in place—politics belonged to the Parliament and the Crown, and commerce would follow rather than lead.

Predictably this principle created economic hardship for the Company as the costs of political and military control, subject to decisions made by Parliament, were forced onto Company accounts whenever possible. The Company now found itself appealing to Parliament for assistance rather than the opposite. In 1813 the British government formally asserted sovereignty over the Indian territories held by the Company and further chipped away at the Company's deteriorating trading monopolies. The trajectory of state preeminence was clearly heading in one direction. The Company was nationalized in 1858, and formally dissolved in 1874. One of the many florid histories put the transformation in these terms:

> If supremacy in Bengal meant that [tax] revenue replaced commercial profits as its financial support, then administration must replace trade as the profession of its employees . . . increasingly

its outbound ships carried more in the way of troops and stores, passengers and European luxuries, then they did of broadcloth. Ledgers became tax rolls, warehouses arsenals . . . an empire was something else. It needed regulation, and in time, regulation meant nationalization.[12]

The primacy of politics and the defiant reassertion of state power is the big theme of this story. The Company was an icon of global reach, borderless commerce, and the precedence of profits. But only for a time, and only for so long as the state would consent.

REPRISING THE GLOBAL IMPERATIVE

The conviction that big is beautiful when it comes to markets might seem so obvious on the face of it as to barely need explication. But placing yourself back in time—for instance, in the shoes of a British East India trading ship captain from 1620 or thereabouts—you might imagine a rather different set of thoughts or at least a rather significant set of doubts. You wouldn't have had the modern language of transaction costs to describe your experience. But when your ship was battered by storms, your crew devastated by disease, your maps (such as they were) shown to be almost completely wrong, and your destinations populated with sometimes hostile foreign peoples for whom trade with strangers was a strange concept, you might have very well concluded without consulting much economic theory that commerce was just as well something that should be confined to the British isles.

In fact it might very well have been your craving for adventure rather than profit that sent you out on your voyage—in which case all these transaction costs might have been the point of what you were seeking, rather than a drag on economic return per se. But the same would not have been true of the investors who bankrolled the voyage. Recall the 8 percent annual dividend paid to shareholders during the best days of the Company. To put that in perspective, the average dividend yield on the Standard & Poor's (S&P) 500 has been below 3 percent for the last twenty-five years (and for most of that time hovering below 2 percent).

How is it that a trading company from a small island nation with a tiny portion of the world's population could generate such high and consistent profits?

Simple Ricardian elements of comparative advantage and trade are, of course, a big part of the theoretical answer.[13] Larger markets enable a more precise and efficient division of labor. Greater demand enables larger economies of scale, at least in sectors where scale is an advantage. But theory doesn't always work out for the best in practice, because larger markets also place greater demands on society, people, and institutions.

Small-scale markets, in contrast, can come into being without very much beyond a source of supply and a source of demand. This "instant market" recipe is probably what it felt like when a trading ship landed in a new destination for the first time. A place to dock, some common elements of language, and enough capacity for violence kept in the background (in case someone would try to cheat during an exchange) might be the only real infrastructure necessary to make a market at that moment.

Going bigger, or even sustaining over time these small-scale exchanges, is a different story. Markets of significant size and scope have always required a wide range of nonmarket institutions in order to achieve economic stability and social-political legitimacy.[14] And this is where the real friction between different scaling phenomena arise.

Put simply, the equation for scale benefits in markets looks different than the equation for scale benefits in *governance* of markets. The precise nature of that difference changes over time, but because each is being driven by its own underlying forces the curves have almost never overlapped for anything more than the very briefest moments.

Let's unpack those statements a little and see if we can simplify them at the same time. In the modern era the principal locus of economic governance has been the national state, with transnational or global governance institutions mainly an outcome of agreements and arrangements made between and among states. And most people have wanted it that way most of the time. To see this clearly, consider the most upscaled imaginable alternative: a global government. Has anyone seriously argued that a global government should be established so that firms could maximize their profits in global markets? Calls for global government, when they happen, have usually been linked to the prevention of war, not the expansion of commerce per se. And, of course, they haven't really been heard for long in that arena either.

The commercial arguments typically step down from the word "government" to the phrase "global governance"—which is different in just a few letters but vastly different in meaning and practice. Global governance has been and remains weak by design. In fact, the principal debate within international relations theory about global governance is whether a minimum viable set of governance services can emerge from international institutions that really have so little power relative to states.[15] It took forty-seven years to get from the General Agreement on Tariffs and Trade (GATT), mainly a coordinating organization with relatively few enforcement provisions, to the World Trade Organization (WTO) with its more meaningful authority and dispute-settlement mechanisms. The United Nations provides quite a lot of space and time for speeches about international cooperation and the setting aside of national differences, but not much concrete institutional action that enables either one. And as I discuss in later chapters, the trajectory in the back half of the 2010s is mostly to revert power and authority back toward the state and away from the global governance institutions that do exist.

The important thing to note about this story, is that it happens not just because power-hungry people with anachronistic mind-sets inside national governments are selfishly desperate to hold on to dysfunctional power—though that might be part of the reason. It happens fundamentally because people on this very big planet don't all want the same things from governance of their economies, to say nothing of their politics—and they never have. Perhaps they never will. As Dani Rodrik put it in the context of what he called "the globalization paradox," "differences in history, culture, levels of income result in divergences in needs and preferences."[16]

But what's the paradox, really? Rodrik's crisp statement of difference applies not only to what used to be called the high politics issues of territory, religion, and nationalism but to commerce as well (what used to be called low politics). Trade might create wealth but it also creates winners and losers around the distribution of that wealth. New technologies place former ways of life at risk, even if the future ways of life they promise might seem vastly preferable, at least to some. Concretely, not everyone believes that a world where robots drive cars and trucks is a better world than the one where humans do the driving. People have different points of view and belief systems about how the tradeoffs of commerce and wealth creation ought to be managed, sequenced, and—ultimately—governed.

These differences are neither rational nor irrational, but are simply primordial. If there's a paradox, it is that observers, commentators, and scholars have from time to time made arguments to the contrary. Those arguments should really be seen as normative, not analytic—in other words, referring to what some people *wish* to be true rather than what is *actually* true or why.

My point is that the fundamental friction between the scaling function of markets and the scaling function of governance that I described earlier is not going to resolve in any meaningful fashion. Rather the friction simply will manifest in different ways at different times. And the dimensions and characteristics of that friction are not a sideshow—they are the main show. They compose the fundamental feature of the landscape on which the aspiring global organization has to figure out and deploy its organizational strategy.

THE MODERN MULTINATIONAL

The modern multinational corporation has been remarkably, if unevenly, successful at this task. It's easy to lose sight of the way in which these organizations are awe-inspiring achievements of human imagination. Consider GE (what used to be called General Electric). The firm is well over a hundred years old; it has locations in about 170 countries and more than 300,000 employees. Or consider the more recent miracle that is Alphabet (the parent company of Google): founded in 1996, incorporated in 1998, and listed on the public stock market in 2004. The firm had over seventy offices outside the United States and more than 85,000 employees at the end of 2018. And it is the number one search engine in all but about ten countries around the world. It's a recent phenomenon in human history to be able even to conceive of organizations this massive in size and influence, much less to operate them as profitable enterprises where people and machines communicate and exchange ideas, coordinate their actions, and ultimately work together to serve a shared set of goals.

Global reach is an anything-but-guaranteed outcome of making those things possible and getting them right. There is, of course, no single formula for success or a standard organizational template that makes it all work. The modern multinational has had a core logic that reflects its embeddedness in late twentieth-century political economy and technology. That core logic is made up of three basic stories. The first is about growth; the second, about operations; and the third, about culture.

The growth story is the simplest and has been largely consistent over time—it has been first and foremost about markets and scale. As I said earlier, the bigger the market, the better. And for much of the twentieth century, bigger has in practice generally meant a focus on developed and relatively rich countries because that was where the money was, along with the distribution, payment, service, and other auxiliary systems as well as the political and regulatory stability that allows commerce to function smoothly.

The operations story has been first and foremost about managing complex internal systems so that connections between steps in a production process are appropriately coordinated and sequenced. A simpler way to say this, is to imagine the operations aspect of the multinational as a large and geographically distributed factory assembly line, where a division of labor has to be designed and implemented so that whatever is being built, can be built in a very efficient manner. The product doesn't have to be a physical good that could be dropped on your foot, of course—it could just as well be software. The challenge then would be for the organization to decide which modules of code should be written by whom within the organization, in what place, and how the work gets divided and the pieces put together.

And finally the culture story, which is the most imprecise but also the most important part of the puzzle. The multinational, for all its aspirations to reach the world, did not during the twentieth century detach from—or really even aspire to detach from—its national origin, which included elements of culture. Practically, it was assumed in almost all conversations that GE was an American multinational; that Toyota was

Japanese; that Siemens was German; and so on. These labels meant something more than just where the company had been founded and where its headquarters was located in respect to "foreign" offices and factories. It also said—or at least intimated—important things about corporate culture. And this is where some of the most important differences might lie.

In fact, one of the more contentious and interesting arguments about multinational firms in the second half of the twentieth century was precisely about this impact of national origin on firm behavior. The intuition was straightforward: it seemed that an organization founded in a particular national setting would inevitably be shaped by the regulatory environment, business practices, and overall culture of its "home-country" setting. Those influences might not be indelible, but they would be sufficiently strong to shape how the multinational organized itself and acted when it went outside its home national borders to reach "host" countries and foreign markets.[17]

Raymond Vernon in 1993 cut through these arguments with a different perspective.[18] Multinationals in his telling did in fact organize and act in distinct ways, but they did so more as a function of the characteristics of the *product markets* in which they were operating rather than the home country in which they were (sometimes nominally) based. If it was the *host* country rather than the home or headquarters that mattered, then the expectation would be for a kind of convergent set of behaviors based on market location. An American and a Japanese multinational both operating in China, for example, would become more alike. It was a simple perspective twist, but one with very important implications for the narrative of how the multinational had evolved and would evolve as the twentieth century moved toward the twenty-first.

To see this clearly, it's useful to take a small step backward toward the era of Pax Americana in the immediate aftermath of World War II. US-based firms grew their global footprint rapidly in the postwar period. The opportunity drivers were familiar: technologies for communication and transport were fast improving (container shipping, telex, reasonably priced long-distance telephony) and the attractiveness of scale in industrial production, particularly given the physical damage and loss of capacity in Europe during the war, was significant. It was set to be a golden age of exports from home facilities, supported by Washington's political commitment to be the financier of faster recovery, greater consumption, and economic growth with political stability in European states that might otherwise be vulnerable to communist infections.

But US firms found themselves soon playing defense against meaningful competition, particularly in sectors like machinery and chemicals, where recovering European firms had long been excellent. After 1960 with the impact of the evolving Common Market, the European multinationals no longer had to worry about being shut out of other European markets; but they did have to contend with increasing competitive pressure from US firms. The initial strategy of the US firms was often to seek restrictive market-sharing arrangements and attract their European competitors into these agreements. But that approach was itself vulnerable, to new US companies as well as antitrust rules and other competition policy constraints. And though phone calls and air travel were getting cheaper, they were nowhere near as cheap (or free) and run of the mill as we experience them in the twenty-first century. The logistical complications and transaction costs of setting up joint ventures and partnerships with local firms across a big ocean like the Atlantic were still substantial in the 1960s.

A better move in many cases turned out to be to establish foreign subsidiaries of US firms in growing markets, which in turn could essentially implement their own versions of restrictive market-sharing agreements and insure against local competitors locking up either raw material supply chains or access to local markets. In the 1960s the establishment of foreign subsidiaries made sense for a number of reasons. It was perceived as reasonably efficient, since European markets were big enough and growing robustly enough to support continental economies of scale in production. It was a useful hedge against a perceived and, ultimately, quite real threat in some places—that local governments would be tempted to restrict imports in order to subsidize the growth of domestic producers, particularly once US firms lost the technological lead. And it appeared to manifest also a kind of copying phenomenon, in the sense that once a few big firms started to move in this direction others tended to follow in "best practice" mimetic fashion.[19]

These strategies evolved over the course of the 1970s and 1980s, particularly as the prominence of the Japanese economy rose. US firms sought to establish foreign subsidiaries in the protected Japanese market not only to gain (some) access to that market and gain (some) control over technology transfer, but also to learn and acquire new skills from Japanese organizations and experiences like Toyota that were leading with innovations in what came to be called lean production.[20]

In consumer electronics, firms like IBM and Texas Instruments found themselves needing to be in Japan in order to be close to local technology supply chains for memory chips and, later, microprocessors. This was a form of defense against delayed access to fast-moving innovation at or near the technology horizon. It was about avoiding the downside scenario that John Zysman and his colleagues at the Berkeley Roundtable on the International Economy articulated as the risk of getting late access to critical components of fast-moving markets in consumer electronics, where a disadvantage of even a few months could make a crucial difference in the ability to design and deliver the most profitable new products.[21]

By the late 1980s these pieces were coming together, and an early manifestation of global integration through cross-national production networks was coming into focus. Foreign subsidiaries could be used not only to serve local demand but also to fill requirements for components that would feed into the global network. Not all requirements were equal, however. It was still essentially an article of faith that "crucial" high value–add activities should remain at the center, in the home-country national context, and not be sourced from elsewhere. For some sectors this was design and marketing; for many it was the more advanced research and development (R&D) functions. Intellectual property (IP) in particular had to be nurtured and defended at the home-country source for both immediate and longer-term competitive advantage.

In the 1990s a semi-consensus model of global reach on this basis included a few foundational elements. First, autarky or anything close to it was not a meaningful option for modern economies. Second, governments were playing the role of "market shapers" as they sought to exert leverage over crucial outcomes in the distribution of jobs and taxes, as well as balance of payments, and—more than anything else—technology trajectories and technology leadership. Third, the largest and most attractive stakes still lay in other industrialized and developed regions, and not really in the developing world—with China as the critical and massive exception.

Linked to these consensus points was an unfolding debate between a post–Cold War vision of globalization and the possibility of a new form of regionalism. With older, politically motivated "spheres of influence" models having been a 1989 casualty of the Cold War's end, the major conceptual competitor to a globalization mind-set was a regional bloc mind-set based on moderate market scale and scope. This alternative idea was that regional blocs could be structured at sufficient scale and scope to internalize many of the benefits, while remaining just manageable enough for a major geopolitical power to dominate bargaining with the medium-sized and smaller players within the bloc. The medium-sized players in particular might have preferred to operate on a "flatter" global stage, where they would be in a better position to bargain big powers off against each other, but they didn't have the power and influence to create that stage. The biggest uncertainty in the regional bloc proto-model was simply where the boundaries would be plausibly drawn: Was Japan going to be part of the US-led region? Would former Soviet states, now independent, find sustainable growth paths within a European region? And where would the emerging "factory China" manufacturing powerhouse fit?

Clearly these weren't marginal questions—not for political leaders, corporate strategists, or academic observers and analysts who were trying to make sense of the landscape. But in practice, the globalization mind-set and model won out in theory and in practice. In many respects the "new regionalism" perspective served as more of a cautionary tale about what could go wrong in an evolving global system, than as a coherent conceptual model in and of itself. And so it often sat in the background, which had the effect of fortifying the attractiveness of the emerging globalization visions during the early part of the 1990s.

THE INTERNET GLOBALIZATION PERIOD: THE 1990S

If there's a single day that marks the end of the Cold War, you'd have to say it was November 9, 1989, when the Berlin Wall fell. With what we know of history unfolding since that day, it's tricky to recapture the "end of history" ambience that grasped imaginations at that moment in time.[22] But it's important to try because the story of how the global enterprise evolves in the next decade depends on it.

The collapse of the Soviet empire and—just a short time later, the Soviet Union itself on December 26, 1991—made the world seem a much smaller and more open place. The ideological and institutional barriers that were the Communist bloc had in effect been the twentieth-century equivalent of a vast mountain range in the 1500s or a huge ocean in the 1600s, an impermeable membrane that stood in the way of global reach. And then it felt as if a sudden jolt had turned the vast mountain range into a flat and well-paved eight-lane freeway with no traffic jams and no tolls.

The word "globalization" was coming into its own. Former Soviet and East European states were now rebranded as "emerging economies" open for global business to restructure, invest, produce, and sell. China was more than a decade into its market-reform process. And the internet was escaping its roots as a science experiment linking Defense Advanced Research Projects Agency (DARPA) research sites, to become a communications network that even the most imaginative science fiction authors a decade earlier would have been challenged to foresee.

It was a coincidence of history, but 1989 was also the year that a British scientist at CERN named Tim Berners-Lee created the first "website." It described the basic features of something that Berners-Lee would call the World Wide Web, and it instructed others how to set up their own servers and access others' documents through a "linking" protocol. In the spring of 1993 CERN placed the necessary software in the public domain. It was also in 1993 that a team at the National Center for Supercomputing Applications (NCSA), led by Marc Andreessen, released Mosaic, the first widely used web browser. Mosaic was reliable and easy enough for almost anyone with a personal computer to install and play with. As important, it had the defining feature of what we now take for granted as the Web: displaying images inline with text instead of in a separate window. Robert Metcalfe (the inventor of the Ethernet protocol) famously described the experience this way:

In the Web's first generation, Tim Berners-Lee launched the Uniform Resource Locator (URL), Hypertext Transfer Protocol (HTTP), and HTML standards with prototype Unix-based servers and browsers. A few people noticed that the Web might be better than Gopher.

In the second generation, Marc Andreessen and Eric Bina developed NCSA Mosaic at the University of Illinois. Several million then suddenly noticed that the Web might be better than sex.[23]

These two core ingredients of 1990s economic geography overlapped in time and space in a rather unique way, setting the stage for the mid-1990s "Cambrian explosion" of dot-com companies and sole superpower geopolitics.[24] It was a heady mix of Coase theorem thinking from economics and "distribution of power" thinking from international relations theory, and it set the stage for global reach for most of the decade.

Put simply, the Coase theorem is an argument about what it takes to get efficient allocation in markets. The theorem states that in a situation where property rights are well defined and transaction costs low enough, it doesn't really matter who owns an asset at time $t = 0$, because the asset will be traded up to the owner who can extract the most value from it. As I said in Chapter 1, Coase was invoked to sketch out some features of a world in which the internet supposedly would drive transaction costs in many sectors and places and interactions toward the ultimate asymptote of zero. This would in turn enable the creation of markets that would function effectively and efficiently to optimize situations that people had assumed were just stuck the way they were.

I remember Kevin Kelly, the founding executive editor of *Wired* magazine and later the author of *New Rules for the New Economy*, delivering a poignant speech around 1993 or so, in which he pointed to a seat in the auditorium and proclaimed (this is a paraphrase) "right now, someone sits in that seat for the random reason that they arrived here when they did. In the near future, that seat will have a real-time price. Anyone will be able to bid for it at any time, and it will find its way to the person who most values sitting in that particular seat at that particular moment." It was a stunning vision of hyper-efficient Coase-type resource allocation, revolutionary and actually deserving of some of the hype it was generating. And that's true regardless of whether on reflection it felt like human beings would want to actually live in a society or world that allocated (more or most or even all?) resources in that fashion.

Sole superpower thinking about the distribution of power in international politics had its own somewhat less stunning but still compelling story. When the Cold War ended, what disappeared with it was a bipolar distribution of power in which two superpowers, roughly matched, were far ahead of the next most powerful states.

In his 1979 book *Theory of International Politics* Kenneth Waltz had explained why bipolarity would paradoxically generate international political and military stability, mainly through the reduction of uncertainty about the balance of power. In a different world, with multiple very powerful states trying to match and deter each other from aggression, countries form alliances to try to enhance their power—but alliances are for the most part unenforceable promises that might or might not be fulfilled when push comes to shove. That kind of uncertainty in international politics breeds miscalculation of risk, and miscalculation of risk is a primary cause of war.

In contrast, bipolar distributions of power are terrifically clarifying. As Waltz put it, in bipolar worlds "it is clear who will oppose whom." That kind of clarity creates a robust competition that is actually stable competition, since neither superpower can harbor illusions that some third party or ally could join a conflict between them in a way that would make any significant difference. Bipolarity also has the effect of minimizing interdependence, at least between the two superpowers who would rationally seek to limit their exposure to influence from each other's economic and political maneuvers. And again, low interdependence would be a cause of stability, by reducing vulnerability to external shocks and highlighting the importance of self-help.

In that telling, the sudden collapse of bipolarity might have been a troubling signal of instability to come. American political scientists, however, quickly created a new narrative that centered on a concept of "unipolarity," an awkward term that was really just a description of an international system where one country stood in a vastly greater power position than all others. Unipolarity had its own stability argument attached, but it wasn't a structural one tied to an impersonal distribution of power. Instead, it rested on the ability and willingness of a particular country, the United States, to sustain and extend what was supposedly a rule-based liberal international order from what had been only a part of the world (the "free world," as it was called in Cold War rhetoric) to essentially the entire world.

To engage on this newly open playing field, emerging economies had to accept wholesale the package deal of Washington consensus macroeconomic policies and liberal democratic political processes (or at least point themselves in that direction). This was the real manifestation of TINA ("There Is No Alternative") that Margaret Thatcher had proclaimed, prematurely, a decade earlier.[25]

I have another memory that captures this part of the story linking Coase and unipolar international politics. As a political consultant to the president of the European Bank for Reconstruction and Development in 1992, I was responsible for assessing the likelihood that former Soviet republics, now suddenly independent sovereign countries, would meet the terms of the bank's political conditionality for lending (which included a clause about democratic elections).[26] We erred on the side of optimism, which in retrospect seems painfully naive when it came to countries that had no history or culture of democracy, no relevant institutions in place, and so on. In fact we weren't completely blind to those realities in the moment. But in 1992 it seemed like a plausibly hopeful bet to place, given the magnetic attraction of the unipolar moment and the very concrete material incentives and disincentives that the reduction in transaction costs made possible.

I have one last personal anecdote that can serve to summarize the landscape of the time. In 1993 I joined a small boutique consulting firm in Emeryville, California, that was an intellectual spinoff of the Royal Dutch Shell Global Business Environment unit, which had become known for the use of scenario planning in the energy sector. Our business proposition was to develop and extend scenario methodology so that it could be used more broadly for strategic planning in other sectors as well as in nonprofits and government agencies. The founders named the company Global Business Network (GBN), which turned out to be remarkably prescient. If there were three words that best described the political-technology landscape of the 1990s, they were in fact probably these three: global (capturing unipolarity and the end of the Cold War divide); business (capturing the perceived triumph of liberal capitalism and the more positive reputation of large multinationals at that moment); and network (capturing both the emergence of internet technology as a critical driver of economic, social, and political change, and the cultural trope of the time that celebrated more broadly the potency of "networks" in contrast to hierarchies and bureaucracies to innovate and navigate change).

The 1990s thus created some distinctive conditions around the state and the technology landscape that would set the stage for global reach. The state was supposed to have settled into its primary role as a facilitator of market interactions, the umpire of the playing field (rather than an active player on that field) whenever possible. The number one job of government would be to enable and promote the growth of markets across barriers and borders, whether as public policy maker, technology investor or subsidizer, or as procurement machine that by virtue of its size could influence technology trajectories and standards. The equation boiled down to this: Coase plus unipolarity equals a clear trajectory toward a global playing field unencumbered by the detritus of earlier history.

If that equation was right, then many multinational firms would find themselves, strangely, with inadequate or inappropriately configured government relations offices. It wasn't that these organizations as a group generally lacked lobbying capacity (though many of the new information technology firms founded in the 1990s did, and by intention). It was that the lobbying capacity would be focused in the wrong functions and places. The political environment was now an extremely auspicious one for businesses' global reach; government relations could move toward a more opportunistic stance where finding ways to proactively advance the cause of global reach would be at least as important as preventing detrimental regulation and the like. Put simply, the new government relations mind-set would have to be "seek the upside" rather than "prevent a downside risk," a better job in many respects but still a very different one.

The technology environment was at least as auspicious in its own way. Again it may be hard to recapture the memory, but the 1990s information technology revolution narrative was a dramatically optimistic story about higher productivity, improved services, and new business creation feeding each other. Complex issues that would appear later around the downsides of disruptive innovation, polarizing discourse, self-selecting filter bubbles in politics, social media privacy concerns, and the like were barely on the radar screen at that time. Labor-market displacement and the loss of jobs were mainly theoretical concerns. Surveillance was a niche anxiety, at least until the events of September 11, 2001, changed the game.

IT in the early to mid-1990s was seen as an upside engine of growth and organizational transformation, whose potential was yet to be convincingly demonstrated in productivity and other metrics (Robert Solow famously said in 1987 "you can see computers everywhere except in the productivity statistics").[27] As such, it had a relatively low political profile, at least in comparison to today. But there were a few key issues that were emerging as foreshadows of greater concern.

One was about how large-scale trading partners, in particular the United States and Europe, dealt differently with overcapacity issues. This wasn't a new issue or for that matter specifically about the IT sector. But given the timing of the immediate post–Cold War recession and the explosive growth of exports from Factory China, what was distinctly visible in industries like steel production had consequences for global reach in other sectors as well. To oversimplify a bit, Europe was organized to deal with overcapacity by using government support to organize rationalization cartels that were supposed to manage downsizing in an organized manner. The United States was more likely to let market competition run, which in effect meant externalizing some of the costs of adjustment to the rest of the world (including, of course, Europe) through trade channels. And that was destined to create friction in the multilateral trade regime that could not be readily managed through WTO processes.

A second issue loomed around the inefficiencies, instabilities, and perceived inequities of IP rights systems that were increasingly prominent and critical to profit-making in modern business models. Directly in the case of sectors like pharmaceuticals and software, and indirectly in many other major sectors, competitiveness and the ability to protect and advance it through monetizing intangible value was seen to depend on legal regimes around IP. But much of the world found itself confused, ambivalent, and in some cases resentful regarding the protection of IP in the digital age (more on this in Chapter 4).

It is no coincidence that Napster—a peer-to-peer file-sharing system that was principally used to make music MP3 files available to pretty much anyone who wanted them, without payment—was released as software for download in 1999. At its peak Napster had about eighty million registered users, most of whom were treating music under copyright as if it were in the public domain.[28] In the fall of 2000 I asked this question to a lecture hall of three hundred undergraduates at UC Berkeley: how many of you believe it is appropriate to pay for music? I didn't say "legal" and I didn't say "ethical" and I didn't say "fair," and that was intentional. I was looking to pose the question with a word ("appropriate") that felt least emotional and most neutral.

Fewer than ten hands went up in response. Importantly, this wasn't because the students lacked knowledge about IP and the economic arguments for copyright; I had taught them the basics earlier in that same lecture. It wasn't because they didn't care about the law or the livelihood of musicians. It was simply a reflection of mainstream thinking at that moment, and the confusion and ambivalence that IP in digital form engendered.

Was IP overvalued or undervalued, and how could anyone actually tell when piracy machines like Napster went mainstream? Was it ever sensible to treat ideas or for that matter almost anything digital as excludable property, particularly if it could be copied an infinite number of times at essentially zero cost? Who, exactly, was being hurt when a UC Berkeley student used Napster to download and listen to a couple of new songs, particularly if she never would have bought the album in any event? If Pfizer's IP was infringed by an Indian pharmaceutical company (for example), was this a foreign policy issue for governments, or a business model issue for firms—and who had the right to decide?

This might have remained a somewhat obscure or at least technocratic legal and economic issue that wouldn't have engaged much of the world's public opinion. It might have been compartmentalized as a copyright and entertainment issue, a fight over music and movies pitting consumers against lawyers and millionaires in Hollywood and the like that would be fought out in the courts. But in another coincidence of history, the HIV / AIDS epidemic changed the game.

HIV transformed IP rights into something quite different: a widespread public debate about humanity, common sense, compassion, race, discrimination, and even modern-day colonialism (more on this in Chapter 4). The fact was, tens of thousands of people were dying in less-developed countries because they could not afford the sky-high prices of antiretroviral therapies created and sold by "Western" pharmaceutical companies under the protective umbrella of IP patent regimes. After all, these were mostly small molecule drugs, which cost pennies or at most dollars to manufacture.

But, of course, it was also true that those same Western pharmaceutical companies had spent billions of dollars to fund the R&D that discovered, created, and tested those drugs. Apart from their claim to deserve an adequate return on capital already invested, they argued that without IP protections and the massive profits that went along with that, they would be unable to fund the next generation of R&D to create better therapies for HIV and other horrible diseases.

But how much profit was enough, and how much suffering could today's patients possibly bear in order to incentivize shareholders to invest in the potential good of future generations? It might not have been a matter of life and death when similar questions were posed to the software or music industries.[29] But the conceptual arguments for and against IP were much the same, and the answers just as confused and ambivalent. As the decade progressed, it became increasingly uncomfortable for IP-intensive sectors, just as it was becoming increasingly profitable as well.

The third big issue emerged toward the end of the 1990s as global and particularly US equity markets soared into what was at the time uncharted territory. A few selected numbers help to contextualize just how rapidly and boldly what turned out to be a "castle-in-the-air" theory of enterprise value boosted stock-market valuations into the stratosphere.[30] The NASDAQ composite index rose 500 percent in the five years between 1995 and 2000, to reach at its peak a price-earnings ratio of around 200 (roughly seven times the historical average for the S&P

500 over the last hundred years). In the single year of 1999, Qualcomm shares rose by over 2,000 percent. A number of companies sold initial public offering (IPO) shares without having any revenue at all, much less profits on their books.

There was at the time, as is generally the case with castle-in-the-air bubbles, an explanation for why this all made perfectly good sense. It was called "the new economy" and it rested on the proposition that corporate profits were irrelevant, at least for now. What supposedly mattered to enterprise value instead was the speed with which customers could be acquired for the new goods and services that the World Wide Web made possible. The formula was pretty simple: get big fast and even more importantly get network effects going. Monetization and profits would come later, in some (often unspecified) fashion.

It's almost too easy in retrospect to make fun of some of the wild claims and even wilder businesses that were built on this proposition. My personal favorite was pets.com—as the owner of two extremely hungry cats, I couldn't help but love the experience of ordering their food and their litter on the Web at prices that were substantially below what I paid at the brick-and-mortar store in my neighborhood, and then have these heavy items delivered to my front door the next morning by FedEx—for free. Somewhere in my gut I knew it didn't quite make sense . . . as did many others. But it was much easier to stay in the moment, enjoy the subsidized consumption, let my cats do the same, and attend the audaciously expensive and elaborate IPO parties in San Francisco (the cats didn't get to go to those) than it was to let my inner Scrooge spoil the fun.

The dot-com crash started in the spring of 2000. By the time it was over, the NASDAQ composite index had fallen 78 percent, and a large number of new-economy businesses had become new-economy bankruptcies. The silver lining, of course, lay in the now underutilized and underpriced assets that were rushed onto fire-sale markets to raise cash on an emergency basis. I bought a nearly new Aeron chair, the favored office furniture of dot-com businesses, for less than $200 at a bankruptcy sale (the retail price at that time was over $500). More important were the underpriced IP, highly skilled technical labor, and "dark fiber" (unused fiber-optic bandwidth and switching capacity in the internet backbone).

The Coase theorem never said that to watch new technologies re-shuffle property would be easy or fun. Unipolar international politics was never a promise that political volatility and disruption wouldn't test the boundaries of instability and conflict. And in the real world, volatility was the result. The dot-com bust broke a lot of hearts as well as destroying a lot of retirement plans, for young entrepreneurs and for older investors alike. But it laid the foundation for a rapid move to a new model of global reach, which would start to emerge in the wake of the financial carnage. The other important foundational element materialized out of a different carnage, which took place on September 11, 2001, in downtown Manhattan and changed the theory and narrative around unipolarity. Together, these new dynamics of state power and presence along with digital technologies set the stage for a new model of global reach, what would become known in the mid-2000s as the globally integrated enterprise. Chapter 3 discusses how this came to be and what it would mean.

3

THE ERA OF THE GLOBALLY
INTEGRATED ENTERPRISE

THE GLOBAL POLITICAL ECONOMY SPENT the first few years of the 2000s balancing on a tightrope. The dot-com crash and the 9 / 11 attacks together were more than sufficient to undermine simplistic visions of a "new economy" untethered from classic constraints of scarcity and a new global politics free of ideological, religious, and nationalist divisions. But the fundamental driving forces that had brought those visions into being were in many respects as robust as ever and in some ways even more so. The seemingly relentless march of Moore's law, the expansion of internet connectivity, the ongoing Doha round of trade negotiations—none of these forces of 1990s globalization were undermined or reversed by the dot-com and 9 / 11 shocks. Paradoxically, as this chapter argues later, these underlying forces were probably strengthened overall by the turmoil and volatility of the first years of the new millennium.

An organization aspiring to reach the world in 2002 or 2003 faced a fundamental dilemma. Technology appeared to be pushing relentlessly toward a borderless network where barriers and boundaries were destined to be temporary phenomena, ripe to be overcome by innovation and creative business models. International politics, in contrast, seemed like it had taken a step backward toward religious or even "civilizational" conflict, with the United States in a central defining role.[1]

One of the key strategy questions of the time captured that ambivalence. The question was at once simple and profound: was it now a good thing, or a bad thing, for an aspiring global organization to be an "American company"? This had the potential to become a particularly vexing issue for some of the most prominent "American" mega-brands—Coca-Cola, Ford, Apple, and the like. Whether the label "American company" really had a precisely defined meaning for firms like these (more on that later), it was certainly a perceptual reality that many people *believed* to have meaning. And thus it was a serious question that needed an answer, and to be of any use that answer had to carry with it with a set of actions an organization could take if it wanted to either strengthen or weaken that perceived association.

A few organizations chose to reject the question entirely. And not because it was inconvenient or because it was troubling or because leaders weren't sure what they could do with the answer. Rather, because in a new formulation the question could be rendered unnecessary to answer, by having a strategy that made the conversation about it simply irrelevant.

The clearest articulation of this new argument about how to reach the world came from another iconic American mega-brand—IBM—and its charismatic CEO at the time, Samuel Palmisano. In a 2006 *Foreign Affairs* article titled "The Globally Integrated Enterprise," Palmisano put forward a set of distinctive propositions that sketched IBM's vision of modern economic geography and how global organizations should configure themselves for that landscape.[2] This article wasn't just the typical marketing fluff or abstract "thought leadership" written for external consumption. It was a powerful argument that crystallized years of work that IBM had undertaken to revamp its strategic posture, and the firm was seriously at work following its prescriptions.

This chapter describes the logic of the globally integrated enterprise (GIE) model and situates it within the economic geography of the moment. It is a story about how the looming disequilibria of the 1990s would be managed in the context of learning from the end-of-decade shocks. It is also a story about the continuing, extraordinary vigor of the internet's borderless-world narrative and the power of a seductive phrase like "the world is flat" to capture imagination. Like most good stories, it has within it heroes who jump in with courage and conviction, as well as wannabe heroes who act as enablers by blissfully cultivating ignorance of blind spots in the narrative. And like a TV series that sets up a sequel for the next season, it ends by sowing the seeds of its own demise.

The GIE was a bold and brilliant idea whose time window would turn out to be startlingly short. That was no fault of IBM. But the irony of the decade was that when Palmisano crystallized IBM's view and presented it to the public clearly and elegantly in 2006, the economic geography that had enabled GIE was already at an inflection point, and the end of the model was just around the corner.

AFTER 2001

The winter of 2002 should not have been a particularly positive and hopeful time for the world economy. The dot-com bust was still working its way through financial and business systems. And the United States (along with the rest of the world) was just beginning to digest the implications of the largest modern terror attack on the US homeland. What was most immediately visible was a war in Afghanistan, but this was only the leading edge of a massive reorientation of US foreign, military, and intelligence policy to confront Al-Qaeda, as well as organizations and governments that were thought to be in league with or financing and enabling that movement. Samuel Huntington's "clash of civilizations" argument, which many saw as an extreme point of view when it was first written in 1996, didn't seem quite so radical anymore.[3] The sense of vulnerability and weakness was exacerbated by a series of anthrax attacks through the mail that started only a week after 9 / 11, and the anthrax-laden letters ultimately killed five people and infected seventeen others.

If a fiction writer had put together a pitch for a dystopic novel with just those several elements, it's likely that her editor would have said "too dark and too implausible to publish." But that feeling of impending doom, which people who lived through late 2001 and early 2002 in places like New York City will never forget, was entirely real. And it didn't last long.

Two important ideas began to surface in the early months of 2002 that would turn the tide of mood in a different direction. Predictably, one was first and foremost about technology; the other was about the state and particularly the American state, the nature of American power, and global presence going forward. Together, these two ideas set the stage for the GIE organizational synthesis.

The first idea, or really, set of ideas, belonged to Venezuelan economist Carlota Perez. In *Technological Revolutions and Financial Capital: The Dynamics of Bubbles and Golden Ages*, Perez put forward a sweeping argument about boom-and-bust cycles of technology innovation, fueled by speculative finance, that mirrored and extended some of Marx's and Schumpeter's central logics while nearly matching their massive ambition to find and explain recurrent patterns related to technology in economic history.[4]

Situating the dot-com bust in a broad narrative of five modern cycles (starting with the classic industrial revolution; then steam and railways; steel, electricity, and heavy engineering; oil, cars, and mass production; and finally modern information and communications technology), Perez argued that "productivity explosions" and "financial excitement leading to economic euphoria" were interdependent phenomena that together created a recurrent pattern. At the highest level, her model suggested that it would take decades (not years) to see the "maturing" impact of a major technological revolution like the internet, and that the disruptions and turbulence of the interim years (felt so distinctly in 2002!) were entirely expected. The pain of transition was, in semi-Marxist terms, an innate consequence of a mismatch between the old socio-institutional framework, which had evolved to meet the needs of a previous generation of technologies, and the new technologies, which needed a different set of institutions to achieve their potential. Perez's model was particularly distinctive because it highlighted the role of financial capital in exacerbating this mismatch to start; it later provided the energy to heal it and bring the new system into being.

She modeled this pattern in four distinct phases: irruption, frenzy, synergy, and maturity.[5]

- *Irruption* describes the intense excitement or "love affair" with a new general purpose technology, recalling (from Chapter 2) what Bob Metcalfe said about Mosaic, the Web, and sex. The leading edge of financial capital becomes obsessed and throws money at the new technology, building "castle-in-the-air" stories that also lead to the de-funding of older technologies and assets.

- A *frenzy* period follows, where a second wave of financial capital pushes the market value of new technologies and the firms that employ them outside a zone of reality, into what is commonly called a bubble. This "decoupling" (as Perez called it) sets the stage for an inevitable crash. That in turn sets the stage for . . .

- A period of *synergy*, where production and profits return to center stage and financial capital is brought back into line with real wealth creation. This is the basis of what Perez called "coherent growth." That evolves into . . .

- *Maturity*, the stage in which standard investment and profit dynamics dominate; finance looks to scale, scope, and new markets; and the system settles down into normal technology deployment and growth. Speculative finance capital begins to look elsewhere, toward the possibilities for the next big technological discontinuity.

By weaving together the logic of finance and the logic of technology development and deployment, Perez created a theory with some very important insights for the first decade of the 2000s. The first insight was about "institutional recomposition," another semi-Marxist argument about how the financial crash between frenzy and synergy would be resolved through redesigning institutions, not just working off bad debt. Put simply, the crash was a signal to rethink in some fundamental manner how firms, governments, and even societies organize themselves, which is a much more ambitious agenda than just cleaning up the financial detritus of overeager investors.

The second insight was about the opportunity that underpriced assets present during the crash period itself. A financial crash is different than simply a correction because it implies a significant downside overshoot, which in turn means that valuable assets (through fire sales or bankruptcy or the like) will find their way onto the market at prices that are below, and sometimes massively below, their potential value. The poster child for this in 2002 was "dark fiber," a huge amount of communications bandwidth that had been built out a few years earlier but was not now being used and could be "lit up" at a very low price. This was painful for the equity and bond holders who had financed the creation of all that bandwidth . . . but it was manna from heaven for new firms that could access critical inputs to their new business models at almost unimaginably low prices.

It would be too much to say that the dot-com crash was good news. But if Perez was right, silver linings were now there for the taking.

The second big idea of the early 2000s was a newly audacious perspective on American power and presence in the world. This might have been even less expected in the wake of the emotional shock that was 9 / 11. Recall the unipolarity narrative of the 1990s: the United States was back then the "sole superpower" and the "indispensable nation" (as President Clinton's Secretary of State Madeleine Albright put it).[6] This wasn't just about outsized US military and economic capability; it was also about what Joseph Nye called "soft power," the supposed attractiveness of American ideas about political-economic and social order to people all over the world.[7] It may sound like a cartoonish oversimplification, but it isn't: it seemed *to many Americans* in the late 1990s that most other countries and societies wanted to emulate the United States. And that those who didn't would soon realize the error of their ways, or could be brought into line if need be with coercive force as a last resort. Right or wrong, this is what many American elites believed almost as an article of faith at the time.

9 / 11 shook that narrative to its core—for a few months. October and November 2001 saw the rise of an alternative narrative, or at least a set of big questions about American power and presence in the world, that expressed foundational doubts about unipolarity in both hard and soft power. "Why do they hate us?" was the simplified version of a very serious and important question that was, for the moment, being asked and talked about in diverse circles. The deeper question was, what is it about the nature of American power and presence in the world that has created such profound animosity that could motivate groups like Al-Qaeda to plot an attack that would amount to murdering roughly three thousand innocent civilians at the World Trade Center and the Pentagon, two icons of American power and identity?

It would be too much to say that the United States underwent an introspective dark night of the soul. But there was some serious soul-searching, and not just among liberal Democrats living on the two coasts.

And then the mood seemed almost suddenly to shift. It's hard to specify the exact moment that this happened but it was somewhere around December 2001 to February 2002. While American special forces deployed to Afghanistan, the mainstream political discourse began to reject the "why do they hate us" question as self-immolating, a "blame the victim" expression of weakness. The question "what is it about the nature of American power and presence in the world?" was challenged and essentially replaced by a different question: what is wrong with the Muslim world? In January 2002 Bernard Lewis argued in *What Went Wrong?* that the problem lay in Muslim civilization and that it was their fault, pure and simple. Debased politics and a lack of freedom among Arab states were the roots of the problem, not anything having to do with outside influences and most definitely not American power.[8]

By the late spring of 2002 the introspective moment had passed, and America was in its own mind back to being the sole superpower, indispensable nation, city on the hill, and magnet of soft power, with hard power deployed halfway around the world in newly aggressive overt and covert operations to dismantle and defeat terrorist networks on a global basis. Confidence in the robustness and moral righteousness of US power now seemed to double-down. The phrase of the moment was "American empire," and it was used by both Republicans and Democrats, conservatives and liberals alike. They might have had different valences around the word "empire," but what they shared was a renewed assessment of the potency of American leadership, even more resolute now that it had been so directly challenged.

President George W. Bush said, "Every nation, in every region, now has a decision to make. Either you are with us, or you are with the terrorists."[9] With that statement, he put the United States and American power right back firmly at the center of a Ptolemaic geopolitical universe, with the United States at the center of everything. If unipolarity and sole superpower status means anything, it means that the options others face and the choices they get to make are defined by what the United States chooses to do.

Bush's assertion might have been a particularly bold formulation of this position, but it wasn't out of line with what most American elites had come to believe by the spring of 2002. The challenge to an American-led world order was going to be met with an even more aggressive defense of and insistence upon that order. If this was triumphalism, so be it.

These two ideas together set the stage for a new theory of how to reach the world.

FOUNDATIONS OF THE GLOBALLY INTEGRATED ENTERPRISE

In the early 2000s a group inside IBM led by Bruce Harreld was charged with an ambitious strategic task: to figure out how to expand and extend the reconfiguration of the company, which had begun to adopt open-source software solutions, in the context of the global political-economic challenges visible at the turn of the century. The team was given a great deal of latitude to think broadly and concoct a set of "what ifs" that were in some cases heretical. As part of their work, they brought in resources from outside the company, and I was lucky enough to be a part of that initiative for several years. It was some of the most intellectually challenging and stimulating work I've ever done, in large part because I knew that the C-suite was listening, and that our work could be part of an inflection point for one of the world's most storied technology firms if we got it right.[10]

Three high-level principles emerged from these discussions as central to the project. The first was simply that the world really was now integrating in a meaningful and sustained way and that business models were changing, sometimes dramatically, to take account of that trajectory. The second was about first-mover advantage: first movers on that landscape were creating and capturing a high proportion of the economic value that could be generated from the integration process, so waiting to learn from others' mistakes or playing fast-follower was not a winning proposition. The third was about the dynamic of accelerating benefits, demanding a mind-set of "go faster to get better."

Years before Mark Zuckerberg told his early Facebook employees to "move fast and break things," the IBM strategy team had created an essentially similar construct inside one of the world's largest companies with one of the more storied histories of conservative corporate culture. That was a revelation, of a kind. But the notion of moving faster to get better does not by itself tell a firm in what direction it ought to move.

IBM sought to answer that question with a comprehensive analysis of the emerging geopolitical and economic geographies of the decade. The foundation for the GIE argument had three components, which together defined for IBM a fairly precise and usable definition of contemporary globalization (or what the team liked to call the flat world, adopting the catchy title of Tom Friedman's popular 2005 book), at once a structural, operational, and cultural construct.[11]

Ideas

This included particularly the decline of economic nationalism as an idea among the most important governments and societies in the world economy.

This wasn't starry-eyed naïveté or blissful ignorance of the fact that the supposed global economy was still conceptual, and that the actually existing global economy was more like a set of national economies (each with its own government, companies, cultures, currencies, regulations, and so on) playing out on a global stage. But it did focus attention on a very important vector of change in core beliefs and practices in a globalization trajectory. China's economic reform program was now in its third decade and showed no signs of slowing. India seemed to be heading in a similar direction, if more slowly and tentatively. A decade into the post–Cold War disruption, the former Central and East European states were for the most part headed in the same direction. Growth rates were picking up in major sub-Saharan African economies, and not only because of commodity exports. In 2006, "emerging markets" achieved an average GDP growth of 6.5 percent, more than double that of "developed" markets; and for the first time in the modern era they would account for over half of total world demand.[12] The precise numbers, of course, depended on the particular category definitions and the quirks and imperfections of statistical models and agencies . . . but they still signaled something important about a shift in center of gravity.

The notion of a full-on convergence around "Washington Consensus" ideas and "there is no alternative" mind-sets would have been a step too far ahead of the evidence; progress was certainly going to be uneven as it always is, but the directionality seemed clear.

Information Technology

This point particularly related to the massive reduction in the cost of coordinating complex activities that were separated in time and physical location.

This was in IBM's view the most consequential impact of the modern IT revolution and particularly the business-to-business (B2B) Web. A basic truth of the division of labor, at least as long as human beings are involved, is that coordinating economic activities of any complexity is a hard thing to do. Markets may set prices in some sense, but markets don't tell you where or from whom to buy a part that you assemble into your car, computer, or couch. Markets don't automatically transfer knowledge about how to modify the design of that part when some other supplier modifies the design of the part to which it connects. Markets don't collate and distribute knowledge about why a particular part wears out, or how to improve the design or material or maintenance procedures so that it doesn't do so as quickly or as expensively. And so on.

All of those coordination functions involve communication, of complex and granular (often tacit) knowledge that sits in human minds. Even when some of that knowledge is systematically recorded in database fields, it still needs to be communicated and understood by people. And so things like geography, time zones, language barriers, and the general complexity of human communication about complex subjects create barriers that shape the location and character of economic activity.

In an era where container shipping had so dramatically reduced the purely physical costs of moving heavy objects from place to place around the world, it was possible to argue that in many production systems it was now information coordination costs that in effect limited global reach. In concrete terms, the costs of moving an automobile engine from Japan to an assembly plant in Thailand might very well be less an issue than the costs of locating precisely the right engine in the right place at the right time, transferring knowledge about how to best assemble the car around it, tuning the engine's control systems for that particular build, learning how the engine control software would function under different environmental conditions, and the like. And this is exactly the barrier that was being dismantled or at least substantially lowered by 2000s IT and in particular B2B web-based technologies.

In IBM's worldview this would be transformative. Cheap physical transportation (container shipping) was the lifeblood of the 1970s and 1980s multinational, because it allowed for concentrating production and exploiting economies of scale and cheap labor while later shipping products out into faraway global markets. In the 2000s IT certainly enhanced that part of the story by making transportation even more efficient and cheaper. But it had the much more profound effect of reducing coordination costs for complex production systems, whether the thing being built was a physical product (like a car) or a digital product (like a software package).

And that, for IBM, meant that globalization was more than a way of reducing the costs of inputs. The new global organization could do a lot more than source cheap labor and increase the efficiency of production. It could also begin to meaningfully tap expertise and ideas among talented people—engineers and scientists, artisans and designers, coders and user interface experts, and beyond—in China, India, Brazil, indeed anywhere that human talent might happen to be at that particular moment.

If you assume that talent is more or less randomly distributed among the roughly seven and a half billion human beings that live on this planet, this signaled an incredible potential for innovation. Sourcing *ideas* from anywhere in the world and coordinating them within complex economic activities was the goal—a much bolder and more revolutionary notion of global integration than sourcing a physical commodity, or labor, or really any other input.

Business-Process Standardization

Innovation at any meaningful scale rests on some shared foundation or basic infrastructure within which new ideas and new processes can fit. The TCP/IP protocols that underpin the Internet are a perfect example— by creating a standardized means of communication among diverse systems, TCP/IP freed up the endpoints to experiment. Too much standardization extending too widely would have limited that creative energy, but too little would have limited the scope for scaling good ideas and innovations that work. In IBM's view, the early 2000s had hit on a kind of Goldilocks moment when it came to business processes writ broadly, and in particular to many of the backend business functions that are sometimes invisible but essential to any value creation process.

It was an important part of the IBM view that while business-process standards are good, when it comes to global reach, *open* standards are better. That was anything but an obvious conclusion for a firm that had, not many years ago, built its business on proprietary standards, particularly in the realm of operating systems for mainframes, where IBM hardware and IBM software were intricately interconnected and had been sold as a package.[13] The remnants of this kind of thinking were famously satirized by Ridley Scott in what is likely the single most renowned commercial of all time, the 1984 Apple advertisement that portrayed IBM as an Orwellian Big Brother whose control over the minds of the masses to enforce conformity of thoughts was going to be smashed to bits by the new Apple Macintosh.[14]

By the early 2000s, IBM had a very different mind-set and had developed a surprisingly close relationship with key parts of the open-source software community, especially the Apache and Linux communities. This grew partly out of an effort to extend the market reach of IBM's "Websphere" software package, which in turn prompted an outreach from IBM to the Apache Group in 1998. Around the same time, IBM developers had been quietly experimenting with porting Linux to IBM's top-of-the-line mainframe, System 390. In December 1998 IBM chairman Lou Gerstner brought these strands together in a historic announcement of a company-wide initiative to bet on open-source software as a key part of the firm's strategy.[15]

Open source and open standards are, of course, quite different things, and there are many gradations of "openness" in both that matter a lot when it comes to the precise terms of property rights and usage rights. But the argument about intention and directionality once again was clear. IBM's GIE model would build on progressively more open standards in business processes, which in turn would enable "componentization," followed by seamless integration to build complex systems.

Here's what that awkward phrase means in plain language. When coordination becomes easy enough, it makes sense to seek out the "right" suppliers wherever they may be. But "right" isn't always the same as "absolute best." In some cases, the kind of flexibility this enables means that "good enough" suppliers may be the right business choice. One of the benefits of an open standard is that the system integrator doesn't need to place a huge bet on which is which—the costs of that bet are largely outsourced to the network of possible suppliers who are "bidding," in effect, to get into the production system.

This kind of coordination is probably easiest to envision in software. Imagine that you are creating, for a client business, a customer relationship manager package (CRM) that connects to a sales tracking system and a call-center management system. Open standards means that IBM could assess a customer's needs and put together an efficient solution that integrated an IBM piece of software with others' software (including de facto competitors' software, if that was the right component for the job), depending on what was suited for the particular use case. You could swap out components if and when needs change or when upgrades made sense. You could promise the ability to scale the system relatively easily if that need arose. And you could, as IBM, start to build "verticals" that created internal scale in particular components that you could use as part of a solution offered in custom configurations to many potential customers.

Much of that story would a decade later become obvious or close to it, as the modal business logic for cloud computing. In the early 2000s, it was inventive, nonobvious, and somewhat audacious, particularly for a company with the history and culture of IBM.

In sum, the foundation for the GIE had three pillars: the decline of economic nationalism along with liberalization of trade rules and evolution of intellectual property (IP) regimes (more on that particular IP issue later); massive reduction in coordination costs with the IT revolution and particularly B2B internet and Web; and standardized business processes enabling scale along with interoperability through open standards.

"WHEN EVERYTHING IS CONNECTED, WORK FLOWS"

It was a penetrating analysis of modern economic geography for the first decade of the twenty-first century—but what did it mean for IBM in its aspiration to reach the world? Palmisano put forward a bold answer to that question. It was at once an explanation for the quite radical changes in strategy, organization, and culture that IBM had been engaged in for the last several years; a rationale for pushing those changes further throughout IBM; and a call to action for other organizations to move in the same direction.

That last part could have been interpreted as either self-serving or self-immolating—after all, if you have the "secret" recipe for success on a complicated global stage, why share it with your competitors and why try to convince them to do it faster and more thoroughly? The answer (as I'll explain in more detail) is that IBM's view was bigger than a conventional corporate strategy seeking advantage in a well-known game. Its intention was a redefinition of the rules of the game. To be clear, it wasn't a naively positive-sum picture where somehow everyone would gain from the new model of competition. But it was an articulation of a system in which a rising tide could lift many boats at the same time and create an enormous amount of new economic value, which would also have the effect of advancing the underlying globalization pillars that enabled the GIE in the first place.

Put differently, the proposition was to establish a positive feedback loop between GIE value creation and the political-economic-technology landscape that made it possible. That may have been the greatest blind spot in the model, as the later part of this chapter and the next explain; but for now, let's stick with the upside and aspirational story about what the GIE would mean in practice.

The intellectual fulcrum was when everything is connected, work flows to where it will be done best. It sounds on the face of it like an unsophisticated globalization mantra, but think again.

Globalization in the previous decade—and really for about a hundred years prior—was a story about the causes and consequences of increasing mobility of goods, ideas, money, and people. For most of human history these things stayed quite close to where they were created. Mobility had been increasing gradually for some time, and the speed with which it increased rose dramatically toward the end of the twentieth century. But it was still a world of borders and barriers, and both the political economy and corporate strategy questions around globalization were about the interaction between mobility and borders.

In the language of *stock and flow,* it was still at least as much about the stock (what you own in a particular place) as it was about the flow (what is moving). The question of how much water there was in the bathtub remained at the center of the story, as compared to how much water was flowing out of the tap and down through the drain.

The radicalism of the GIE vision was to shift the focus directly and decisively from stocks to flows. When everything is connected, the flows of work become more central to value creation than the stocks of work—or factors of production—that you have on your balance sheet. Phrases like "integration of production and value delivery worldwide" take on real meaning. Work flows to where it can be done *best* supplants, at least in principle, the search for low-cost inputs and low-cost labor—where work can be done *cheaply.* And to repeat the point, firms organize on a global landscape not simply to gain access to markets but also to gain access to local talent and ideas, in order to serve the entire global market.

That is one reason why the phrase "emerging market" had to be rethought and ultimately replaced, since developing economies were more than markets in which to sell goods (or production locations in which to make goods cheaply). They were to be nodal parts of a global production network.

The simplest way to envision this was later articulated by Richard Baldwin: think of a factory that is distributed without regard to geography or borders, a factory that exists almost on a third plane elevated above physical space (a plane of flows, if you will). Then each "location," whether in the United States or India or Brazil or Indonesia, is like a machine within that factory.[16] No longer would you try to create economic clusters that produce a particular good or service and export it to the world. Instead, you'd seek to create specialized nodes in a global production network that was organized around a particular function. As Palmisano later put it, "Corporations are no longer simple collections of country-based subsidiaries, business units or product lines. Instead, many corporations have become an array of specialized *components:* procurement, manufacturing, research, sales, distribution, and so on."[17]

Michael Porter's classic competition model gets turned upside down here.[18] In Porter's cluster model, the region around Shenzhen would (at the limit) build consumer electronic devices for the global market. In the new model, a region around Bangalore might write device drivers for every IBM software package and for other firms' software packages as well.

The fundamental feature of GIE is decomposition of the value chain and the movement of pieces of it to anywhere in the world, where work can be done best. Work happens without regard to physical geography, and the products of work are coordinated by the GIE firm to serve a global marketplace.

Taken seriously, this is a radical proposition. A GIE firm should no longer be organized around concepts like business units or product lines. It should instead organize around functional components: manufacturing, research, sales, and the like; with each function serving the entire enterprise.

And once you pull together functions in this manner, the concept of "openness" comes to mean something different. It would be a natural next step to open each function up to a variety of collaborative relationships with different partners, including other firms. Thus you arrive naturally at an operational model of open innovation. Consider a concrete example where the human resources (HR) function is now a single massive vertical that covers all of IBM's employees around the world. Why not then offer HR services from that vertical to other firms, who have similarly decomposed their production networks along GIE lines?

More radically, why would you not invite competition from other firms *into* the components of your HR vertical? That competition could come from another firm; it could come from an open-source software community; it could be crowdsourced. It hardly matters where it comes from, it only matters what it can contribute. That is, of course, what open innovation is fundamentally about—the ability to mobilize assets that you neither own nor control for the purposes of value creation within your globally integrated enterprise.[19]

IBM's decision to locate its Global Business Solutions Center (GBSC) in Bangalore was an important signal. The Bangalore location certainly took advantage of the fast-growing domestic Indian market for IT services, but that was not its primary rationale. This initiative meant transforming what had been essentially a back-office support center into something much more pivotal and central to the GIE strategy. The GBSC was to be a business innovation hub for hardware, software, and consulting services and other new capabilities that would serve IBM's entire global business. And this meant significant investment in both funding and people, as well as reconfiguration of other parts of IBM's business so that teams around the world could effectively interface with and make use of the projects being carried out in Bangalore.[20]

The final element in this radical vision was about a new degree of alignment between firms and governments with regard to basic global public goods that underpin international order. These are the foundations that lie *beneath* standards, the nonrival and nonexcludable (thus public good) footings that stabilize the world political economy and make it possible for integration to proceed apace. Firms and governments were supposed to be clearly aligned now around basic goods like the absence of great-power conflict, freer trade, managing climate change, and pandemic preparedness. As with most public goods situations, not everyone could be expected to be on board—some would free-ride on the contributions of others, and some might even try to undermine public goods for the sake of short-term unilateral advantage. Economic and other kinds of nationalism didn't have to go all the way to a zero asymptote to make this work; it just needed to go far enough.

Call it "good-enough global public goods." Despite the measured language, this too was a pretty radical idea, at least in comparative historical terms. To assume even the most basic global public good, the avoidance of major war between great powers, would not have been a good bet for most of human history. And the GIE vision needed more than just that, even in the good-enough public goods articulation. It needed highly skilled talent, which is at least in part a product of education, much of which was going to be provided in the public sector by governments. It needed some basic global regime rules around the valuation and protection of IP, a huge hurdle in practice (about which more later). And somewhat more abstractly, it needed a sense of trust and confidence among the global business elite, a belief that governments would stay with the program for more than just a few years. And, of course, most importantly, that they would stay with it through both the ups and the downs of business cycles.

One last component of the GIE model—at least as important to the people who designed it as any of the others—was cultural. Global meant global to them, and IBM took that word very seriously as being different than globalizing or multinational or even transnational. The notion of a home country and host countries or foreign offices was going to be passé. I remember very clearly stepping on some toes in this regard, when in a conversation with some IBM senior executives around 2002 I referred to IBM as an "American transnational company." They corrected me politely but firmly. IBM, they said, was a global company, with headquarters that happened to be in Armonk, New York. I suspect the response would have been precisely the same if I had been at an IBM facility in Bangalore and remarked on the huge number of IBM employees working in India. Global meant global.

As a summary, the GIE meant the following:

- setting up functionally decomposed production systems without regard to physical geography
- moving the work around to where it can be done best
- integrating the resulting components, to serve a global market
- opening parts of the value chain to a variety of external partners
- making the most of interest alignment with governments around global public goods

In 2017 I asked several members of the original strategy team what they thought it was that had made this bold reconfiguration possible at that particular moment in IBM's history—in other words, not the longer-term causes and enablers but the immediate sources of the sense of urgency (and possibility) in Armonk. Some pointed to immediate macroeconomic drivers and particularly the fast growth of emerging markets not limited to China. Some pointed to the intense uptick in competitive pressure on IBM's access to conventional sources of talent, as Google and other Silicon Valley firms came into their own. Almost all pointed to the particular wisdom and courage of Palmisano as a CEO who was deeply grounded in the organizational values but not the current processes and ways of doing things at IBM. One person put it this way: "Sam was impatient with process, intolerant of processes that try to eliminate risk, he saw process as an evil necessity."[21] Others pointed to Palmisano's faith in pushing decisions downward within IBM to put greater choice and control in the hands of individual employees, in return asking them to take on greater responsibility for those choices and for their own ability to continuously deliver value to the enterprise.

The GIE concept and its strongest articulation might have been distinctive to IBM, but the general strategy ideas associated with it were more widely accepted and put into practice in various ways by other global firms. Take Procter and Gamble (P&G) as an example. The mid-1990s P&G—generally seen as the world's premier consumer products and branding organization—had been organized on a regional basis with production facilities and offices all over the world. Its GIE-style move in the late 1990s was to reorganize around product-based, global business units, each of which had global profit and loss (P&L) responsibility for the product. The firm also created a new "Global Business Services" organization to provide shared IT, HR, and data services, which in turn opened some of its verticals to external partners in the quest to lower costs and improve quality of service.[22]

P&G made a particularly bold and public push to open its research and development (R&D) processes to external partners. The firm went out of its way to report that more than a third of new products had involved outside R&D partners, and that the new-product success rate had concurrently risen to 90 percent (from 70 percent) in the period 2001 to 2007. The organizational change seemed to be paying off: after an average annual net earnings per share rise of 5 percent between 1997 and 2000, earnings increased 17 percent annually between 2001 and 2006.

The Mexico-based building-materials company CEMEX was another important example. Heavy building materials like cement and concrete are mostly too low in their value-to-weight ratio to export at scale, but the business processes and the knowledge that enable the production and delivery of those materials in exactly the right way at exactly the right time to building sites around the world are a perfect substrate for the GIE model.[23]

CEMEX pursued its GIE strategy mainly through acquisitions in foreign markets and particularly through a distinctive postmerger integration process that came to be known as "the CEMEX way."[24] That meant the familiar goal of standardizing business processes, technologies, and organizational structures across geographies.

But more importantly it also captured a method of integrating knowledge from acquired companies into the CEMEX system as a whole. Following acquisition of a foreign firm, CEMEX would send a newly formed ad hoc integration team, made up of functional experts drawn from existing CEMEX operations around the world, to visit the newly acquired company for weeks or months in order to do two things. The team was responsible for bringing CEMEX's standardized business practices to the new acquisition, as is generally the case with postmerger integrations everywhere. But the team was also explicitly tasked to identify practices *from* the acquired companies which could be brought back to CEMEX as a whole and incorporated across the global enterprise.

One industry observer estimated that something like fifteen to thirty practices per acquisition were judged superior to existing CEMEX practices and were then brought back into the center and distributed out to the firm as a whole. That's a small but significant number, and as one analyst noted it sent the message to the acquired firm that "we are overriding your business processes to get you quickly on board, but within the year we are likely to take some part of your process, adapt it to the CEMEX system, and roll it out across operations in [multiple] countries."[25] Like P&G's emphasis on the percentage of new products coming from R&D partners outside P&G itself, CEMEX was proud to estimate that something like 70 percent of its business practices and systems had been adopted from acquisitions.[26]

A THEORETICAL INTERLUDE ON THE MODERN DEVELOPMENTAL STATE

With so much emphasis on the GIE's IT underpinnings and the globalization narrative, it's important to step back for a bit and situate the model within a workable concept of the contemporary state. In 2006 that might have seemed a retrograde argument, because most of what one needed to understand about the state was commonly thought to be subsumed into the logic of globalization. With 20/20 hindsight it's easy to see that this was wrong. It was possible to see it back then as well, if you just looked closely at the oversimplified premise, that there was somehow a zero-sum relationship between the state and globalization.

Put differently: the (faulty) premise was that what globalization gained, the state would lose. Or that the progress of the global economy would come at the expense of state influence and state power. It wasn't so. The basis of the Reagan-Thatcher neoliberal state synthesis was that societies needed the discipline of the market to control and constrain national politics, but that was necessary precisely because national politics were still very much in play. (This in contrast to the social welfare state synthesis of the pre-1980 period, where political systems were supposed to control and constrain markets, largely through regulation, for the good of society.) States were central pieces of the globalization puzzle, and the GIE needed a particular kind of state carrying out a range of functions to enable its evolution and growth on the global stage. This section lays out the rationale for the GIE developmental state.

But wait a minute—doesn't the term "developmental state" call up an image of the 1970s state-led Asian Tigers, the South Korea/Taiwan-style sprint up the industrial ladder? The developmental state of that era was fundamentally about two things: capital accumulation needed for industrial development, and interpersonal ties between key state institutions and a modernizing elite that made up a narrow but crucial part of society. Capable, meritocratic, and (relatively) noncorrupt public bureaucracies were the linchpin, enabling governments to convince business elites that they were committed to a long-term economic growth project, not short-term extraction of rents. That, in turn, supported close ties with the private capitalist elite of entrepreneurs who took that conviction as a collective national good and built on it, to mobilize accumulated capital for investments in industrial growth. This is what Peter Evans called "embeddedness." The opposite side of the equation was "autonomy"—the developmental state had to remain sufficiently robust and independent to avoid political capture by the private capitalist elite, who might have otherwise slipped into their own rent-seeking and consumption rather than capital accumulation for longer-term developmental goals. Thus, "embedded autonomy."[27]

This developmental state model was successful in some respects, in limited circumstances for a few select countries and for a particular moment of the global economy. The many qualifiers in that sentence are intentional. By the time of the East Asian Tigers' rise, the underlying conditions that had made their rise possible were already corroding. Manufacturing was beginning to show signs of the productivity explosion that would become a much greater challenge in the twenty-first century (more on this in Chapter 4)—the challenge of productivity growth outpacing demand and thus leading to a reduction in employment (as with agriculture a century earlier). In South Korea, the manufacturing sector peaked at around 25 percent of the workforce in the early 1990s and declined from there as manufacturing productivity rose (in contrast, from 1840 to 1940 Britain's manufacturing sector employed more than a third of the workforce). This was never going to be big enough to create on a global basis the kind of middle class that had been the American Dream and to some extent a reality during the 1950s and 1960s in the United States and the industrialized North.

And it was also vulnerable on political grounds. As compelling as it was for students of economic development to observe political institutions and bureaucracies that could overcome short-term rent seeking and corruption dynamics to set collective goals for a country, it was equally true that the formula for doing so required financial and political repression of most of society other than that small swathe of capitalist elites. Labor, for example, had to be "convinced" to participate in this long-term project of capital accumulation and wealth creation. Other elements of civil society had simply to be excluded. These ingredients of the equation were sometimes seen as necessary evils, a kind of coerced societal investment in a better long-term future for the very people that were the (short-term) subjects of repression.

This dynamic (and the ambivalence of academics who studied it) was captured in the two acronyms that were often used to describe this version of the developmental state. One was to call them NICS, which stood in a plain vanilla fashion for "newly industrializing countries." The other and more descriptive acronym was BAIRS—"bureaucratic authoritarian industrializing regimes."

The twenty-first-century developmental state consistent with the GIE model was obviously going to have to be a different animal. What academic economists called new growth theory was now the basis of the argument.[28] The fundamental tenet of new growth theory was to put ideas rather than land, labor, and capital at the center of the growth and productivity equation. It was going to be changes in the stock of ideas, rather than stocks of traditional factors of production, that would drive economic growth. The ability to generate and circulate ideas but even more importantly to sort out good ideas from bad ideas (about which much more later) would be a critical determinant of competitive advantage. In that story, growth would be much more dependent on human capital and knowledge, the accumulation of good ideas more so than traditional capital accumulation.

Innovation was the linchpin—the use of ideas, both new and recombinant, in the service of creating new value (my definition). The point was that to throw more land, labor, capital, or energy into an existing production process had run up against limits, including but not only limits on how much carbon the Earth's ecosystem could absorb. In contrast, the economic potential of ideas might be unlimited. It was certainly in part about the value of intangible assets made up essentially of ideas—things like brands and images and even software-defined goods like badges and tokens in video games. But it was also about the application of ideas to very conventional production processes making heavy things that you could drop on your foot. After all, any reasonably complicated factory production line would have thousands to millions of actions coordinated with each other before the widget came out at the end of the line. A very big good idea could generate an entirely new way of making the widget. A big good idea could remove a million unnecessary steps. An incremental good idea might apply to any single one of those discrete actions and improve that tiny little step in the process—and once you change and improve one production step, that might open up new possibilities for improving others. Ad infinitum. . . .

The stretch toward infinity is precisely the point—there are, in principle, no limits to this kind of innovation-led growth. The limits in practice were set by the ability of human beings to generate ideas, separate good from bad ideas, and incorporate the good ones. The GIE developmental state needed first and foremost to do the things that markets would not do by themselves to support that ability. Two functions then seemed paramount. The first was the perennial public good, education. It wasn't just that better educated people would be advantaged and get better jobs in the knowledge economy; it's that educated people were its lifeblood.

The second and more controversial function was the provision and enforcement of an IP rights regime. If ideas were the most important source of value, the creators of ideas (whether they be people or firms or anything else) would seem to need some incentives to invest in their creation. That need became acute when the ideas in question could be expressed or encoded in digital form, because that, of course, made possible instantaneous and infinite copying.

The precise terms of IP protection were and remain highly debatable, and they were in fact debated at length in theoretical terms, as well as in practical terms regarding enforcement particularly across national borders. I'll have much more to say about the nature of these debates and how they evolved later. The immediate point is that any IP regime and particularly an IP regime in a digital era is almost necessarily a political undertaking, now of critical importance to the GIE synthesis.[29]

The GIE developmental state had other interesting possibilities, such as subsidies for R&D that could increase economic growth rates by boosting incentives for innovation; or economic cluster-enhancing policies that would improve the conditions for positive externalities and spillover effects among firms, which in turn would accelerate learning and improve overall performance in the all-important separation of good and bad ideas. These were nice-to-haves, not must-haves, and were mainly expressed as opportunities for developing countries to accelerate their growth rates and become even more attractive locations.

After all, if works flows to where it can be done best, then investments that help create a location where work can in fact be done best (not necessarily most quickly, most cheaply, or even most efficiently in a narrow sense) are good investments. But if you were a person naturally skeptical of public-sector development schemes, or ideologically suspicious of government, or just looking for minimum viable politics to support the GIE scheme, then all of this was actually very good news. Because what the GIE story actually *needed* from the state was comparatively minimal: support for education and a sensible global IP rights regime.

Unspoken in that equation was a kind of trust in the sustainability of even those relatively minimal public goods. Aspiring GIE firms would obviously need to believe that these enabling conditions weren't subject to short-term political reversals, or liable to be undermined by the success of the GIE model itself over time. It seemed like a workable agenda, not too much for the political ideology of the time to bear at least in some countries . . . and if you really believed in the basic logic of the model, then you could reasonably conclude that GIE success would reinforce the sociopolitical foundations for the public goods functions of the GIE developmental state. A positive feedback loop of sorts is what every economic growth model seeks, and the optimistic case for the GIE model was that it had landed on a realistic one.

With 20 / 20 hindsight, it's easy to see where this went wrong. To unravel that story and explore precisely how it was connected to the GIE model itself is the task of Chapter 4. But it's important to note that the proponents of the GIE even in 2006 weren't starry-eyed. They saw at least some of the vulnerabilities and volatile assumptions that were in play within the model.

YOU WOULD HAVE TO BELIEVE . . .

A good way to think about the strategic coherence of a model is to continually ask yourself this question: what do you need to believe, in order to believe that your next move in accordance with this model is in fact a rational one? The GIE model was sufficiently well articulated that to apply this test was relatively straightforward, and the basic dependencies were quite clear at the time.

To believe in the GIE model, you would have to believe that early 2000s-style globalization was fundamentally robust. More precisely, that talent, capital, and information flows would continue to grow in an increasingly unconstrained fashion. And that the internet would be an increasingly open network through which those flows would pass. Trade would almost have to continue its seemingly inexorable march upward as a percentage of global GDP. And the obvious friction makers—things like security initiatives, terrorism, war, and major cultural backlash—would remain mainly in the background, even as they surfaced occasionally and episodically in particular places and discrete events.

The key to success would be to see those episodic surfacings for what they were, and not to panic or overreact about the alternative interpretation: that these were harbingers of a deeper globalization halt. A more general way to see this assumption would be to say that the GIE model depends on IT having a relatively low *political* profile and mainly a positive one. Governments would be customers more so than regulators. The IT sector would be seen principally as a source of economic growth not first and foremost as a source of military power or national security risk and advantage. Being deeply embroiled in political, cultural, and, of course, national security issues would start to put real pressure on this assumption (and if it today seems naive to have held the belief that IT could maintain that kind of splendid isolation, remember my earlier recounting of why it did not seem so naive in the context of the early 2000s).

To believe in the GIE model, you would have to hold the related belief that IT would continue to be a massive driver of economic growth and productivity. Part of the reason you'd have to believe that is because it allows you to have confidence in the notion that customers of IT and IT-related services would continue to bear the lion's share of the risks associated with IT investments because the upside was so big. That was never a fact of nature—it's just as possible to imagine sharing risk in different ways. Or for that matter putting most of the risk on the supplier. IBM's customers could have said, "If you are confident that your business-process outsourcing systems will save us $100 million a year, why don't you pay for the systems to be put in place, and then you can take

75 percent of the savings as your ongoing revenue from it and we'll pocket the other 25 percent?" You'd also have to believe that the magnetism of IT-enabled growth would keep supply chains relatively open and global—and that just-in-time and just-right-for-purpose would continue to dominate "just-in-case" and "lots-of-backup" mind-sets around sourcing and supply chains.

These beliefs are neither mutually exclusive nor comprehensively exhaustive. They overlap in some respects. And there were certainly other identifiable shocks that could have sent the GIE model into a downward spiral (for example, a massive technical failure of the underlying internet architecture or the like). The point of this kind of exercise is not to identify everything that can go wrong; it is to identify the most fundamental assumptions and systematic sources of potential failure, and then assess whether you can take those as just-given-enough to proceed. In the early 2000s, IBM's answer and the answer of many other aspiring global organizations was "yes."

Was the GIE model all just a naively hopeful castle in the air? I didn't think so at the time, and I still don't think so. Some of what undermined the model came from outside its realistic purview, shocks that could reasonably be labeled exogenous and thus a kind of unfortunate historical accident. But not all. The GIE model did have within it intrinsic contradictions that started to surface faster than almost anyone could have expected. These are the subject of Chapter 4.

4

WHAT WENT WRONG?

IN FEBRUARY 2007 I was invited to organize and facilitate in Salzburg a scenario thinking exercise for a group of national trade negotiators and World Trade Organization (WTO) officials who were meeting offsite away from the daily bustle of Geneva. Their goal was to generate behind-the-scenes momentum for a final push that would get the Doha round trade deal over the goal line after six years of grueling negotiations. The mood was mainly positive and hopeful, in part because of the proximity of this meeting to the annual World Economic Forum enclave, which had just a few weeks earlier highlighted completion of the Doha round as a priority next move for the business / government elite that coordinates at Davos.

My job was explicitly not to be a Doha cheerleader; most of the people in Salzburg had their fill of that kind of stuff, and some of them were cheerleaders themselves. I was asked instead to help the delegates develop coherent logical scenarios of what could go wrong, and then use those scenarios to wind-tunnel and fortify the positive policy and negotiating agendas, in order to make them more robust and increase the chances of getting it right and closing the deal. I brought with me Naazneen Barma, one of my most talented Berkeley PhD students, a woman of Indian ethnicity who had grown up in Hong Kong (and whose father had lost his senior government position in the handover to China because of his ethnic origin). She had gone to college at Stanford, worked in the interim as an economic development specialist for the World Bank in Laos and Cambodia, and more—a person who had lived firsthand a broad swathe of the vectors of global integration that for many government officials were still abstract forces. We wanted to use her intelligence combined with her experience to keep it real, or at least that's what we had hoped would happen.

In fact, none of it worked. The group devoted a full day to the scenario exercise and, predictably given the quality of the people assembled, developed smart and insightful scenario arguments that could have formed the basis for better strategies going forward. But from an advisory perspective it was a complete failure—because those arguments were simply put aside and ignored come the very next morning. It was my worst nightmare as a consultant. My clients had used the work simply to make themselves feel better about their existing approach by reassuring themselves that they had considered alternatives, and then they left all possible lessons of that behind. To make it even worse, Naazneen and I were then socially ostracized, as if we had somehow been the bearers of bad news. The meeting devolved from that point mostly into familiar tactical stuff about the intricate negotiations, which struck me at the time as a bit sad and a lost opportunity but not really a tragedy.

What was tragic was the closing speech of the conference. A leading official (I won't name this person here) stood up and made a "see no evil, speak no evil, hear no evil" argument for free trade in almost exactly these words: our strategy is that we just have to keep telling ourselves and everyone else that the Doha round is good and that the world will be a better place for everyone when the deal is done. If we hear any doubters, we simply have to say the same thing over and over again even more loudly and more forcefully. Confront questions with assertions, was this person's call to action.

It was a very long flight home. To make it a little less painful, Naazneen and I wrote a memo for the organizers that tried, one more time, to make plain and evocative arguments about where the Doha round had gone off track and how it could be revitalized.[1] We reminded everyone that the trade round had originally been called the "Doha Development Agenda" and that the "development" aspect had somehow been lost in the years of negotiating process. We argued that the reigning idea of a "single undertaking"—a trade deal that would achieve balance across all issue areas in one master stroke—was inconsistent with a modern dynamic view of economic change, and thus while it might be simpler in principle to negotiate, it risked locking in cross-sectoral, cross-silo bargains in an unsustainable (and potentially unfair) manner. We called attention to the participants' own articulation in the scenarios of growing economic nationalism and asked what the Doha round was going to do about that. We pointed to the embeddedness of trade in security, environmental, and technology pressures, and called out the lack of attention to these cross-cutting issues in the existing negotiations. And, finally, commenting on the opening keynote speech that was delivered to the group by Pascal Lamy, Director-General of the WTO at the time, we wrote,

> Lamy's message—that we all know the right "technical" details of the deal, and the stumbling block is the "politics"—may be an instrumentally useful argument for the next few months in getting to a deal, but is a risky attitude on which to build the foundation of a sustainable trade regime. "Asking for forgiveness not permission" is not a forward looking strategic approach. It might have been plausible fifteen years ago (leaving aside the question of whether it is ethically or politically responsible). It is no longer plausible in the hyper-politicized domestic and international political environments in which we live today.

And that was 2007.

Writing the memo made us feel a little bit better and made the flight home more tolerable. We sent it to the meeting organizers and a few trusted companions, and received some polite thank you notes in response. But it too failed utterly to change anyone's mind or anyone's actions. There's little solace in having been right on the arguments when we couldn't get anyone to listen.

It was about nine years later that Sam Palmisano wrote a compelling retrospective on his globally integrated enterprise (GIE) argument for *Foreign Affairs*.[2] (It's worth emphasizing that Palmisano published this piece in October 2016, roughly a month *prior* to the election of Donald Trump as president of the United States.) Much had changed in the intervening years, and a few things hadn't. The Doha round was still in limbo, de facto not even on life support anymore but just plain dead.³ Economic nationalism had come visibly to the fore in mass politics and in several major political regimes around the world. The global financial crisis (GFC) had undermined confidence in the technocratic consensus that we had hit our heads against so painfully in Salzburg. Security, environmental, technology, and other pressures were bearing down on the foundations of the GIE's sociopolitical order. And while some global enterprises (particularly those at the upper echelons of the IT sector) seemed to maintain social license to "ask forgiveness not permission," that kind of freedom and flexibility was a wistful memory for most big firms.

Palmisano's diagnosis of what had gone wrong was and remains penetrating. At the highest level, he argued that the GIE story he told a decade earlier had spawned imbalances that built up below the threshold of attention and were not managed by business or government alone, and certainly not by a coalition of both together. One of his most trenchant observations was about a failure of corporate strategy leadership, that the GIE model had been narrowed and distorted by short-term strategies and a lack of vision.

> Over the last ten years, many managers have responded to the challenging economic environment by focusing on just one element of the Globally Integrated Enterprise model: reducing costs by optimizing existing structures and arrangements. Other elements, such as pursuing growth and increasing agility (which could help accelerate scaling up, market entry, product design, and most importantly reach and satisfy new demand) were mostly ignored.⁴

The article goes on to say that the digital and physical worlds had become increasingly connected in practice but were still treated by most firms as separate realms with their own distinctive rules. And while technology had indeed brought diverse generations, communities, nationalities, and perspectives into much closer contact with each other, the results of that contact had created more friction and conflict than they had understanding and integration. Put those elements together, and the GIE model was in real trouble by 2016.

Palmisano put forward in his article some rough and general elements of an agenda to rescue it. But reading the piece objectively, one wonders whether he himself believed it could be saved. Ending with a call for "enlightened leaders to develop and continually modernize models for business and government" as the necessary corrective didn't inspire great confidence in the fall of 2016 and it doesn't inspire great confidence now.

If the GIE model was right but only for a decade or less, that would make it a historical anomaly as the global reach model with the shortest life span by far. The question this chapter must answer is why. Why was its season so short?

The answer ought not to focus on assigning blame. But it is fair game to ask, was business at fault? Was government at fault? Was it a failure of coordination between the two, or a failure to agree on a division of labor in responding to looming imbalances (which in a classic shirking manner, governments might see as business model issues for firms, and firms as policy issues for governments)? Did the GIE transformation move too quickly for societies to handle—or perhaps not quickly enough to get over the inevitable rough experiences of transition? Had global integration gone too far—or perhaps not far enough, leaving itself stuck in the "dangerous middle"?[5]

Whatever went wrong, the higher-level question has to be, was it endogenous to the model itself, a logical consequence of the GIE that proponents had simply failed to foresee? Or was it possibly a story about historical accidents—exogenous forces—that fell outside the scope that any reasonable model could address?

Unraveling these arguments is more than an exercise in historical counterfactuals. And even if it were only that, the relevant counterfactuals are complicated to parse and would be harder still if not impossible to validate. For example, it's an intriguing question as to whether the GIE model would have performed better minus the GFC of 2008–2009. But is it possible to logically construct an alternative history that includes the GIE model but not the GFC—or are the two interlinked as particular manifestations of some of the same underlying causes?

Some economic historians have argued that what should have been a moderate downturn in the autumn of 2008 was tipped into a historic crisis by a policy mistake: the failure to bail out Lehman Brothers. If so, perhaps a different outcome (with a bailout and a much less severe crisis) can be constructed as plausible alternative history. Maybe . . . but it's a long road from that already somewhat heroic counterfactual to a consequence counterfactual history where the GIE survives and thrives as the predominant model of global reach. It would be a weak foundation for what matters most, which is to take the lessons of failure and transfer them to what comes next as a strategy for global reach.[6]

In any case the point of this chapter is not to try to rescue the GIE model with counterfactual histories. It is to better understand what went wrong in the actual history, in order to develop a new model that is optimized for the next decade as the GIE was for its decade. And as an aspiration, to design a model that is set up at least as far as we can logically see, to reinforce its own foundations, not undermine them as it moves forward.

A GLOBAL FACTORY

The place to start is with Richard Baldwin's pathbreaking analysis of globalization's "second unbundling," an argument he developed in a 2011 paper and later expanded in a 2016 book.[7] I say this because in all the massive writing about globalization and its impact on the world economy, Baldwin's work provides the single best big-picture argument and lens for assessing what the GIE model could and could not be expected within reason to achieve. He may not have intended it for that purpose. The 2016 book is titled *The Great Convergence* because it is first and foremost concerned with explaining the catch-up in share of world income and particularly in share of manufacturing by emerging economies to developed economies in the last two decades, and the economic development strategies available to countries as they seek to grow within that context. But his core insights about the modern phenomenon of "unbundling" and the metaphor of the "global factory" which it reveals will tell us a lot about why the GIE was such an attractive idea, and also a lot about why it fell apart so quickly.

The "first unbundling" in Baldwin's parlance is what most people in-tuit when they think about the globalization process: the gradual sepa-ration in space (geography) of production and consumption, which was enabled by increased mobility of goods, ideas, money, and people.[8] It's important to keep in mind (again) that for most of human history, life in general and economic activity in particular were largely concentrated in small geographic spaces. People had little if any interaction with others outside of a tens-of-miles radius from where they lived. As transport got cheaper, that radius began to expand and as it did so production and consumption unbundled from each other. It became possible for people to consume things that were made somewhere far away, and producers could sell at scale what they made in markets beyond the village or city in which they made them. Modern trade and the first generation of glo-balization were the incremental results.

But (as Baldwin highlights powerfully) through much of the twen-tieth century the *relative changes* in mobility of goods, ideas, money, and people were very uneven. The price of moving goods and in some cases money across large distances fell dramatically, while the costs of moving people and ideas fell much less. Because ideas and the people who car-ried them in their heads stayed closer to home, innovation tended to cluster in self-reinforcing pockets of concentrated activity, which in turn enjoyed increasing economies of scale in production. The formula for the first unbundling was made up of low trade costs and high commu-nication costs. Put these ingredients together and you have a simple recipe for the twentieth-century model of industrial clusters in a rela-tively small number of places, that serve much larger markets through scale production and export.

Now fast-forward to the internet era where the cost of moving ideas suddenly falls, even faster and more dramatically than had happened earlier with goods. It becomes possible in principle not only to divide up complex activities into discrete pieces, but also to coordinate many of those pieces at a distance from each other by communicating about them instantly and nearly for free. Innovation spurred by new ideas doesn't have to stay anywhere in particular. It can move, most inter-estingly in the 1990s and early 2000s, to places where the cost of labor is relatively low (because the mobility of people remains relatively constrained, both by national law and resistance to immigration, as well as the primordial desire of most human beings to stay close to their language, culture, and religious and family roots).

This is the formula for Baldwin's "second unbundling"—the creation of global value chains, which can just as easily be thought of as taking apart a physical factory and putting various pieces of it in different locations around the world without much regard for distance or borders. In the new economic geography, you would no longer think about "competitiveness" as a characteristic that attaches to a country. You would think instead about competition between international production networks delineated in turn by the functions and the organizations that coordinate them.

IBM's GIE model maps directly onto this landscape. Baldwin provides a sports analogy that makes the point elegantly:

> Imagine two soccer clubs sitting down to discuss an exchange of players. If a trade actually occurs, both teams will gain. Each gets a type of player they really needed in exchange for a type of player they needed less. [That's the first unbundling and the rationale for the traditional political economy of globalization.]
>
> Now consider a very different type of exchange. Suppose on the weekends, the coach of the better team starts to train the worse team. The outcome of this will surely make the league more competitive overall and it will surely help the worse team. But it is not at all sure that the best team will win from this exchange—even though their coach will profit handsomely from being able to sell his know-how to two teams instead of one.[9]

And thus the logic of the GIE as "coach."

The analogy is a bit imperfect in an important way with regard to the advantages that still can accrue to the better team. The better team is almost certainly better for a number of reasons, not just because it has a better coach. Possibly it learns faster as a team from experience as the game evolves. Likely its players can adjust more quickly and comfortably to unexpected and surprising plays that other teams might try. And if the system is working well, the coach isn't just transferring knowledge in one direction—bringing ideas from the better team to the not-as-good team. She is also bringing new ideas back home from what she learns in the process of training a not-as-talented team in a different playing environment.

The general claim looks like this: if we are in a game that is highly contextual and the playbook evolves through practice and exposure to all kinds of different competition and field conditions and so on, then in the course of training the not-so-good team, the coach is going to learn some very important things about her own playbook. These are things that she can bring back to her home (better) team to make it *even* better, and do so faster, than others.

It's a lot like the logic of open-source software business models in this respect. The source code may be available to everyone, but deep expertise and diverse experience with implementation and execution in different contexts are major competitive advantages. The GIE by analogy plays on a global landscape but even if its "source code" equivalent is open, that does not mean that every piece of the global factory is going to be equally competitive and equally able to create outsized value by using it. That said, it still ought to be a better deal for the less developed parts of the world than was the first unbundling, since the combination of excellent know-how and ideas with low-wage labor (or what IBM in its GIE model called good-enough human capital) should produce excellent growth and returns in locations that become attractive to the GIE. And that is exactly what Baldwin's model describes.

In practice, the most attractive locations weren't actually that many. They still needed in most cases to be close—an easy airplane flight—to the home enterprise. That was because of what we all know intuitively: the internet for all its communication-cost savings was still not able to transmit efficiently the kind of tacit knowledge, experience, and trust that comes from face-to-face interactions among managers and technicians. And so these people still had to travel on a regular basis among the key nodes in the cross-national production network. India was the notable exception in large part because the business services in which it specialized were less dependent on tacit knowledge transfer. But even if a relatively small number of *countries* benefited directly from the second unbundling, they were big ones—including China, of course—which means that a very large number of *people* (roughly half the world's population) were part of it.

And for those who weren't, there were still knock-on growth benefits, in part via the "commodity super-cycle" that was the result of booming demand for raw materials in the growing industrializers. There was a saying in the late 1990s that went like this: everything China makes is getting cheaper, and everything China uses is getting more expensive. And China was using lots of raw materials—food, fuel, metals, minerals, chemicals, cement, and the like—both as inputs to its factories and as development, growth, and building materials for its cities and infrastructure. Many locations in sub-Saharan Africa, for example, might not have been immediately integrated into cross-national production networks as machines in the global factory. But they still benefited greatly from selling raw materials to feed that factory at prices that were multiples of what would have otherwise been the case.

This sounds like a pretty sustainable system on the face of it. Of course, no positive feedback loop runs forever, and it's certain that the GIE model on this landscape would have run into limits eventually. But if you can pretend for a moment as if you didn't know what actually happened in the next decade and place yourself back around 2006, you can probably capture the feeling of excitement and optimism that this narrative engendered. A rising tide never really lifts *all* boats and not equally, but this could reasonably have felt like something close to the rising tide that would have come as close to that as possible, and certainly closer than any other model for global reach in modern history.

In his 2016 book Baldwin does an exemplary job of summarizing in six key points how the second unbundling helped to create a new economic geography for the early twenty-first century. Some of these arguments will reappear later and in more detail as sources of instability, but for now a very high-level summary looks like this:

- National economies are impacted with a "higher degree of resolution," creating a very complex and unpredictable scatterplot of winners and losers.

- The rate of change is much faster, undergoing a kind of accelerating acceleration along with the pace of information and data technology (IDT).
- The importance of competitive advantage attached to *countries* (as I discussed earlier) declines, with competitive advantage increasingly becoming a function of global firms.
- The "social contract" or "compact" between rich-country workers and rich-country firms comes under pressure, or simply ruptures.
- The role of physical distance changes but doesn't disappear, because the internet can move bits instantaneously but not people, and not highly contextual ideas.
- Government economic policy options that worked during the twentieth century don't work in the same way, and new modes of regulation and intervention need to be developed.

This certainly sounds like a challenging landscape for firms, governments, workers, investors . . . everyone to adapt to. *But there's no logical reason or necessity why that adaptation was doomed to fail.*

For example, a higher resolution scatterplot of winners and losers might at first glance seem like a harder political-economy problem to manage. But it certainly doesn't have to be. Instead of an entire region (say, the "old industrial Midwest of the United States") undergoing decline, the new landscape might have both winners and losers arrayed in the same geography. Instead of a particular sector (say, consumer electronics) or a particular skill group (say, machine tool operators) undergoing broad decline, the new landscape might have some winners and losers in both categories. It's true that policies aimed at helping losers would need to be more granular and nuanced in this setting, but is that really an impossible task for governments to manage? And isn't it equally possible that the unpredictability of impact itself would foster greater political willingness to act?

As Baldwin puts it, "No matter what sector you work in, you cannot really be sure that your job won't be the next to suffer or benefit from globalization."[10] That is actually as close to John Rawls's "original position" view from *A Theory of Justice* as we are likely to get in this world.[11] If you cannot know from behind the new globalization's de facto veil of ignorance whether you will be a winner or a loser, you might very well find your rational self-interest pointing toward a more accommodating social welfare stance. You might be less likely to point a finger of blame at losers who can't keep up and less likely to conclude that it is their own personal failure.

It's obvious with 20/20 hindsight that this isn't what happened. But that is precisely what needs to be explained and understood, and without the fatalistic sense of inevitability that is not really justified by either theory or history.

SYSTEM FAILURE

The GIE system did not have a single point of failure: it had many. It's tempting to try to isolate from that story a single master variable of sorts and describe a causal chain with one big link that we could claim "if not for" the failure of that big link, the chain might have very well held together. Tempting, but most probably wrong. If you are a fan of using the mnemonic STEEPM (social, technical, economic, environmental, political, military) to keep a checklist of the range of variables that might be in play, then what stands out from the actual story is that four of the six categories held important points of failure. And even the two exceptions—environment and military—might have come into play in a longer-run history of GIE had we gotten there. Put differently, it's a reasonable speculation that carbon accumulation and traditional geopolitical conflict might have become rate-limiting functions for the GIE in the 2020s or 2030s—but neither really constrained the GIE in the 2010s. What did get in the way was a range of the other four elements—social, technological, economic, and political variables—and in a complex mix. In the rest of this chapter I isolate three key points of intersection that together doomed the GIE model.

If there is a single big theme that unites those three points in a narrative of failure, it's this simple statement: the system couldn't bear the tensions and stressors that the GIE model placed on it. GIE asked too much too soon of political economy, of individual human beings, and ultimately of the internet infrastructure itself.

Hypercompetition

The political-economy part of this narrative was signaled by the increasing use of the phrase "hypercompetition" during the early and mid-2000s.[12] It sounds like one of those banal phrases that grace the covers of airport bookstore books, and it was certainly that . . . but it also captured something quite real about the lived experience of many senior managers during this period.

There's no precise definition, but what hypercompetition came to mean was a combination of speed and intensity on shifting market playing fields that add up to *unsustainable competitive advantage.* There might have been some quick wins by fast-moving firms, but no real long-term wins and no chance to rest, recoup, and enjoy a bit of outsized profits. Here's an indicative description of the feeling that the phrase was trying to capture: "executives have watched the intensity and type of competition in their industries shift during the last few years. Industries have changed from slow moving, stable oligopolies to environments characterized by intense and rapid competitive moves, in which competitors strike quickly with unexpected, unconventional means of competing."[13] There's more than a little of the "good old days" nostalgia motif here, capturing the desire of every generation to believe that it uniquely is undergoing the greatest, fastest, most dramatic transformations of all time. It mimics some of the 1990s international politics rhetoric, where pundits and scholars alike indulged in a (bizarre) nostalgia for the supposed good old days of the Cold War when things were simple and clear.[14] But with all that in mind, hypercompetition did capture something real about the lived experience that people were feeling at the moment.

The disconnect was that despite the breathless excitement of the business press and academics talking and writing about hypercompetition, it was not an experience that almost anyone really wanted to live within for very long. And so the biggest and most successful firms, largely but not exclusively coming out of the tech sector, began to find ways to escape, much as Joseph Schumpeter argued would happen almost seventy years earlier.[15] Later I will present some arguments that seek to break out and assess the various means of escape, but for the moment a single piece of evidence describes what actually happened: a small number of very successful firms pulled away from everyone else and earned profits way above anything that would have been consistent with the expectations of hypercompetition.

A 2015 paper by Jason Furman and Peter Orszag presents the data this way.[16] They assess return on invested capital defined as net after-tax operating profits divided by capital invested in the firm, measured on publicly traded nonfinancial US firms from 1965 to 2014.[17] And what they find is that the top decile of firms started around 2001 to pull away dramatically from everyone else, topping out at a return on invested capital of nearly 100 percent.

Return on invested capital of almost 100 percent doesn't sound a lot like what should happen in a hypercompetitive market. If you go down to the 75th percentile, performance drops a bit, but even there firms earn between 30 and 40 percent return on invested capital. What's more, the firms that show up in the upper parts of the distribution tend to stay there over time. (Furman and Orszag point out that of the firms that showed a return greater than 25 percent in 2003, 85 percent *still* show a return of over 25 percent ten years later. In other words, the winners are mostly staying in the winning camp.) If hypercompetition means unsustainable competitive advantage, it surely wasn't an accurate description of the reality that these firms were living through.

Precisely why this is happening—for example, whether super-normal returns are justified by the super-normal risk these firms are taking—is debatable. But the phenomenon itself really is not. Two-thirds of the nonfinancial firms that earned more than 45 percent on invested capital between 2010 and 2014 were either in IT or health care, so there is at least some relationship to particular sectors—but only the first of these can plausibly be said to generate outsized productivity growth.

The bottom line is that there is some relationship to consolidation and market power as a means of escaping hypercompetition. Among all the fascination with startup businesses and disruption and the like that dominated popular discourse, a new recognition began to surface in the data that corporate America was actually becoming *more* concentrated.[18] The *Economist* in 2016 looked at just under nine hundred sectors of the US economy and found that fully two-thirds of them were more concentrated in 2012 than in 2007; and that the four leading firms in these sectors saw their weighted average share rise from about 26 percent to 32 percent.[19] Just under 10 percent of the US economy lay in industries where the top four firms held more than two-thirds of sales. Global return on capital for US companies overall was, at around 16 percent, higher than it had been in forty years; and profits as percentage of GDP were at or near their all-time high. At the other end of the size continuum, new business formation has actually declined over the past thirty years (despite the popular hype about startups).[20]

That also doesn't look on the face of it much like hypercompetition. There certainly is a robust debate to be had about why concentration has been increasing. It may be partly the result of political influence such as lobbying, regulatory capture, and other nonmarket behaviors. It may be partly a secondary consequence of the power of large institutional investors. It may be partly the result of network effects in particular industries. Of course, it could reflect a period of extraordinary innovation and risk taking that is rewarded with outsized profits at least for a time. But it is almost certainly not *only* a return on innovation, as evidenced by the widespread sectoral preponderance of both higher profits and merger and acquisition activity, and by the persistence of advantage for large incumbent firms whose mega-profits aren't frequently competed away by new entrants or other forces.[21] In retrospect it seems that the 1990s were a much more intensely competitive period overall for American firms, not the 2000s or the 2010s.

This matters because it challenges a central tenet of the GIE narrative—that benefits would flow broadly to firms that could contribute within global value chains without regard to geography or (mostly) to size. A hypercompetitive world might not have been easy or comfortable for managers to live within, but it would have been more consistent with the upside of the GIE model, including its implied promise of meritocratic growth and spreading welfare. It also would have been more consistent with the implied mechanisms pushing the GIE to continuously upgrade its performance by searching boldly for places where work could be done best, not just most inexpensively. And it would have felt more like the economic equivalent of democracy's fundamental promise—that today's winners would not necessarily be tomorrow's winners simply by virtue of incumbency. But that's not the way the world was working either before or after the GFC.

Intellectual Property

A second element of systems failure that was fundamental to political economy but also had immediate ethical and societal dimensions lay in developments around intellectual property (IP). The substantial moves that IBM made toward the use of open-source software during the late 1990s was a key part of the GIE foundation as much as it was a competitive strategic move on the part of one company.[22] Open source mattered because it represented the software element moving up the stack of the open internet infrastructure, that would enable global integration and the fluid movement of work to where it could be done best. It was essential to IBM's vision of creating open architecture business-service verticals where specific functions could be outsourced at scale for efficiency around the world. And it (like hypercompetition) was part of the meritocratic narrative that was supposed to attract emerging economies and startup businesses into this new system, by charting out a relatively unobstructed pathway to growth and success.

Put simply, the ethos of the open-source movement (and it was something of a movement at the time) told the right story for the GIE—with source code open and available for use by anyone who can build value on top of it, the software industry would advance more quickly, spread its value more widely, and be set up for competition where anyone can prove their worth and advance by writing excellent code, regardless of their academic degree, their company affiliation, their nationality, or anything else. Incumbents have no advantage other than their superior knowledge of the code that comes from using and improving it; and if they slip in the accumulation of that knowledge or try to protect their advantage in ways that exclude others, the code was openly available for a new prospective leader to recruit followers and jump out ahead.

In an earlier book, *The Success of Open Source,* I tried to capture the essence of this software story with two idioms. The first was simply that in the open-source model leaders need followers more than the other way around, putting the burden on leaders to prove their worth on an ongoing basis. Second, borrowing from Albert Hirschman, I said that the open-source process is a social system that eschews loyalty and extols voice, by making the exit option always available to new prospective leaders.[23] Both as a model for software engineering and as an ethos for business models per se, these idioms were ways of thinking that reinforced the overall GIE narrative as well as its particular manifestation in IBM's strategic plan.

But the story around IP became much more complicated than the move to open source would have had it. Instead of being the glue that held the GIE together, IP became the nexus of intensely conflicting vectors, with too much emotion (not just money and power) at stake to manage, and on the international stage in particular with regard to China.

The first principles of creating and enforcing property rights around something as intangible as "ideas" or "intellectual product" have always been controversial and nonintuitive. If the debate were confined only to economics, at least the basic terms would be relatively clear: how do you balance the incentives for investment in intellectual product, with the potential of distributing that product widely for further development and building upon by others? The modern patent and copyright regimes have evolved as imperfect but internally logical responses—in practice, the modern IP regime is often seen as the worst answer except for all the other possible alternatives.

This isn't the place to engage in a long defense of or attack on IP per se, but it is important to recognize the degree to which the emergence of open source as something of an alternative IP approach set fire to smoldering debates about IP and particularly IP in the digital age. The open-source community's notion of "copyleft" (a wordplay on copyright) turned the core logic of software IP upside-down—now, instead of an IP regime giving you the *right to control* code and exclude others from using it, you could choose to join an IP system that actually *obligated* you to *distribute* code and *enable* others to use it. That obligation was instantiated in what became known as the viral provision of a commonly used open source license, the General Public License (GPL). If you use GPL code, essentially anything that you do with it must also be released under the GPL, which allows everyone else exactly the same open-source rights.

There's an economic logic to this regime as well. In the simplest terms, software that was "free" of copyright restrictions didn't have to be "free" in economic terms. In other words, there was no obligation to make software available at a price of zero dollars. The Linux community liked to explain this (apparent) contradiction by telling people that the words were at fault—and to think of free software more like "free speech, not free beer."

That helped and hurt at the same time. It helped because it reminded people that the freedom to speak didn't mean that it was impossible to make money from selling books, articles, screenplays, or other such things. The words were free, while putting them together in a meaningful and valuable way was certainly worth money. But it also hurt because it invoked, even if subconsciously, a whole set of ideological tropes around free speech, discourse, and openness that were largely a distraction for the use of open-source code in the IT world.

In practice, the open-source model forced monetization onto parts of the value chain other than the code base—companies using open source could charge large sums for integration of software packages, for "solutions" that included software, for customization and service, and for lots of other value around the code, if not for the code itself. And that made sense to some firms, though of course not to all, and in particular not to a company like Microsoft that had built a massively profitable business on the basis of proprietary code (including but not limited to the Windows operating system and the Office suite of applications). It also jumbled a bunch of assumptions—or to be less charitable, near-theologies—about the relationship between value and openness. While much of the community preached an "open good, closed bad" mantra (reminiscent of "two legs bad, four legs good" from George Orwell's *Animal Farm*), other quite sophisticated IP industries and most notably the pharmaceutical industry preached exactly the opposite.

To explore the edges of this debate, Jonathan Sallet and I wrote about eclectic examples of open networks that had created both significant innovation and significant private returns in money for shareholders, such as the express package-delivery companies like FedEx. I experimented in a nonprofit consortium with a group of pharmaceutical executives, their investors, and drug-access nongovernmental organizations

(NGOs) like Oxfam who were willing to go to the edges of thinking through what it would mean to open-source a therapeutic molecule.[24] With a large internet service provider, Sallet and I built strategic models of what a closed overlay network with high-level quality of service guarantees and other distinctive characteristics would look like (in the context of net neutrality legislation it was, of course, a thought experiment, but that was its expressed purpose). And the categories were indeed jumbled up. The point was that for every theory about how an open system or open network would advance innovation and generate profits, there was an equal and opposite theory about how closed networks could and would do as well or better on both.

The bottom line was that there was a clear economic logic to open source, but it was an unfamiliar one to many traditional software industry strategists, and it was a downright scary one to proprietary software incumbents. Predictably, some of those incumbents fought back against open source—in markets, in the political sphere, and in the court of public opinion. Over time, the industry ecosystem would come to embrace open source as a mainstream way of writing code and doing business, but that was still some time in the future . . . while IBM's bold and quick moves in that direction during the early 2000s were extremely hard for the system as a whole to digest.[25]

Two big passion plays around IP that happened during this crucial time of the late 1990s and early 2000s made matters worse. By "passion play," I mean a highly charged public debate that seemed to escape the bounds of logical reason in favor of emotional appeal to large numbers of (in this case) frightened people.[26]

One IP passion play surrounded access to antiretroviral drugs for the treatment of HIV / AIDS. In 1995, the number of HIV-related deaths peaked in the United States at over 50,000.[27] In 1996, the Food and Drug Administration approved the use of combination therapy with antiretroviral drugs (often called drug cocktails) to treat HIV as the standard treatment. The number of HIV-related deaths in the United States subsequently began a long, gradual decline. However, the countries worst ravaged by HIV and particularly in sub-Saharan Africa did not see deaths start to decline until almost a decade later. The principal reason was cost—an antiretroviral treatment regimen in the United States cost around $10,000 to $15,000 per patient per year and this was a price that poorer countries could not pay.[28] Under the WTO TRIPS agreement, pharmaceutical companies had a clear legal right to protect their drug patents in overseas markets, and they did so for antiretroviral drugs under the standard rationale that patent protection was necessary to provide a return on their research and development (R&D).

But humanitarian groups and health activists rejected this, arguing evocatively that the costs of these drugs were condemning millions to unnecessary early deaths. Organizations such as Médecins Sans Frontières (MSF; Doctors without Borders) started aggressive campaigns to pressure pharmaceuticals to "put people above profits" and allow patent licensing, which would bring the prices down, but to little avail.

The passion play quickly escalated. In 1997, with HIV infection rates and deaths continuing to climb in most places outside the United States, the South African legislature tried to route around the patent regime and lower costs by authorizing parallel imports of patented drugs.[29] This led to a major court case where the legislation was challenged by a coalition of thirty-nine pharmaceutical companies backed by the US government.[30] The South African government argued that international trade agreements allowed for patent infringement exemptions in cases of public health emergencies while the United States considered it a TRIPS violation. It was also in 1997 that Cipla, an Indian generic drug manufacturer, announced that it would ignore patent protections and manufacture and provide antiretrovirals for $350 per patient per year to MSF (or $600 to governments).[31] Condemnation for the US stance poured in from all over the world. Three years later and after doing significant harm to their reputation, the pharmaceutical companies dropped the South Africa case.

It's not necessary to take a position on who was right and wrong in these cases to simply observe that the economic arguments about patents barely mattered. It had become a passion play about life and death, humanity, race, and poverty that transcended any arguments about business models or R&D investments.

Less life and death in terms of the stakes but still emotionally intense in the late 1990s were the IP controversies around file sharing in the music industry (this was about copyright, not patents per se, but in a passion play, that distinction doesn't matter). Napster, the extraordinarily popular file-sharing service of the time, was slapped with a copyright infringement suit by the Recording Industry Association of America (RIAA) at the end of 1999. The RIAA won the case in 2001 but it was a pyrrhic victory because it led to overreach. In September 2003 the RIAA filed lawsuits against 261 individuals whom they accused of being "major offenders" in peer-to-peer sharing of music.[32] The defendants included twelve-year-old Brianna Lahara, who apologized and paid $2,000 to settle the suit. Sarah Ward was a sixty-six-year-old Mac-owning grand-mother who was accused of downloading hard-core rap from a Windows-only file-sharing service named Kazaa. An eighty-three-year-old woman who had recently died was named in a similar lawsuit. And the number of cases swelled to 35,000 over the next five years until the RIAA an-nounced it would no longer sue people in 2008.[33] These stories prompted intensely emotional fights that engaged the record companies, the art-ists, music lovers, a group of high-profile academic lawyers who took on the mantle of the defenders of creativity, and others. It utterly es-caped the boundaries of rational argument about the economics of property rights and incentives to become passion plays about art, common human heritage, and even "the future of ideas."[34]

The GIE vision wasn't brought down by melodramatic pleas about the use of Mickey Mouse, music remix, and the global intellectual commons. But these passion plays did help to turn the IP debates away from what the GIE required, which was to tackle these issues on less emotional grounds of what the IP-reliant industries needed to create growth, effi-ciency, and innovation—with "fairness" considerations held firmly in the background. The answer to the question, posed in those terms, still had a lot of uncertainty to it, but the terms of debate would have been grounded in comparable arguments and measurable parameters. In-stead, the IP world found itself wrapped into a high-emotion passion play framed around extremist positions. And that was not a good foun-dation for the GIE to grow on.

A third big set of conflicts emerged specifically about the role of gov-ernments in creating and policing IP regimes and agreements. This reflected in part some of the passion-play dynamics from above, but it was also a function of fundamental economic and strategic considerations about how IP should and could be treated in cross-border foreign economic policy. It was (and remains) axiomatic that governments' role in establishing and maintaining property rights regimes takes on even greater importance when property is IP, and yet more so when that property is in a digital form that can be copied and moved at zero cost. But despite the gut appeal of the slogan "information wants to be free," of course the truth is that information doesn't want anything at all, and that property rights regimes around information are constructed according to human ideas by human action and institutions in precisely the same way as regimes around physical property like enclosure and land ownership laws.

Different countries can choose to do this in entirely different ways. There has never been a uniform set of property rights, intellectual or otherwise, on a global basis. The GIE vision didn't depend on reaching that unreachable apogee, but it did need some reasonable degree of compatibility and clarity to make it work. And it needed to *not* be in a situation where countries were openly and boldly arbitraging others' IP rights regimes to strategically maximize their free-riding capacity. That kind of behavior at any kind of scale would be just as much a barrier to twenty-first-century integration as Smoot Hawley–style tariffs were in the early twentieth, or as massive pirate infestations were in parts of the world during the nineteenth.

So on the variegated global playing field of nationally determined IP rights regimes, governments essentially had to make two important judgments about how to play the game. The first judgment concerned how others were thought to be playing the game—that is, were the differences in approach justified, workable, and ultimately negotiable, as reflections of honest difference in national positions and beliefs? Or were they purely strategic arbitrage plays intended to maximize a free-ride payoff?

The second judgment concerned what a government needed to do or not do about the disagreements and frictions that would inevitably emerge. Put simply for the American case: when it came to the set of problems on the global landscape of and markets for IP, which of these were foreign economic policy problems that governments should engage? And which were business problems that firms needed to handle essentially on their own?

A major reason why the GIE vision faltered here was because key governments, including most importantly the US government, didn't make these judgments and answer these questions clearly and coherently.

The foundational issue for government was really this: what is the perceived nature of the threat to IP rights that justifies decisive international intervention? The answers were fuzzy and undefined. For some, the threat was when foreign *governments* expressly or tacitly appropriated the IP of US companies. For others, it was when *foreign firms* acted to unilaterally revise the scope of US companies' IP in ways that eroded their profitability or tarnished their brand.[35] Another position was that as long as private actors were *bargaining* in legitimate ways for new forms of property rights (as in the case of open-source software) rather than simply engaging in theft, then governments should restrain themselves and in effect privilege markets and bargaining over property rights per se.

On an aggregate view for the US economy as a whole, the last position would have been most compatible with the viability of a GIE model (and I believe it is also the smartest). After all, we don't want governments to prevent people from constructing new IP models in order to learn and experiment—that's called innovation. We want something like the open-source movement to be able to explore the viability of new business models that work when they offer their source code freely (that's different than stealing someone else's proprietary source code and then revealing it). We want to empower music companies to experiment with whether consumers would pay for higher-quality downloads, streaming, or tracks without digital rights management. And we don't want to prevent users from bargaining with IP owners for the revision of traditional IP rules. Consider this example: if all the drinkers of Coca-Cola in the world get together on Facebook and tell Coke that they won't consume the soda without access to Coke's secret recipe, then we don't want a government to stop the negotiations dead in their tracks because the trade secret somehow deserves government protection from bargaining. That's a different proposition than asking governments to arrest a criminal who breaks into Coke's corporate network, steals the secret formula, and threatens to give it to Pepsi.

Another way to say this is, the economy as a whole benefits from a vibrant cycle of learning, experimentation, and bargaining over property rights. It does not benefit if a foreign government through unilateral action (or deliberate inaction in the face of violations) breaks that cycle. It does not benefit if firms use market power to break that cycle. And it does not benefit if criminals engage in theft that breaks the cycle. That is why governments might want to act if Coca-Cola drinkers storm Coke's Atlanta headquarters and steal the secret formula from a filing cabinet.

A high-level summary of this view is that we want governments in effect to privilege markets over property rights per se, and to hold IP owners and users accountable for any behavior that impedes negotiations that take place in the market. That's why unilateral rejection of IP rights recognized under a legitimate regime is theft and not bargaining, and the imposition of monopoly-style market power to avoid bargaining is equally bad.

This all makes sense from the perspective of the economy as a whole. But it's a picture that might be much less attractive to some individual firms and particularly to incumbents with a bunch of traditional IP. It is in this sense a lot like the discourse around hypercompetition—good for the economy as a whole and in the long run, but somewhere between uncomfortable and intolerable for individual companies at any given moment.

Running what is today sometimes called a "high-pressure economy" is what the GIE was all about, but it's particularly challenging for governments to see a clear path to that very dynamic equilibrium when value lies importantly with a newly critical and abstract concept like IP.[36] It's even more challenging when there is a convenient villain on the horizon—which was in this case largely but not exclusively China.

China in the mid-2000s was a major nexus of the United States' struggle to figure out international IP policy. On the government side, International Trade Commission (ITC) border enforcement actions against China on IP issues rose massively after 2000 (between 2002 and 2007, 35 percent of all ITC IP complaints were against the People's Republic of China (PRC); another 20 percent were against Taiwan and 12 percent against Hong Kong, most of which were treated as "Chinese" violations routed through those places). In 2007, the US trade representative filed high-profile WTO piracy cases against the PRC for inadequate protection of intellectual property rights.[37] These actions were the tip of the iceberg, signals of a profound concern in Washington that IP conflicts with China were getting worse, not better over time.

Many academic specialists on IP (which was still a subspecialty at the time, predominantly in law schools) took a somewhat less combative attitude, but with not-so-different consequences. The modal argument was that China had now reached a stage of development where it was "underinvested" in IP protection. The favored proxy indicator was simple but evocative: China was significantly below the level of most OECD (Organization for Economic Cooperation and Development) countries in terms of how many patent applications its companies were filing in other countries when normalized for R&D investment. The contention in effect was that the Chinese economy had advanced to a point where its lax IP protections weren't just hurting American firms or even the global economy as a whole—the lack of IP protection was hurting China itself, by holding back the next stage of development and IP value creation in Chinese firms.

If this sounds a bit like an IP version of what development scholars in the 1960s called "modernization theory," that is because it is.[38] One senior official charged with managing IP in a large American-based global IT firm spent months traveling around China delivering a speech in which he made this argument quite explicitly, portraying on a single slide a set of "stages" for the "modernization" of IP policy through which all industrial economies had supposedly transitioned. This slide asserted, as in modernization theory, that there really is a single equilibrium solution to the question of how to regulate and protect IP, and countries differ only to the extent that they are at any moment on different stages in development along the trajectory. Japan supposedly moved through those stages in the 1980s; Korea in the 1990s; and now it was China's turn. Put simply, this IP modernization theory held that China was "just like the United States," merely a few decades behind, and was somehow destined to travel the same path to the same destination on IP that the United States had.

The clear implication was that it would be good for everyone—the United States, the GIE high-pressure global economy, and, most importantly, China—if that inevitable journey were to speed up a little (or a lot). And that provided a robust platform for consultants and advisors to argue their case to particular firms and industries. The message went roughly like this: as a growing Chinese firm, you want to sell your products on world markets, but your IP stance leaves you at risk of being excluded from key markets and particularly the United States by government trade actions. You want to create high profits, but your IP stance leaves you at risk of sacrificing profits to the royalties and settlements you have to pay to others, as well as having partnerships on unfavorable terms. You want to develop global brands, but your IP stance makes it very difficult or impossible to create distinctive Chinese brands with global recognition. The upshot of this story was that if China didn't move more quickly on the IP modernization train, Chinese companies would become stuck on the lowest rung of the value ladder, doing low-cost and low-profit original equipment manufacturing (OEM) for Western companies. And that was presumably not an attractive long-term prospect for a Chinese capitalist.

If that story had convinced many Chinese firms and, by diffusion or otherwise, the Chinese government, it would have been good for the prospects of the GIE vision. But it largely failed to do so, and for good reasons. It was suspect on basic theoretical grounds, since the overarching modernization trope that underpinned the IP argument had largely been left behind in most other serious development discussions. And even if you believed it had a grain of truth and that economies do in fact evolve along a single trajectory, what was the compelling case for US government policy to force faster evolution on the Chinese economy?

The argument was also suspect on intellectual grounds since, under closer examination, the concept of Chinese underinvestment in IP implied a peculiar assumption about the appropriate mix of factors of production for different economies, and probably was ignoring a very simple insight about competitive advantage. If we think of intellectual product or even simply ideas as a factor of production in addition to land, labor, and capital, then the notion that economies have or should evolve toward having the same mix of factors of production in play at any given moment is at odds with the theory of competitive advantage. Perhaps the Chinese underinvestment in IP was appropriate to its factor endowments, essentially the mirror image of Chinese overinvestment in labor relative to capital at this point in time.

Ultimately the IP argument could not be sustained on political grounds. The Chinese government in the early 2000s was not in a position to shut down pirate DVD factories or to prosecute people who stole music or copies of the Windows operating system. They were, however, in a position to make the argument that this kind of IP "leakage" didn't really affect the economics of Hollywood or Microsoft, since the people who were consuming pirated IP would not have consumed the "real" product if they had to pay the "real" price. Since the IP was digital in form, there was no reduction in its availability in IP-protected markets, and very little if any "re-importation" from China to elsewhere.

The Chinese government never quite made this argument explicitly, but it was reasonable to say that at least some forms of IP infringement in China had little if any impact on the market for IP-intensive goods elsewhere. It was also reasonable to say that for the foreseeable future and in the politically relevant time frame, a full, US-style IP regime in China would increase inequality within China in unacceptable ways. And it was at least plausible to say that for particular firms whose IP was at risk within Chinese joint ventures or local production facilities, that was really a negotiation and business-model challenge for the particular firms, not a foreign policy issue for the US government to solve.

There was a final and quite ideologically charged element layered on top of this already fraught debate, which I previously have called "the imperialism of IP." It wasn't only the Chinese who felt that American policy with regard to IP (and here I mean both US government policy and the business-model practices of large US-based IP-intensive firms) had more than a whiff of imperial attitude attached in two important respects. The first was parallel to the democracy promotion agenda that had climbed up the George W. Bush foreign policy priority list—a kind of blithe assumption that in this case, since US IP law was said to be good for the United States, it was by definition good for the rest of the world, and the rest of the world needed to be shown that fact. The second was a sense of explicit collusion between those large firms and the US government that had its own parallels in earlier decades of more openly imperialist policies.

Put simply, it was a story about US IP policy in the explicit service of the US state. And to the extent that this notion infected the policy discourse in China and elsewhere, it created a grating intellectual and political friction with the concept of the GIE. It wasn't possible that both images of economic geography for the early twenty-first century could coexist.

Industry, Manufacturing, and Jobs

The third major element of systems failure was a stock-and-flow problem around jobs—"stocks" being what you currently have in your possession, and "flows" being what moves among all the stocks. At the highest level, there was in the 2000s a cognitive-political mismatch between a GIE aspiration for an economic geography that emphasized *flows of value*, and an existing mind-set that was still primarily focused on *stocks of jobs*.

For work to move fluidly to where it can be done best means that flows become more salient than stocks. And although new value is created along the way (and thus a particular flow away from one stock and toward another does not necessarily mean that there is a loser and a winner, because it won't be a zero-sum redistribution among stocks), it's still the case that flows have a directionality. If people and political systems focus their attention on stocks of work, not flows of value, then the GIE vision is going to be very difficult to sustain for any length of time, and certainly not long enough to erase doubts that overall jobs stocks can rise despite asymmetry and imbalance in flows—or more fundamentally, that flows are actually more important for economic vitality than are stocks.

And if work means jobs (and for a quirk of history about which I'll say more below, in particular manufacturing jobs), then a cognitive-political focus on stocks of manufacturing jobs that are present in an economy will undermine the intellectual and political foundations for a GIE economic geography. That's precisely what happened.

Employment has, of course, always been important to societies as well as economies. A job is for many people as much a source of individual purpose and meaning as it is a source of income, as well as for societies a source of tax revenue and a foundation of social stability. Labor unions have famously rallied support with the deeply human appeal of "a decent job for a decent wage." No surprise, then, that for most citizens in most countries, the availability of what they call at any given time "good jobs" is the most tangible and tactile measure of an economy's health. GDP numbers and even more so theories of value creation are vague academic abstractions that pale in comparison.

But whose responsibility is it to create those good jobs? It may sound a bit strange to say it this way, but the onus for achieving healthy employment has traditionally (at least in the post–World War II era) rested with governments. The core economic presumption has been that under most conditions, when businesses focus on creating value, job growth generally follows apace. When there are bumps in that equation, or in situations where the supply of labor outstrips demand for it, it's a signal of market failure—and addressing labor-market failure is a signature task for government policy. Politicians in both developed and developing countries, in democracies and nondemocracies have understood for decades that their performance would be judged in large part on the basis of how many and what quality of jobs were created or destroyed under their tenure—regardless of whether their decisions and policies were demonstrably the cause.

Firms, in contrast, have been viewed as actors within the labor market, obliged to follow the rules but, like job-holding and job-hunting individuals, responsible for their own economic interests, not the overall employment landscape. And the central economic interest for firms is the creation of value not jobs. An Apple executive responding to the *New York Times*' questions regarding Apple's employment overseas captured that stance perfectly in 2012 saying, "Our only obligation is making the best product possible."[39] He might have added that if Apple created jobs along the way that was great, but it wasn't the creation of jobs that was Apple's purpose. Jobs (as in employment, not Steve) are not the reason why the world is a better place with Apple than it would be without.

That may seem an overly stark characterization—business leaders have always been aware that firms play a pivotal role in job creation. After all, it is on this basis that firms frequently argue against regulations, taxes, and other policies that increase the cost of doing business and, in their telling, constrain the creation of jobs. Firms regularly bargain with governments for incentives to locate in particular geographic areas with the explicit claim that their location decisions would bring good jobs to people living in that place. But this actually underlines the point: the goal of the firm is to create value, and governments will pay to move that value-creation process from one place to another for the sake of locating jobs.

The upshot of this equation seems simple. Firms would be held to account for the creation of value. Jobs are an input to a company's operations, not an outcome on which it will be judged. Governments are responsible for figuring out how to make labor markets function well in the face of that reality.

It's a straightforward equation but it was coming under severe pressure in the 1990s and 2000s for several reasons. First, it was becoming clear during this period that in modern economies the relationship between robust economic growth and robust job growth was complicated and had diminished in recoveries from successive downturns in the last several decades.[40] (The casual phrase for this phenomenon became "jobless recovery.") More on the deeper reasons for why this is so later, but for the moment it's important to note simply that in the wake of the dotcom crash and recession, the GIE model prescribed that firms should make investment decisions that were less about boosting employment in any particular location and more about positioning to serve new customers in emerging economies. That there should be no conflict between these goals in the long run is theoretically defensible, but politically irrelevant—because as John Maynard Keynes famously pointed out, the long run is not the time frame that CEOs, job seekers, and politicians care about.

In fact, governments themselves were conflicted in their commitment to job creation during this period. On the one hand, there was a growing awareness of just how crucial jobs are to the stability of social order (relevant to cities, regions, and countries) and psychological well-being (for individuals). New studies in developed countries showed strong associations between unemployment and mental disease states such as depression.[41] Long-term unemployment was demonstrating particularly severe consequences, as skills erode and new workers fail to gain a foothold in the labor market. In some countries, youth unemployment reached such shocking levels that many worried about a "lost generation" of labor—and by implication, of people.[42] The Arab Spring came a few years later in the midst of the extreme GFC shock. But its roots at least in part lay in faltering job prospects for young Arab citizens, whose governments were being blamed by the population for that failure.[43] Youth unemployment averaged more than 23 percent around the region (some estimates were much higher), and it affected those with both higher and lower education and income levels.

On the other hand, the intense pressure to boost competitiveness and productivity didn't exactly work to the benefit of labor. Productivity after all is a measure of output per unit of input, and if labor is one of the key and costly inputs, then finding ways to squeeze extra output from each unit of labor is the most direct way to improve productivity. That can work to create jobs as long as economies are expanding, demand is robust, and workers who find themselves displaced from one firm, sector, or geography can redeploy their labor fluidly into new jobs somewhere else. If any of those conditions falter, then the pressure to improve productivity will start to be felt directly in labor markets as a deterioration for the position of workers.

And that is precisely how it was experienced by many workers whose work moved away from them, to where it could be done better or in many cases just more cheaply. The GIE concept was deeply vulnerable on these grounds. In IBM's case, the vulnerability was particularly vivid with regard to the great attention paid to India as a location for outsourcing. As one former IBM strategist told me, the firm and others like it did too much simple arbitraging of labor markets and not enough new value creation to manage this equation. The Y2K (year 2000) bug issue was part of the reason why—IBM (and others) needed to recruit a lot of programming talent quickly and at low cost so that it could handle what was essentially a maintenance issue and a not very exciting business proposition that had little to do with new value creation. But it wasn't only Y2K that biased global firms toward arbitraging labor costs as the quickest route to productivity improvement.

This dynamic was most powerful in the context of a phenomenon that Dani Rodrik would later (in a must-read paper) name as "premature deindustrialization."[44] To really understand the political-cognitive impact of this phenomenon, not just its economics, it's important to see clearly right along with it what I call the "manufacturing fetish" that was deeply ensconced in the minds of many (and continues to be). Premature deindustrialization combined with the manufacturing fetish turned out to be a toxic combination for moving work to where it can be done best.

Rodrik starts this paper by saying that "our modern world is in many ways the product of industrialization." He is absolutely right: it was industrial production that transformed what had been a nearly flat economic growth curve for most of human history into a growth story featuring Europe and the United States to start. It was industrial production that boosted Japan and the Asian Tigers into economic catch-up with "the West" in the 1960s and 1970s. It was industrial production that empowered the Chinese growth miracle in the 1980s. And in developing countries around the world, it is still in the 2010s the baseline belief that an economic development plan needs to be anchored in industrial production and particularly in manufacturing. In my work as an economic development consultant in the Middle East in particular, starting in the early 2000s, it never ceased to amaze me the degree to which clients—both government and private sector—continue to focus the vast bulk of their attention on the question of how to bring manufacturing into their countries. We often talked about services, about the IT sector, about content industries and tourism . . . but when the talking got real and investment questions were on the table, peoples' minds snapped back like a ratchet to manufacturing and factories.

These mind-sets aren't prima facie absurd. The twentieth-century examples of countries using manufacturing to climb up the development ladder are some of the most compelling economic growth stories of all time. Manufacturing in the twentieth century was indeed associated with rapid productivity growth and the creation of "good" or even "middle-class" jobs. Importantly, many of those good jobs were suitable for significant quantities of relatively unskilled labor to enter. Factories typically make physical things that can be dropped on one's foot, and that is still a persistent mental model of real and meaningful value creation. And these physical things are quite often tradeable goods that can enter global value chains and foreign markets. That generally means a more robust and steady global (as compared to national) demand function.

The problem is that these mental models were already close to obsolete in the 2000s, and the manufacturing obsession was more a nostalgic fetish than a reality. Manufacturing has become a victim of its own success. Take the United States as the most prominent example for developed countries. US manufacturing share of total employment peaked in the 1950s and again after a dip in the early 1970s at about 25 percent. In 2017 manufacturing's share of total employment was less than 10 percent.[45] The decline in share of employment has been gradual, steady, inexorable, and not much modified by economic cycles or government policy decisions. Bolstering the argument that this is a secular phenomenon is the striking similarity among advanced "industrialized" countries. The decline in manufacturing as share of US employment over the last forty years—about 15 percent—roughly matches the average decline for the G-7 economies as a whole. It's actually an anachronism to refer to these countries as "industrialized" or "rich industrial democracies" (or really to use the term industrial at all to the extent that "industrial" is taken to mean "manufacturing").

The decline in advanced economy manufacturing employment is a consequence of three simple phenomena: increased productivity in manufacturing; a shift in consumption patterns with higher incomes toward services; and, of course, the move of manufacturing production to parts of the world where manufactures can be made more cheaply.[46] There is a lively debate about the relationship between and mix of these three causes, and that will figure in Chapters 6 and 7 because it has consequences for what to do next. But in the political-cognitive debates of the 2000s that mattered for the GIE vision, the debate was largely irrelevant.

The experienced loss of manufacturing jobs played a massively outsized role in US politics (as happened again, of course, in the US 2016 election). It was blamed for the trade deficit. It was said to be a risk to national security. It was put forward as an explanation for declining research and development funding. It was held guilty for the general malaise in the labor market overall, and for the gritty decline in American rust belt cities and rural towns. Even the opioid addiction epidemic was attributed to the decline in manufacturing employment.[47]

That less than 10 percent of the US labor market could be held responsible for all these evils, and even more so, that people believed (and continue to believe in many circles) that "fixing" this would somehow cure all those ills, is why I use the term "manufacturing fetish." The fixation on manufacturing is mostly a nostalgia for jobs per se, but that doesn't make things better: it makes things worse. Call up in your mind's eye an image of a political candidate standing outside a shuttered factory in a Midwestern US town as the iconic image of a modern American campaign, and you'll know exactly what I mean. With few exceptions, politicians who ignore that fetish have been politicians who lose elections.

And it wasn't, and isn't, just a political nostrum. I recall vividly standing up in a room full of US government economic analysts in 2016 and showing a slide that extrapolated the decline in US manufacturing employment downward over time. I asked the question, what if we were to continue that line along its trend and imagine having an economy with little to no manufacturing—in other words, an economy that stopped trying to reverse the decline of manufacturing and instead adjusted to it boldly and without hesitation. It was a thought experiment meant to probe peoples' beliefs about how far the trend could actually go and whether it by necessity had to be a bad thing. I was stunned by the response. No one wanted to engage in the thought experiment, not even for a moment. The silence in the room was deadening and the discomfort was palpable. People couldn't wait to move on to the next slide in the deck.

What Rodrik pointed to in his premature deindustrialization paper was a parallel process—with possibly even more challenging consequences—for a broad swathe of *developing* countries. Except for just a few out-performers, Rodrik showed that developing countries were experiencing their own decline in manufacturing shares since the 1980s—and not only of employment but also of real value added. Because that decline had begun at levels of incomes much lower than those at which the rich economies had begun to see their manufacturing employment decline, the deindustrialization was labeled "premature."[48]

Again the precise causes of premature deindustrialization are controversial. The modal argument points to technologically driven productivity improvements as more important in the case of developed countries, and globalization / trade in the case of less developed countries.[49] It was actually developing countries, not the United States, that bore the brunt of the trade shock emanating from the massive success of Asian (Factory China) exports. But for the purpose of GIE viability, the distinction didn't matter much because neither causal claim offered much hope for policy to modify in any substantial way. So economic development planners were facing a huge dilemma. If most developing countries could no longer use manufacturing to boost their climb up the development and income ladders, what exactly could they use?

That question was sometimes just too hard to face squarely, at least in the 2000s. So ironically the manufacturing fetish mind-set wasn't undermined by it as it should have been by any reasonable logic. Many developing economies actually became even more determined to beat the odds and "win" a manufacturing race that had already been lost, just as advanced economies were doing more or less the same (at least rhetorically). More imaginative and constructive responses would start to emerge in the 2010s, but, arguably, too late for the GIE model to absorb and benefit from.

It's rather hard to imagine a more zero-sum setting for national economic growth policies to engage with each other on a global landscape in the late 2000s. What the GIE needed was attention to flows of value. What it got instead was political-cognitive obsession with stocks of jobs. Even worse, it suffered an obsession focused particularly on manufacturing jobs, a small and shrinking piece of the economies that were most important to engage in the GIE vision. It was a recipe for failure.

SYSTEM FAILURE REVISITED

This chapter explained the rapid demise of the GIE model as a system failure story at the intersection of technology and the state. The story is made up of three interconnected elements—hypercompetition, IP, and employment.

A world that was actually as "hypercompetitive" as the rhetoric of the 2000s painted it would have been more consistent with the GIE vision and particularly the upside of a high-pressure global economy. It would have come closer to the promises of meritocratic growth and spreading welfare, and put more onus on the GIE to upgrade its performance by boldly moving work to where it could be done best, not just most cheaply. The lived reality of the GIE firm, however, was much less hypercompetitive than the rhetoric. The dynamic tension between those two vectors made for an uncomfortable synthesis both at the level of the individual firm and at the level of the global political economy as a whole.

The IP debate around ownership, property rights, and openness would have been difficult to navigate under the best of circumstances, because it was a subtle and sometimes counterintuitive way to understand a critical source of value. Openness implied that bargaining should be more important than property rights, as long as bargaining didn't slip into blatant theft. Those are delicate distinctions, but they are absolutely central to digital IP in particular. In practice the GIE model of IP asked for too much change too quickly from industry and governments, especially in the context of the perceived threat from China on one side and the perceived IP imperialism from the United States on the other. The global passion plays around pharmaceuticals and digital content like music and movies created mass emotional overlays that made the politics even worse.

The employment issue centered on the cognitive and political tensions arising from a fundamental stock and flow problem. Governments and most workers still saw stocks of jobs as more important than flows of value, while the GIE vision rested on precisely the opposite view. The manufacturing fetish made this tension particularly intense. Fetish is a pejorative term, but it was a belief so deeply embedded in governments of developing and developed countries that it could not be dislodged (and is still largely in place).

It is not my contention that only these three issues brought down the GIE. There were other problematic elements evolving, some of which will come back in Chapter 5 as core parts of the new economic geography for the next decade. It is my contention that these three issues, taken together, were enough to cause the system failure that undermined the GIE vision.

In that sense we've answered the most important question for this chapter—it wasn't an exogenous shock or a set of historical accidents that doomed the GIE. System failure was indeed endogenous to the GIE model in the 2000s. The model demanded too much of people and institutions too quickly. Could that have been foreseen and adapted to? Would slower, more gradual change have produced a better outcome and a longer life-span for GIE? It's impossible to know for certain, and in a real sense such counterfactuals no longer matter. The real history is the real history, and the path dependence of political economy leaves the system where it is at present. The failure of the GIE is now part of the new economic geography with which the next generation of global reach concepts will have to contend.

5

INGREDIENTS FOR A NEW

ECONOMIC GEOGRAPHY

TO SPECIFY THE KEY ELEMENTS OF economic geography for global reach in the 2020s is an audacious proposition. But it's a necessity.

It's audacious because we live in an era where both technology and the state can demonstrably become very different in a lot less time than a decade. You don't have to buy in to the hype of a phrase like "exponential change" to recognize a ground truth, that economic geography changes more quickly now that recalcitrant physical obstacles and barriers are becoming less important relative to things like technology standards and regulations, which are subject to human control. But it's equally necessary because, as I said at the start of this book, even if it is now true that anyone can be anywhere, it is equally true that everybody has to be somewhere. People have to make concrete decisions about where to locate their research and development facilities, where to store and process their data, where to deploy their robots, and so on.

Every decision of this kind represents a bet on a hypothesis about economic geography. Sometimes the nature of both the bet and the hypothesis are explicit and coherent with respect to each other. Sometimes they are implicit, and sometimes the two are less clearly connected by logic. The point of this chapter is to put forward and explain the key ingredients of my hypothesis about the emerging economic geography.

Chapter 6 follows with an explicit argument for a particular kind of bet that I believe makes good sense to place on that landscape, and it makes the logical connection explicit.

Recall for just a moment from Chapter 3 the economic geography foundation of the globally integrated enterprise (GIE) argument. It had three main ingredients:

- the decline of economic nationalism, along with liberalization of trade rules and co-evolving intellectual property (IP) regimes
- a massive reduction in coordination costs as a result of the IT revolution and the World Wide Web
- standardized business operations that reward scale and offer significant efficiency returns

Those ingredients and the foundation that they made lasted for a very short window of time and have since run out. The global financial crisis (GFC) accelerated that process of decline. The economic geography for the 2020s will be built up out of new ingredients, three of which are de facto reversals of the 2000s and one of which is new (Figure 5.1):

- Economic nationalism is rising—in materials, agriculture, and other familiar sectors, but most importantly in *jobs* and *data*. This trend is refracted into explicit political nationalist movements that give voice as populism, and a concomitant decline in global public goods.
- IT-enabled coordination cost reduction is slowing asymptotically; labor costs are converging in the same manner; and transport costs are in a race with the declining costs of local production.
- Business-process standardization is running up against government policies and non-Western rule sets, especially those on procurement and data localization.
- Capital is cheap and abundant, while global demand is soft and fragile. Declining economic growth rates, possibly a secular trend, loom large.

Financial crisis starting 2008
accelerates underlying vectors that are weakening the foundations

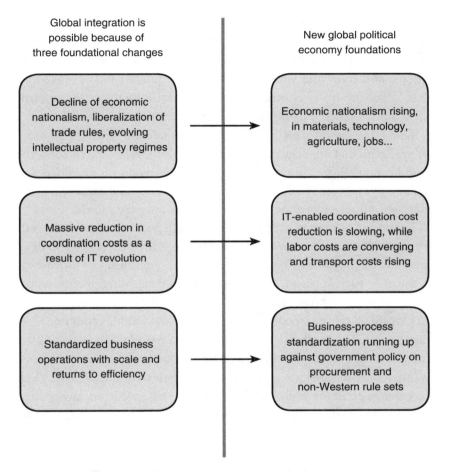

Figure 5.1: The Shifting Foundations of Economic Geography.

As before, there's a lot to unpack about these ingredients prior to figuring out what a robust bet for global reach should look like against
that landscape. The place to start is with slow growth. Slow growth isn't
the root of all evils and is itself the outcome of more fundamental causes.
But if you had to pick one central defining feature that shapes the new
economic geography, slow growth would be at the center.

SLOW GROWTH, SECULAR STAGNATION, AND ALL THAT

There have been over the last several years an explosion of arguments about the sources and consequences of slow growth in the post–financial crisis period (or, as in some arguments, for even longer than that). There is even (as expected) substantial disagreement about the magnitude of the phenomenon and whether it is at all surprising in the wake of a debt-deflation shock. For the purposes of describing the new economic geography, a few key data points and arguments matter most.

One is the global growth shortfall relative to contemporary expectations. Recall that after the massive shock of global recession in 2009, the world economy grew 5.4 percent in 2010. That rebound was aided and abetted by emergency and in some cases unprecedented fiscal and monetary stimulus in just about every major economy around the world.[1]

Economic growth of 5.4 percent is a strong performance—it exceeds by a good bit average growth during the 1998–2008 precrisis decade of 4.2 percent. But it now seems fair to call it something of a dead-cat bounce. In each subsequent year up to at least the start of 2017, global growth has slowed from 2010—in 2016 and 2017 it came in at just about 3.1 percent.[2] And the trend repeatedly surprised credible economic forecasters who seek to predict what will happen in following years. At the International Monetary Fund (IMF), for example, projections made each spring for the following year over the last decade have been almost a half percentage point too high. (At the time I'm writing this, in spring 2019, the IMF has just again reduced its estimates for 2019 overall.)[3] With 20/20 hindsight it is often possible to see where excessive optimism crept into the forecasting models, but the simple observation stands: the global economy has grown more slowly than expected, and expectations have not adjusted overall to conform to that pattern.

With regard to slow growth, the American experience has been anything but exceptional. The rate of growth in US GDP per capita from a decade earlier has been slower in the period from 2007 onward than during almost any other period since World War II (with short exceptions around 1982 and 1961). If you accept the intuition that a decade's experience will sink into the popular imagination and mind-set and make a difference in a way that a good or bad year or two won't, then you can parse the aggregate American experience of growth in a few simple observations. There was a bit of a golden age in the late 1960s and before the first oil shock in 1973, in which the United States experienced a jump of around 35 percent per capita GDP from a decade earlier. After a tough period of adjustment to the oil crises and 1970s inflation, there was another semi-golden age between roughly 1984 and 2007. Even with an end-of-Cold-War recession and a dot-com bust in the middle, Americans enjoyed roughly 25 percent growth from a decade earlier. But the following decade, 2007–2017, was decidedly not golden—with average growth falling closer to 5 percent from a decade earlier. That is the lowest number in the last sixty years.[4]

The difference between 25 percent and 5 percent is a difference that a society can feel, a difference that will pervade daily life, expectations for the future, and, of course, politics. And keep in mind these are aggregate GDP numbers—a measure of growth for the economy as a whole, and not household income numbers, which probably represent the lived experience of people on the ground more accurately. Those household income numbers tell a story that is arguably worse and certainly more vivid. On a real basis, median household income in the United States rose from about 51,000 in 1993 to just under 59,000 in 1999, a huge leap. And then it fell—to about 56,300 in 2004 and 53,300 in 2012.[5] Put differently, the median US household had the same real income in 2012 as it did in 1995—seventeen years later. The recovery to levels last achieved in 1999 happened in 2016, also seventeen years later.

Seventeen years is a long time in the popular American imagination, almost a generation. Seventeen years is four presidential elections and eight congressional election cycles.

It's right to point out that there was growth in the interim that was reversed and lost during downturns—but given what we know about how people experience the pain of losses more intensely than the pleasure of equivalent gains, that economic fact shouldn't cloud what it feels like.[6] It's also right to point out that inflation deflators used to correct nominal to real income don't always account well for some of the quality improvements that impact what real income buys you at any given moment—but that too doesn't change the overall impression that essentially stagnant incomes create. And while it's possible that faster GDP growth overall might not have boosted household incomes—for example, if the fruits of that growth ended up as returns to capital, not labor—it's unlikely that the median household wouldn't have seen some benefits along the way.

There were policy choices available that might have changed the picture somewhat, through even more expansionary fiscal and monetary policies, or redistributive policies, or some combination. Much of the macroeconomic policy community was probably overly fearful of the bold monetary policy moves that the Federal Reserve took in the earlier years of the Great Recession. That flipped nearly 180 degrees a few years later, when many macroeconomic policy experts called on central banks and fiscal authorities to stop worrying about nonevident inflationary pressures and take even more aggressive expansionary actions to boost growth.[7] There was for some a bit of "Monday morning quarterback" play here, as government policies (like various means of quantitative easing) that at one time were labeled as dangerous and unprecedented in their expansionary and market-distorting effects, were later relabeled as "austerity" policies too timid to make a meaningful difference.

But it doesn't really matter at this point what the alternative history could have been. A stark way to sum up the US growth story of the last decade is to say that while it might have been somewhat better, in reality it wasn't. Growth was slow, and household incomes were essentially stagnant. Both might very well have been experienced by most Americans as worse than they really were. This was the first real "social media recession." Those with stagnant incomes (most everyone) were treated to a continuous feed of personal news and pictures about the extravagant lives of the rich and famous, boosted in that portrayal by the social positivity bias that Facebook in particular is known to promote.[8]

In that context, the growth of economic populism and nationalism should have surprised absolutely no one. There are enough potential villains to go around, and enough complexity in modeling the relative contributions of those villains—technology (in particular automation), trade (in particular Chinese manufactures), and policy—to ensure that the vibrant academic debates about causality (some of which have generated brilliant research strategies and measurement techniques) were not going to make that much of a difference in political discourse.[9]

My view is that if there is a surprise here, it is actually that economic nationalism didn't grow more quickly and more infectiously than it has. One of the unfortunate characteristics of economic nationalism is that nationalist mind-sets and policies generate their own momentum—a positive-feedback, tipping-point kind of dynamic on the international stage. Once it appears likely that significant parts of the world are moving in a nationalist direction, it becomes less and less attractive for governments and societies still "on the fence" to hold out and maintain a more open, globalist mind-set and policy stance. The political logic is simple: if the world is moving decisively in the direction of economic nationalism, the last thing you want to be is the last government to move with it. The equilibrium that will emerge (at a higher level of ambient economic nationalism) may not be on aggregate as advantageous as a more globally open alternative—but that aggregate outcome is largely irrelevant to individual governments.

This self-reinforcing dynamic is part of the reason why slow growth is set to continue as a longer-term trend. Another set of reasons is captured in the several "secular stagnation" hypotheses that have evolved over the last several years.

Robert Gordon's is the longest standing and best known.[10] In Gordon's view, the problem lies in fundamental shortfalls in the Solow-Romer factors that generate economic growth—productive inputs themselves, and the efficiency with which those inputs combine to create growth. His argument is often (over-)simplified to emphasize the technology component, and sometimes cartooned further as claiming that contemporary technologies are not as important or revolutionary as were last century's breakthroughs (like electricity, the internal combustion engine, or indoor plumbing). That is a piece of Gordon's argument, but it is more accurate to summarize his view by saying that the technologies that generated outsized productivity growth during the 1930–1980 period were a massive exception, and today's technologies and the productivity boost they offer are closer to historical norms.

Put in those terms, this part of the argument no longer seems quite so surprising. And it is not only technology-driven productivity growth that is slowing—Gordon points as well to four "headwinds" that are reversals of other drivers that were distinctively supportive of growth during the mid-twentieth century. Those are demography (we now have a stagnant population in rich countries, with increasing life expectancy but not an equal increase in working life expectancy); education (diminishing returns now that basic mass education is provided to most rich-country inhabitants); inequality (a rising share of income going to the top earners, who tend to spend less as a proportion of income overall); and public debt (unfunded pensions and health-care obligations for an aging population among other burdens).

It's possible to envision over the horizon a post-Gordon period where advanced machine learning, biotechnology, and other revolutionary breakthroughs overcome all of these headwinds by creating entirely new industries and massively boosting productivity in old ones. That is the optimists' case, and you can read it pretty much anytime you want in *Wired Magazine* and other such publications. But the case at this moment is still unproven, and the history of technology prognostication doesn't tilt in its favor. For what it's worth, I am enough of an optimist to believe in the long-term revolutionary potential of these and other emerging technologies. But I'm also painfully aware of the time and resources it takes for organizations to integrate fundamentally new technologies in ways that meaningfully boost productivity. Even before we get to organizational change, in the realm of pure science it is important to keep in mind that biological systems in particular are more recalcitrant to human design and engineering than we typically admit. Synthetic biology is now real, but evolution is an extraordinarily powerful force for engineering to overcome, which is why drugs have side effects, bacteria develop antibiotic resistance, immune systems reject transplanted materials, and cancer cells mutate away from immunotherapies. Biotechnology applications will need to overcome evolution first, and then organizational inertia. That will take longer and possibly much longer than many think.

When 2050 rolls around, the Robert Gordon of the 2010s may seem to have been blindly pessimistic and remembered in the same vein as nineteenth-century pessimists who believed that invention had come to an end.[11] But 2050 is still a long way off.

In the interim, there is another secular stagnation hypothesis, popularized by Larry Summers among others, that rests on a straightforward

Keynesian argument about persistent shortfalls in demand. In this story, the GFC blew up a debt bubble that had produced an unsustainable and in some sense "fake" level of growth in the 2000s. The crash then led both firms and households to accumulate savings, in order to pay down debt and build up rainy-day cash piles to protect themselves from future dislocations. A self-fulfilling cycle ensues, where demand shortfalls hinder investment, and growth remains stuck stubbornly below long-term potential. Low interest rates and other monetary stimuli become like "pushing on a string." Unemployed and underemployed workers become discouraged and essentially give up hope; they allow their labor skills to deteriorate and eventually just withdraw from the active labor pool. There is evidence for each of these secular stagnation ingredients in the post–financial crisis decade.[12]

These lines of argument are, of course, neither mutually exclusive nor comprehensively exhaustive. A persistent shortage of productivity-enhancing technologies could certainly coexist with Keynesian demand shortfalls and excess savings. The two lines of argument would then complement each other, and that is in my view the most likely description of where the world finds itself as the 2010s come to an end.

If this is something of a vicious circle, there's some comfort to be taken in the fact that it won't go on forever. When Alvin Hansen made his original secular stagnation argument in 1938, he did raise that possibility, but he also did not foresee the imminent world war and the postwar economic growth dynamics that such a massive discontinuity sets in play. Nobody would wish for large-scale war to be the next decades' mechanism of escape from stagnation (though it can't be ruled out). Technologically induced productivity would be better for human beings than would, for example, a global pandemic that remade labor markets because of the mass death of workers. A scripted combination of policy moves that generated sufficient stimulus without creating too much concomitant financial instability might thread the needle as well.

We don't yet know how this period will end—and that is precisely the point. The most likely outcome is that it won't end soon, and that searching for growth in a low-growth world will be the leitmotiv for both corporate and government strategy for some time to come.

THE RISE AND FALL OF PERMISSIONLESS INNOVATION

But wait a minute: what of the impact of "innovation," which seems to be the buzzword for just about every business and government initiative taken over the last several years? Remember the quip that computers were showing up everywhere except in the productivity statistics—could the same be true of innovation more broadly?[13] To understand how innovation fits into the new pillars of economic geography requires a little bit of intellectual history of the concept, because that underpins an assessment of why it is now moving in different directions in different parts of the world. Those divergent pathways are now a second critical feature of the emerging economic geography.

This starts with an observation from around 2017 when the phrase "responsible innovation" creeped into the lexicon of industry, government, and technology, most noticeably in the United States.[14] There's no formal and agreed definition of that phrase, but the concept of responsible innovation has a sentiment behind it that is pretty clear. The core idea is that when you do something innovative and new, it's important to seek a balance between the potential value and good you can create, against the risks of downsides and losses you might also create, for yourself and for others.

In most conversations I've had with people whom I ask to define what they mean by responsible innovation, they end up talking about three categories of things that innovation programs should take into account: externalities, unintended consequences, and general risks. There's some overlap between the three, of course, but together they suggest a threshold or at least a filter for what kinds of innovation a firm or an industry should decide it wants to go forward with. Responsible innovation seems to imply that you should consider the external effects on others (which are known but for which you don't bear financial or legal responsibility); consequences that are unintended or unplanned in some sense, regardless of where they land; and a general risk profile that goes even further into the realm of conjecture (though it's not precisely clear how far).

Imagine, for example, that you were aiming to build a machine learning system for diagnosing depression though real-world evidence, drawing from diverse data streams about a person's risk factors, communications, work outputs, sleep patterns, and other digitally observable behaviors. The notion of responsible innovation recognizes the enormous potential value here, given that depression is an underdiagnosed and undertreated condition that causes immense human suffering.[15] But it also asks for balanced consideration of externalities (like how will this impact the conventional psychiatric profession, or pharmaceutical companies?); unintended consequences (like what would happen to people who were diagnosed but could not access any treatment, perhaps because they simply can't afford it); and general risk (what if it turns out that 25 percent or even more of the US population suffers from some form of depression—what would the health-care system and society more broadly do with that knowledge?).

It's fair to ask, precisely what does a responsible innovation doctrine say you ought to *do* with those considerations now that you have *thought* about them, and ultimately how do they affect your decision to proceed? The answers are unclear, but the intention seems clear, that it is incumbent on the innovator at least to *consider* these issues as part of her decision-making process.

Now wait a minute, once again. Isn't this all very obvious? Shouldn't we assume that people act this way? Apparently it isn't obvious. Did anyone ever believe in anything other than responsible innovation? In fact, they did. It wouldn't have been called "irresponsible innovation," of course; it's just that the notion of responsibility really was not present in the same way. A less polemical way to ask these questions is this: how did we get to a place where responsible innovation is a new notion that people need actually to state out loud? Or, *precisely what concept is responsible innovation supposed to replace?*

The answer, in short, is the concept of "permissionless innovation" that the IT industry promoted for decades. The simplest definition of permissionless innovation is that you should be free to innovate in essentially whatever way you can imagine contributing value, without having to secure the permission of gatekeepers whether they be regulators, incumbent firms, or people with mind-sets that fear change. Notions of responsibility to something other than the innovation process itself are just too vague to be a part of the equation.

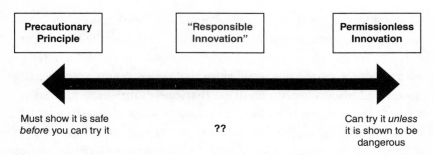

| Precautionary Principle | "Responsible Innovation" | Permissionless Innovation |

Must show it is safe *before* you can try it   ??   Can try it *unless* it is shown to be dangerous

Figure 5.2: Philosophies of Innovation.

Another way to put this is to say that permissionless innovation represents the polar opposite of the precautionary principle.[16] In a precautionary principle setting, you essentially have to prove that something is safe in order to move ahead. In a permissionless innovation setting, the burden of proof is flipped, and you ought to be able to go forward *unless* there is clear proof from uninterested parties that your innovation is positively dangerous. It's a bit of an oversimplification, but the continuum looks like Figure 5.2.

With that bit of context the question then becomes, how did this concept of permissionless innovation come to the fore and become the mantra of a particular time? And if responsible innovation is now a riposte, what does that imply about the economic geography landscape with which innovators will now have to contend going forward?

The modern intellectual history of permissionless innovation comes in three distinct phases, moving from technical to organizational and finally to societal. I place the founding moment in a somewhat obscure 1997 paper titled "Rise of the Stupid Network" by David Isenberg, a quirky and self-proclaimed "telephone company nerd" at AT&T.[17] Isenberg in this paper anticipated and made tangible many of the most important business-model implications of TCP/IP, the central protocol that routes packets around the Internet. He argued that it enabled a "new network philosophy and architecture . . . engineered for intelligence at the end-user's device, not in the network." This was the end-to-end principle, and it would spell the decline of monopoly power situated within the network itself, which would now be a "stupid network" where "the data on it would be the boss."

At the end of the paper, Isenberg offered a spirited opinion that the old telephone monopoly (whose value proposition rested in intelligent network services and bureaucratic control) could certainly remake itself for this new architecture, but that it probably would not do so "as long as their senior managers prefer to talk with lawyers, regulators, consultants, and financiers more than with experts in their own employ."

That language won him no friends inside AT&T, but it did instantiate the idea that pushing innovation out to the edges of the network would undermine the ability of the lawyers and regulators and the like to control and constrain innovation. Instead of having to ask permission from a monopoly to connect a device to a network or run an application on it, the stupid network would simply do what the devices and the applications asked it to do. This, at least in principle, went even further than the idiomatic "don't ask permission, ask forgiveness" mind-set. You wouldn't even have to ask forgiveness from the stupid network, because the technology had driven the system toward the de facto state of permissionless innovation.

The second big technical move toward the permissionless mind-set was the evolution of WiFi—something almost everyone in much of the world now takes for granted. The story of WiFi begins even earlier than Isenberg's paper, with a 1985 decision by the US Federal Communications Commission (FCC) to open several bands of radio spectrum in the 900-Mhz, 2.4-Ghz, and 5.8-Ghz ranges (these were known as "garbage bands") to unlicensed use. This was a radical decision at the time, because the radio spectrum had long been thought of as scarce, valuable, and thus regulated with very few exceptions (such as citizen band ham radio channels). The decision to unlicense these garbage-radio bands was an experiment prompted by a staff engineer named Michael Marcus, who in some sense was to wireless what David Isenberg was to the traditional telephone network.

Not much came of the experiment at the beginning, as various firms built radios for this spectrum that used proprietary and incompatible standards. It wasn't until 1997 that a committee of the Institute of Electrical and Electronics Engineers (IEEE) agreed on a common 802.11 standard. It took a couple more years for that common standard to be developed and simplified, and in 1999 the cascade of innovation took off. Working with Lucent, Apple introduced WiFi into its laptop computers and offered a home hub called AirPort. WiFi access points quickly found their way into coffee shops, hotels, airports, and other public spaces. WiFi cards were put into home consumer electronic devices like TVs, video recorders, and eventually security cameras and thermostats and, of course, smartphones (which otherwise in the early, pre-4G LTE years had to rely on slow cellular connections that made activities like mobile web browsing infuriating and almost impossible). This was precisely the virtuous circle of supply and demand that the unlicensed spectrum experiment had hoped to set off, and it spawned a cycle of innovation that made easy what had just a few years before seemed like impossible things—for example, piping music around your house or streaming video content into a living room TV without opening up your walls to rewire your home with Ethernet cables.

There were many lessons to be drawn from this success story, but one of the most important and influential was the dynamic power of permissionless innovation to change the world. To see this, simply imagine the counterfactual: a world in which the FCC had stuck to its normal mode of operation and required WiFi devices to pass a licensing regime and pay a fee. Imagine the cellular network operators lobbying the FCC to tighten that regime (which would have had the effect of forcing more data traffic onto their expensive cellular data plans). Imagine that Ethernet cable installers and drywall contractors had a say. If WiFi innovators had been forced to ask permission all along the way or to prove that their products were 99.999 percent reliable before deployment, we'd be living in a world without connected homes, without wireless printers, and with a small fraction of today's smartphone apps.[18] Perhaps we'd all still be buying CDs and DVDs. It seems almost impossible to imagine that world now, which is indeed one of the reasons why permissionless innovation became as important an idea as it did during the 2010s.

At some point this mainly technical principle of permissionless innovation joined up with an organizational principle that pointed in the same direction. The key moment here was the publication of Clayton Christensen's book *The Innovator's Dilemma* in 1997 (just before the "stupid network" paper). There are very few "business" books that have been the subject of quite as much praise and critique as this one.[19] The critiques notwithstanding, Christensen's theory of disruptive innovation had a massive impact on organizational mind-sets related to permissionless innovation.

Christensen's model is less about technology than it is about organizational incentives. Strong and successful incumbent firms too often lose out to startups in sectors with rapid innovation not because they aren't aware of what's going on, but because their innovation processes essentially block them from taking advantage. The incumbent firm is focused on serving its existing (and profitable) customers, giving them more of what they say they want. A disruptive innovation technology, to start, is an alternative that underperforms the existing technology, and so it offers "less of what customers in established markets wanted and so could rarely be initially employed there."[20] But the technology is disruptive because it has the potential to improve at a much steeper rate than the existing technology—and at some point in a future projection, the curves will cross.

Now even if the incumbent firm recognizes the potential of the disruptive technology to ultimately win the race, a decision to jump onto the new technology curve early would mean accepting lower profit margins and redirecting research and development resources away from "sustaining innovation" investment, which aims to improve on the existing technology curve, and to meet the expressed needs of the firm's existing customers. That's a very difficult decision for a highly successful firm that operates with normal organizational processes to make. In contrast, betting on disruptive technologies is the best and sometimes the *only* decision available to scrappy startups. And so the deck would appear to be stacked against the incumbent, who ironically in Christensen's turn of phrase is set up to do precisely the wrong thing by doing what it thought it was supposed to be doing, which is listening closely to what its most important customers say they want.

Could the decision turn out differently—that is, could a successful incumbent make the leap and embrace disruptive technologies? Of course it could, in theory. But it will most likely need leadership with a clear understanding of the dilemma, a distinctive corporate culture, as well as organizational structures and processes that would allow these counterintuitive decisions to be made and implemented.

This is where the permissionless innovation mind-set becomes critical. If there are people and business units within the incumbent that see the potential and want to make the leap, there are systems and processes that will do their best to block them or shut them down—most obviously through budgeting but also through more subtle means of dissuasion. *As long as the internal disrupters have to seek the permission of the normal corporate hierarchy,* they are at a structural disadvantage to startups that have nothing to lose. And so part of the solution is to create protected pockets within the incumbent where permissionless innovation can thrive—for example, in units sometimes known as "skunk works" that are financially, organizationally, and physically separate from the rest of the firm.[21]

This is the organizational component of permissionless innovation. It is a means of instantiating a version of Max Weber's notion of charismatic leadership, a way of creating spaces for breaking through the systems and processes that bureaucracies would otherwise use to control innovation: a protected refuge where disruption gets a chance to prove its worth.[22]

In 2011 Marc Andreessen coined the phrase "software is eating the world" as another way of expressing this organizational dynamic.[23] The move to software-based competition, which Andreessen put a label on here, both requires and enables a permissionless innovation environment.

It requires something close to permissionless innovation because software of any complexity is a beta product—imperfect and evolving, generally on a fast cycle. The best way to accelerate software-based innovation is to release software into the wild early in the product cycle, and long before anything like all bugs and other problems have been worked out . . . and then improve the software on a rapid iteration timeline as its interactions with the world reveal what is broken.

To see this clearly, consider another vivid counterfactual, an imaginary world in which software would be subject to the kinds of regulatory approval processes that the US Food and Drug Administration applies to prescription medications. Most new medications have to be proven efficacious and safe (not quite but to nearly a precautionary principle level) through at least three separate stages of clinical trials and thousands of pages of filings, involving hundreds or thousands of employees and costs that are usually in the hundreds of millions of dollars. No modern software product would survive even a fraction of that level of precaution. You can't imagine an "app store" model of platform growth in that world because it wouldn't exist; the model requires something much closer to the other end of the spectrum where only software that has been demonstrated to be positively dangerous is restricted from the market.[24] And sometimes even that kind of software sneaks through.

Software-based innovation also enables permissionless innovation by vastly reducing the costs (directly) and other barriers (indirectly) to starting new software-based businesses from scratch. The late 2010s manifestation of this is, of course, the cloud services model, which has reduced startup costs for software-intensive firms by at least ten times and possibly more. The permissionless innovation mind-set builds on that enabling cloud technology to support a broad presumption that no other major barriers to entry should be allowed to offset that development.

Two concrete examples show just how important this has been. Consider autonomous vehicles, which moved in less than a decade from the basic research stage to lab settings and, in the second half of the 2010s, onto live road testing in many locations around the world.[25] Cars and trucks are some of the most highly regulated tools that people use; and the companies that make them are some of the largest and politically connected incumbents on the globe. In that context, the innovation environment around autonomous vehicle development has been for the most part closer to permissionless than to a precautionary principle, and much more like a software-eating-the-world environment than most observers of the motor vehicle industry would have expected.

Another set of examples comes from what is called "fintech," a range of firms that provide financial and banking services on top of the basic banking infrastructure that the (highly regulated) large incumbent banks still control. The 2015 revised European Payment Services Directive (PSD2) required incumbents in 2018 to open significant parts of their systems and data through application programming interfaces (APIs) to fintechs that offer software-based services to customers, while guaranteeing access to the underlying financial infrastructure that makes those services usable and valuable. It's quite a lot like the opening of the basic telecommunications infrastructure that took place in the United States over the course of the late 1970s and 1980s, which was in many respects the beginning of the internet revolution and the stupid network model itself. But now it's happening in financial services, which (given the fact that it deals with people's money and the most basic societal infrastructures for the storage and exchange of value) is again where a precautionary principle mind-set might have been expected to linger.

That is what "software eating the world" really means, and when you think about how quickly sector-redefining shifts around autonomous vehicles and fintech have been allowed or even encouraged by governments to move forward, it looks like not much of an exaggeration from a technical and organizational perspective.

Where permissionless innovation ran into meaningful trouble is when it took a third big step and quietly transformed into something much more like a *societal principle*—a way of thinking about remaking not just technology foundations or firms or even sectors of an economy but actually something larger, that touches on broader social structures in which technology and organizations are embedded. One place to see this in practical terms is the story of Uber.

The remaking of personal transportation as Uber conceived it is a societal-level project, not just a business model or a sectoral initiative. Put differently, the company had no intention of simply replacing medallion taxis with private vehicles and independent drivers who could be summoned on a smartphone, despite how important and valuable that simple idea turned out to be. The intention was to fundamentally reimagine the process by which an individual gets from one place to another, *starting* with the remaking of the taxicab sector and the individual ownership of motor vehicles.

Thinking about the latter half of that reveals the "societal remake" proposition, which is far more revolutionary. Look around your daily life for a moment and focus on how much of your physical space, your financial resources, and our overall economy relate to the simple fact that many individuals own their own cars. If you live in the United States, you might very well have a garage for your car(s) that is bigger than your living room and kitchen. You probably spend more on your car than you do on your health or education. Your neighborhood is dotted with gas stations, body shops, and parking lots (one estimate is that nearly 14 percent of Los Angeles real estate is taken up by parking lots).[26] And what do you get for all that? Perhaps a form of personal mobility—if you are willing to put up with traffic jams and other such things. What you get for certain is a big lump of metal and chemicals that represents a fast depreciating asset as it sits in either your garage or a parking space— which it probably does for at least 80 percent of the time that you own it. And you get a nontrivial probability of being in a serious accident at some point in your life, which could leave you and others injured, maimed, or dead.

I'm not trying to argue here that personal car ownership is an evil thing or even necessarily a bad bargain from a utility perspective. It might not be either, if the kind of personal mobility that it offers is valuable enough to people. My point here is simply to point out how large the personal auto looms in the way in which many people live at the individual and aggregate level. That is why reimagining personal transportation as Uber aspired to do is a societal-level project. And projects of that magnitude are going to encounter obstacles at many different levels, as they go far beyond the corporate or regulatory bureaucracy or the planning models and mind-sets that Isenberg and Christensen explained. It wasn't just taxicab commissions, insurance companies, municipal road authorities, and the like whose vested interests were aligned to slow down or stop the Uber trajectory. These ingredients of regulatory capture and material capture by themselves were massive roadblocks. There were also elements of emotional capture. Many people and not only in the United States have extremely strong emotional ties to the personal automobile, as a symbol of financial achievement, individual freedom, and even artistic expression. These forms of capture naturally interconnect and reinforce each other. Consider, for example, the degree to which the advertising industry depends on automakers promoting cars to individual buyers. How did a company like Uber have any chance of getting past these powerful incumbent interests?

The answer was a societal-level application of the permissionless innovation mind-set, adopted now as an explicit corporate strategy. The strategy was to get Uber on the road as quickly as possible without worrying too much about its status in law or regulation. Call it a "ride-sharing" service or a "sharing economy" platform, to buy just enough time. Play an aggressive form of regulatory arbitrage that says confidently "we are going to do this until you find a way to stop us." In the interim, race to create a product so compelling to users that the customers of Uber would overwhelm the regulators if and when they tried to stop it.

Put simply, the core idea was that if the company could get to sufficient scale quickly enough to generate so much consumer satisfaction with and demand for Uber, that when regulators sought to step in they would be fighting not with Uber per se but rather with Uber's users who literally could not imagine living without it anymore, then forms of capture would fall away.

The strategy worked brilliantly, until it didn't. It was here that permissionless innovation as a societal concept really ran up against its limits. The backlash began to gather around 2014 in a number of different countries (Australia, Belgium, Denmark, France, Germany, and others). It was something of a landmark moment when in 2016 Uber withdrew from providing services in Austin, Texas, rather than comply with a city ordinance that required drivers to submit to fingerprinting and background checks. To be clear, the backlash against Uber was not only about protecting the incumbent taxi companies and the like. It was more broadly about labor markets and the "gig" economy; about urban planning and road use; and about many of the other societal-level implications of remaking personal transportation.

It surely didn't help that Uber was led (until June 2017) by a publicly abrasive personality (Travis Kalanick) who become known for his arrogance and abusive behavior toward employees and others, nor did it help that some of Uber's means of operationalizing its strategy went beyond the realm of anything that could plausibly be called arbitrage and into the realm of the illegal.[27] But even if Uber's leadership had been kinder and gentler and the company had more carefully skirted the line between arbitrage and illegal activity, it's likely that the backlash would have been more or less the same. Permissionless innovation is challenging to sustain at the level of technology; it is even trickier at the level of organizations. When it tested the boundaries by evolving into something more like a societal principle, it hit a threshold that it couldn't overcome.

That doesn't mean the political economy of technology is about to go in the 2020s all the way backward to a precautionary principle mindset (though there are certainly prominent voices on issues like AI safety and algorithmic decision making that at the end of the 2010s are calling for essentially that). It more likely means a move toward the middle, something like the notion of responsible innovation that I defined (loosely) earlier in this chapter. The looseness of that definition is intellectually unsatisfying and difficult to deal with from a strategy perspective, in part because the fuzzy boundaries of what is and isn't responsible are likely to be quite different in different societies around the world. It isn't as easy to work with as would be a uniform global standard or consensus. But those very complexities make up the second major feature of the new economic geography landscape for global reach.

PLATFORM BACKLASH

The third major feature of the new economic geography is the gathering storm around intermediation platform businesses, and the associated return of governments to the playing field as increasingly central players, not just light-touch referees. These vectors relate to the decline of permissionless innovation, but stretch further in both cause and consequence.

Before the second half of the 2010s, it would have been reasonable to start a discussion about the relationship between platform firms and government with observations like these:

- Platform firms are wildly popular among consumers and loved or at least admired by politicians for their technological wizardry and explosive growth.
- Antitrust and competition policy concerns might loom somewhere in the background, but they aren't really more than a theoretical issue that might arise at some point in the (distant) future.

- Information and data technology (IDT) is about productivity and new services, and thus will generally have a low political profile relative to its overall importance in the economy. Government involvement in the industry is moderate; weaker in the United States and stronger in Europe and China, but not enough in any case to merit sustained attention.

Assumptions like these were never on as firm a ground as Silicon Valley wanted to believe. To see why requires another little bit of history, because one of the most important elements of the foundation for their business models—the 1998 Digital Millennium Copyright Act (DMCA)—was seriously flawed from the outset.

It's striking in retrospect that the DMCA could have been passed by a unanimous vote in the US Senate, but that is what happened. While copyright law wasn't always the most exciting area for internet evangelists, there was a recognition that digital rights management systems had reasonable arguments at their core and that if the overall copyright regime for protecting some kinds of IP were to survive, then simply allowing anyone to "break the lock" and make infinite copies of music, movies, and other digital products without any real restrictions was not a logical way to proceed. The DMCA therefore made it illegal to create and distribute tools that could break digital locks; it also made illegal the simple act of circumventing a digital lock, regardless of whether any copyright infringement followed.

Later these were seen as overly harsh and in some respects impractical provisions, even by many people and firms that had sympathy for their underlying goals. But the more important and long-lasting consequences came with an accompanying set of provisions that carved out in Title II of the law special exceptions for what were called OSPs (online service providers). The OSPs (which included internet service providers, or ISPs, but also what would later become known as platforms) were granted copyright liability exemptions in a safe-harbor arrangement for user-generated content.[28] Put simply, if a customer of an ISP or a platform engaged in copyright infringement on the ISP or platform, it was the *customer* who fundamentally was at fault and could be held liable, not the ISP or platform.

Proponents of this position had the force of a simple analogy in the story of the photocopy machine. That machine is an incredibly useful invention with many legitimate uses. Now imagine that someone uses a Xerox machine to make unauthorized paper copies of a book, above and beyond fair use. Who is liable for copyright infringement? Surely it is the person who made the copies, and not Xerox that is at fault. As a society we don't want to restrict photocopy-machine innovation by holding Xerox at risk. We want to restrict copyright infringement and that is about targeting the person who used the machine for illegal ends.

In the case of the DMCA, the firms didn't get off scot-free—they had to meet a set of requirements for safe harbor, which included setting up processes to block or remove infringing material when a copyright holder notified them. But in 1998 those processes were mostly manual and clunky, while the users' ability to upload infringing content was nearly seamless and instantaneous. The imbalance had a predictable effect. In 2005, it massively hit the world of video in the form of a startup company called YouTube, a "video-sharing" website that within six months of launch became the preferred place for internet video, where more than 65,000 videos were uploaded and 100 million views were being recorded each day.[29]

YouTube uploaders were shown a message that was supposed to discourage copyright infringement. But the responsibility and liability lay squarely in the hands of the users, not the company in accordance with the safe-harbor provisions of the DMCA. Very quickly it became an open secret that YouTube was a massive trove of copyright-infringing content, whether pirated music videos or full TV shows and movies (some of which were recorded with video cameras from the seats of regular theaters) and the like.

You don't need to attribute nefarious intentions to anyone simply to recognize that YouTube's business model was heavily dependent on the DMCA safe-harbor provision (the counterfactual here is that if the burden had been on YouTube to verify that uploaded videos were appropriately owned or licensed, the story of the company would surely have been very different). As it was, YouTube grew at such a breakneck pace that the raw numbers are almost impossible to comprehend. One estimate had it that YouTube in 2007 consumed as much bandwidth as the entire internet had in 2000. Various estimates for upload rates exist—a plausible one is that by 2011 forty-eight hours of video were uploaded *per minute* and by 2017 the upload rate was nearly ten times that. No one knows precisely what proportion might be copyright-infringing, but whatever informed assessments we now have depend on video forensics and other sophisticated technologies that can automate at least some detection. These technologies did not exist in 2006.

For OSPs like YouTube, the safe-harbor provision did restrict three things: that the OSP should not make money directly attributable to infringement; that the OSP could not look the other way if it knew about the infringement; and that the OSP would have to remove the infringing material expeditiously once the owner identified it and notified the OSP with a takedown notice.

In practice these were complicated and ambiguous provisions that could be readily side-stepped, regardless of intent. Financial benefit would be hard to assess in a startup business likely showing losses overall. When it came to not looking the other way, that was not a tall order since the platform was not required to actively monitor its system or "affirmatively seek" infringing material.[30] As for expeditious takedown, there was lots of room to interpret what in practice was an expeditious process, and how that could be appropriately balanced with a counternotice process in which the uploader (and purported infringer) could contest the infringement claim.

It was inevitable that some of this ambiguity would be worked out in the courts and not just in markets. Just a few months after Google acquired YouTube (in November 2006), Viacom filed a $1 billion lawsuit (in March 2007) alleging "massive intentional copyright infringement" against Viacom content, citing upward of 150,000 video clips being hosted on YouTube. Google and YouTube predictably invoked the DMCA's safe-harbor provision as a defense. A series of judgments and appeals followed over the course of more than six years and at the end of the process, what stood was the core logic of the safe-harbor provision. The courts awarded no damages and reaffirmed that YouTube was not liable on the basis of "general knowledge" that users had infringed copyright.

It's important to recognize that YouTube did not simply try to hide behind the courts and ignore markets and technology as part of a solution. Rather, it invested heavily in systems (such as Content ID) that were designed to proactively identify copyright-infringing uploads and support the copyright owners in their business decisions about how to respond.[31]

Ten years after the Viacom suit was filed, it was reasonable to argue that a dynamic equilibrium of a kind had been reached. YouTube was enormously successful; copyright holders' interests had been managed to a fair-enough result; innovation had been spurred in both technology and business models; and the world had access to an unprecedented and almost unimaginable trove of video content ranging from cute cats to educational videos and just about everything in between, which it would not have had otherwise.

The problem was, this dynamic equilibrium wasn't stable. This is because it had emerged in an unbalanced manner and even more so because it fostered further imbalances of power on the part of the platform firms. It's good in competitive situations to win and even better to be able to proclaim that a rising tide is lifting all boats. But when some boats are consistently being lifted much higher and amassing even more relative power for the next competition, the equilibrium at some point is destined to break down, for political reasons. And that's exactly what began to happen in 2017, which may very well be remembered as the year that the world and particularly the United States fell out of love with the platform firms.[32]

It wasn't any one thing but a concatenation of events and developments that lay behind the disillusionment. Edward Snowden's 2013 revelations certainly set the stage. It's notable that the first major classified program Snowden exposed (named PRISM) was a system that provided for court-approved access to Google and Yahoo accounts.[33] PRISM was not the most shocking thing that Snowden revealed, but for the American internet platform firms it was a significant public relations and perception predicament. What it showed was that the IDT firms were far more deferential to the US government and particularly to law enforcement than their messaging and self-conscious self-conception had led their employees and customers to believe. Counterculture and libertarian roots and rhetoric notwithstanding, the IDT firms had become part of "the establishment," and no amount of branding was going to hide that fact for long.

By early 2017 the Silicon Valley fairy tale of small startups born in garages was looking threadbare in comparison to the reality of massive global firms with profits and market capitalizations among the very largest companies on earth. Phrases like FANG (Facebook, Apple, Netflix, Google) began to appear regularly in the popular press. Farhad Manjoo in the *New York Times* coined the term "Frightful Five" (adding Microsoft to the list) and in January of 2017 wrote, "The world's governments are newly motivated to take on the tech giants. In the United States, Europe, Asia, and South America, the Five find themselves increasingly arrayed against legal and regulatory powers, and *often even against popular will.*"[34] Manjoo's stories caught part of the wave of perception change; he rightly emphasized the wrenching loss of innocence when founding myths disintegrate. People had for years loved the tech giants as "forces of innovation and delight." The companies had, at least in the common narrative, "gotten huge just the way you're supposed to in America—by inventing new stuff that people love." But this made the loss of innocence yet more poignant. One reason Manjoo pointed to was that "familiarity breeds contempt"—the idea that "as technology wormed deeper into our lives, it began to feel less like an unalloyed good and more like every other annoyance we have to deal with."[35]

Maybe that was part of it. What was equally visible in the public mood was disaffection of a more fundamental sort. Silicon Valley was increasingly being talked about (even in the San Francisco Bay Area) as an insulated island of self-congratulatory privilege where brashly rich young ideologues built products for other privileged people and told themselves that by doing well for themselves and for people like them, they were doing good for the world. It was increasingly common in Berkeley, even for those sympathetic to the IDT world, to hear people talk derisively about the best minds of a generation going off to build technologies whose success was ultimately measured by getting people to click on more advertisements.

And, as was inevitable, the dilemma of relationships with law enforcement deepened. When the FBI in 2016 demanded that Apple assist in accessing the iPhone of a suspect in a mass shooting in Riverside, California, it set off a spirited public debate about encryption technologies, security "back doors," and privacy in which the IDT firms struggled to articulate a position that was both technologically realistic and politically defensible.[36] Their best efforts to explain cryptography and security in terms that made sense to nontechnical people failed. A small majority but still a majority of Americans came to the conclusion that the FBI was right and Apple was wrong.[37]

There were other reasons, some long-standing, for the IDT firm backlash. Arguments about cultural homogenization that had been made in the previous decade resurfaced: the best-known platform firms (outside of China, and more on that in Chapter 6) were after all American firms, and to the extent that Lawrence Lessig's classic argument that values become embedded in software code was increasingly obvious, these were "American" values or possibly even more narrow "West Coast American" values that weren't clearly shared.[38] The 2016 election heightened some perceptions, particularly in Europe, that the American values aspect of IDT firm power was even more complex and worrisome in relationship to populist sentiments in the US electorate (more on that in Chapters 6 and 7). I've referred to this unease previously as GAPAD, or "Generalized American Power Anxiety Disorder," and what was new and distinctive about it here was the degree to which it now attached to the FANG or the Frightful Five, not the US government.[39]

Fundamentally it never made sense to believe that IDT could sustain a low political profile. The sector wasn't just about building productivity and services for economic growth. It was self-consciously blurring boundaries as it moved into close contact with government, politics, and—crucially—*public* services. Business-process re-engineering in the public sector is never apolitical for long. Corruption (and using technology to try to reduce corruption) can't be apolitical. Government agencies moving to commercial cloud services isn't apolitical. The IDT sector wanted to portray these things as simply moves to enhance efficiency, security, and accountability, but that was never going to stand up to opinions and perceptions once the public was aware of and focused on what the IDT firms were doing.

The story of the British East India Company from Chapter 2 is instructive when it comes to the reassertion of government power in taxation, security, what are thought of as public services, and ultimately forms of territorial sovereignty. Nothing guarantees that governments win these fights, but nothing guarantees that they lose them either. What's certain is that nobody is throwing in the towel. Every generation has its John Perry Barlow and its own version of the Declaration of Independence in cyberspace, or death of the nation-state, or crumbling pillars of Westphalia.[40] And then it experiences a pendulum swing. The pendulum certainly seems to be swinging more quickly over the last several hundred years. What this means is that economic geography is still fundamentally political-economic geography, and that the IDT firms can't avoid being at the center of the debate.

In that context, the emergence of cybersecurity as a major public concern in 2017 was the final trend to consider, pointing in the same direction for the platform firms. The internet itself as well as most of the devices and applications that run on it have been insecure for decades, in a manner that experts have known, understood, and feared for nearly all that time. So-called hacks of high-profile websites and data repositories started making headline news at the start of the 2010s. (The use of the word "hack" itself demonstrated the lack of seriousness with which many people still treated these events—"hack" connotes an element of mischief, playfulness, or even clever inventiveness, whereas these events should have been labeled simply and appropriately as attacks, frauds, crimes, and assaults.) The 2014 discovery and disclosure of a massive attack on the US Office of Personnel Management, in which the extensive personal information of millions of present and former government employees with security clearances was stolen, was in one sense just another in a long list of major data breaches. But it was also a powerful demonstration of how Weberian bureaucracies seemed incapable of securing their data against determined adversaries.[41]

The assaults on data sets and network security were overshadowed in many respects by the attacks on content in the 2016 Brexit and US presidential votes. The ensuing debates about "fake news" highlighted from yet another direction the massive power of internet platform firms to shape discourse and political life. What this means and what to do about it is a hugely complicated issue that I'll have a few things to say about in Chapter 7.

For now it's sufficient to point out how the fake news issue at a very basic level became a lose-lose one for a firm like Facebook. Facebook's business model depends on high levels of user engagement, and fake news articles are designed to achieve exactly that. Fake news succeeds.[42] Yet Facebook wants to be an open platform that connects people around the things they care about; it does not want to be a media or news company that edits, fact-checks, and verifies truth from fiction. It seems that very few people want a company like Facebook to become a censor that decides which stories are valid enough to share and which are not. But very few people are happy with the neutral platform approach and the status quo either. While a great deal of very sophisticated effort is being put into trying to find ways of managing this problem (and may succeed to some extent), the basic dilemma of the platform firms remains exposed.

You don't have to make or agree with big philosophical arguments about the place of IDT in modern life and society to recognize that the platform firms would eventually be subject to the same social and political concerns and pressures that have previously focused on sectors like food, transportation, or energy. With hindsight, the surprise really ought to be that such a high degree of splendid isolation for these firms lasted as long as it did. This is particularly and obviously true with regard simply to their size. You cannot be among the ten or so most valuable firms in the world and avoid being at the center of debates about power and influence for long. In Chapter 6, I'll introduce a new and yet more politically sensitive argument about size, power, and positive-feedback loops of a modern technology paradigm, all of which make the intensity of this emerging pressure even more profound.

ECONOMIC GEOGRAPHY IN MOTION

Slow growth, a changing innovation environment, and pushback against the US platform firms are remaking the foundations of economic geography. In each case I've argued here that the trending directions are visibly related, and that if there is a surprising element to all this, it

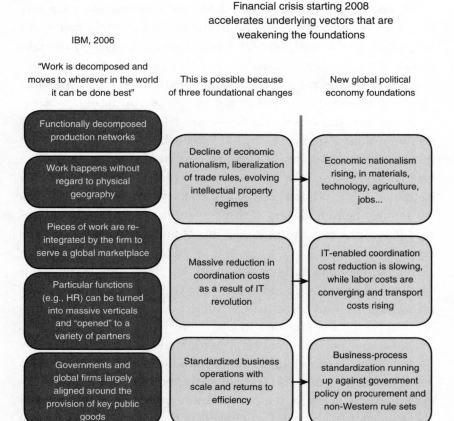

Figure 5.3: Logic of the Globally Integrated Enterprise, Reprised.

ought to be only that these trends took as long to develop and manifest as they did. That puts increasing pressure on the foundations of the GIE model from Chapter 3:

- declining economic nationalism, liberalization of trade rules, evolving intellectual property rights regimes
- massive reduction in coordination costs across geographically distributed production networks tied together with IDT
- increasingly standardized business operations with scale and returns to efficiency

These, to repeat, were the building blocks on which the GIE model could thrive, by decomposing "work," moving pieces to wherever in the world it can be done best, and then reintegrating the pieces fluidly to serve a global marketplace. In that world, functionally decomposed production networks facilitate work being done without regard to physical geography. Particular functions would be turned into massive vertical businesses and opened to a variety of partners who contribute modules and IP. Governments and global firms would largely align themselves around the provision of key public goods that would keep the system vibrant.

Now fast-forward to the post-GFC era, where slow growth, responsible rather than permissionless innovation, and platform backlash make up the new pillars of economic geography. The dynamics that these three vectors create point in a very different direction for the next decade. Economic nationalism rises, in domains from technology to jobs and (as Chapter 6 explains in detail) most consequentially in data. Political nationalism and populism lead to a decline in global public goods and a fracturing of many of the synergistic interests that did exist in this space between firms and governments. Coordination costs for distributed production networks may not be rising per se, but neither are they falling at anything like the rate at which that happened in the previous decade. Business-process standardization is running up against government policies, what I will explain as "non-Western" rule sets, typified by data localization and re-nationalization of technology research, development, and infrastructure deployments. Demand shortfalls and secular stagnation still loom over this landscape and likely will for some time (Figure 5.3).

To reach the world that is shaped by these new forces is a very different proposition. The rest of the book will answer the question of how an aspiring global actor can best do that, with a new template for an organization that makes sense going forward. The most important aspect of that template is how it deals with the flow of data through the organization, which in turn will be a function as ever of technology and the actions of governments. Those are the subjects of Chapters 6 and 7.

6

HOW TO ORGANIZE

THE WORLD IS always more complicated than it used to be. Or so contemporary observers are apt to say. In 1992 and thereabouts, it was common to hear the Washington, DC foreign policy elite pine for the "good old days" of the Cold War when the rules of the game, the stakes, and the most important players were supposedly clear and simple. It's a natural human tendency to engage in what I call "flattening out the past," which means imagining in retrospect that very hard decisions from the past were much simpler, and a great deal of historical contingency that seemed to be present wasn't really all that contingent.[1]

Yet I seriously doubt that John F. Kennedy felt during the Cuban Missile Crisis that his decisions were simple, or that history could not have unfolded in radically different ways depending on what he and Khrushchev chose to do. Similarly, I doubt that leaders of aspiring global organizations in 1776 or 1977 or 2005 had it all that much easier than their counterparts do today. Was it self-evident for eighteenth-century British capitalists to construct an overseas colonial empire for triangular trade at distances that were weeks or months of travel away? Was it so obviously a great idea for major Western firms in the 1990s to rely for production of goods on an unprecedented cluster of manufacturing facilities in a poor, developing country ruled by a Communist Party?

No, it wasn't. And so it doesn't help anyone to make today seem more complicated by understating the complexity of past decisions, nor the yearnings for clear conceptual frameworks to guide them at the moment they were being made (rather than in retrospect) and the wish for a

360-degree view of the facts. But leaders don't get that luxury in advance. We make do with the best hypotheses we can construct and a highly imperfect and incomplete set of facts, to build a conceptual framework that, if we are lucky and tough-minded, gives reasonably clear guidance about strategy and a set of indicators to judge whether things are playing out the way they should if the hypotheses are right.

This chapter's and Chapter 7's hypotheses build on the previous chapters' propositions about the emerging economic geography of the 2020s. The point is to place a bet on that landscape, by sketching a template for an aspiring global organization to reach the world. I will show that the template that makes best sense is a regional one, but with a delineation among regions that is less about physical geography and more about politically determined boundaries that manifest in technology standards and rule sets. The new global organization that functions effectively on this landscape will have several copies that operate within these regions and are relatively self-contained when it comes to design, production, and distribution. Cultural fit and government relations will matter more than they have for decades. I don't think it matters particularly what label is given to this template—whether it ends up being called a new phase of globalization, a new form of regionalism, or something else. What matters is understanding where in physical and political geography things happen and why, and how data flows within and among these places to connect them together. This chapter will make each of these variables explicit in the form of a bet, and then begin tying the logic of that bet to the core characteristics of the economic geography landscape on which they are suited to succeed. Chapter 7 completes that process and then explores what else is happening in a world that is organized along these lines, with explicit arguments about what is better and what is worse, what is more peaceful and what is more conflictual, what is more fair and just versus the opposite, than the world we knew in the 2010s.

The place to start is with a concrete example, from an economic sector and a country where the late 2010s stakes are understood by all to be extremely high. How is China evolving its position as an aspiring global leader in information and data technology (IDT) and particularly machine learning (ML)?

CHINA'S AI RACE AND WHAT IT SIGNALS

Living in the San Francisco Bay Area, it is easy to assume that global leadership in ML is unquestionably centered somewhere between Menlo Park and Sunnyvale, California, with an outpost in Seattle. The predominant big firms (Google, Facebook, Amazon, Nvidia, and a few others) are complemented by a vast ecology of smaller and more specialized firms, domain-specific ML firms (working on autonomous vehicles or computer vision for medical imaging or similar applications), and research outposts of other companies from around the world that have located in Silicon Valley in order to get a seat at the table or at least an up-close look at what the ML leaders are doing.

Because ML sits atop a rapidly advancing set of digital technologies and practices that revolve around open-source code, sometimes shared algorithms, and intensive scientific exchange between and among academics, industry researchers, and pre-competitive collaborations, it is also easy for Americans to assume that US-based companies and in particular the West Coast Silicon Valley and Seattle clusters will naturally be at the forefront going forward. This is part unmitigated ethnocentrism and part an extension of the technology cluster arguments made in AnnaLee Saxenian's iconic study of Silicon Valley, *Regional Advantage*.[2] It is also an extrapolation (sometimes subconscious) of what American students of modern economic development have argued for decades: that open societies and liberal democracies have a distinct advantage in these IT-driven development paths, and that it is essentially impossible to have a nondemocratic, state-led leader *at the digital technology horizon* (as compared to being a fast follower).

But Chinese companies and the Beijing government aren't convinced that any of these arguments will hold up. They see instead a set of fundamental advantages that are propelling China ahead in what the government unambiguously describes as a full-on competition *between countries* for ML leadership. China's advantage starts with a pure mass of internet users—nearly 800 million, which is more than twice the population of the United States in 2018. It continues with mobile phone subscriptions (more than 1.5 billion in China in 2018), which is yet more important because a much higher percentage of the Chinese population accesses the Internet more commonly on mobile devices.[3] These mobile users are in many ways more sophisticated and advanced in their app use—for instance, they are fifty times more likely to use their phones for payments than their American counterparts.

Consider the example of TenCent, the Chinese social media giant that owns WeChat, sometimes called "China's App for everything." WeChat probably crossed the 1 billion user mark sometime in early 2018. Half of WeChat users spend more than ninety minutes on the app daily. They use it for "push to talk" speech as well as text; they publish bloglike posts to it; they share their GPS location with their friends over it; and they use it as a payment service (by some estimates, more than a third of Chinese mobile payments go through WeChat).[4] This adds up to an extraordinarily rich data set that may be unmatchable anywhere.

These are just a few reasons why many Chinese and an increasing number of outside observers believe that because advances in ML will depend meaningfully on large, diverse, and rich data sets, then China is starting with major structural advantages that it will be hard for anyone to contest.[5] Other advantages are policy-driven. The Chinese regulatory environment is likely to remain highly favorable, particularly when it comes to ML experiments and applications that aid the state in social and financial control (these will often be precisely the kinds of experiments and applications that will be constrained in the United States and the European Union over privacy and equity concerns). In an area like autonomous vehicles where many different regulatory, insurance, and legal players have to coordinate, the Chinese state probably has a significant industrial policy advantage over the complex and fractious US environment. That policy advantage extends to massive government commitments at both the national and municipal levels to early stage funding for startups, and the luring with resources of some of the world's most talented scientists.[6]

Two major policy documents from 2017 illustrate the intention and capacity of the Chinese state to further press these advantages. The first, labeled a "cybersecurity law," is actually a widely scoped foray into an unabashed techno-nationalist agenda. Among other provisions, it includes data localization regulations that appear to permit the government enormous latitude in requiring companies (those designated as "critical" or subject to breaches that could "harm peoples' livelihoods") to store the data of Chinese citizens in Chinese data centers. It also provides for "national security reviews" of digital products, which would include access to software source code. Like a series of such laws that have been developed regularly by Beijing over the last twenty years, many of the specifics and implementation details of this law are vague in the writing. In principle the cybersecurity law would constrain domestic Chinese firms just as it does foreign firms. But the history of these kinds of laws and how their terms and practical enforcement evolve over time lead to a clear expectation of selective and strategic enforcement that will in practice focus on foreign competitors and aim for domestic firms' advantage.[7]

The second policy document, Beijing's AI Development Plan from summer 2017, also reads as an explicit declaration that artificial intelligence (AI) will be a national power resource and the nexus of competition between countries for the next decade. China's stated ambition in this document is to match US capabilities by 2020; to produce major original breakthroughs that will drive economic transformation over the following five years; and to become the world's leader in AI by 2030. The government will "foster a new national leadership and establish the key fundamentals for an economic great power"—language that unambiguously signals the yoking of AI and ML technologies to the power of the state, both domestically and in the international economy.[8] Reminiscent of Japanese economic development planning through the Ministry of International Trade and Industry (MITI) in the 1980s, the Chinese Ministry of Science and Technology even designates particular companies that will lead individual sectors (Baidu for autonomous vehicles, Alibaba for "smart cities," etc.) and commits a multibillion-dollar investment initiative to the effort.[9]

This is all the language of aspirational economic planning, and, of course, more than a grain of salt is warranted in projecting what it will actually achieve. But the point here is really about intentionality and the mind-set of the state that is being signaled, a form of ML mercantilism that envisions this technology yoked to the purpose of state power.

Aspirations to technology leadership in ML connect inexorably to a presumptive Chinese rule set that is starting to emerge on the global account as a serious mercantilist-leaning alternative. When ML is seen as an essential resource of state power and the international economy is seen as a set of national economies playing out on a global stage, then great power national rule sets around regulation for ML safety, ethics, privacy, competition and the like will contend to set the logical boundaries of cross-border trade and investment. China's model for governance, ideology, and economic growth won't be the only competitor in that game, but it clearly will be one that matters a great deal. And this in turn will set the terms for how aspiring global organizations will have to navigate on the ML-enabled landscape.

HIGH DEVELOPMENT THEORY: HOW TO GROW

As I argued in earlier chapters, countries need to boost growth in the next decade in order to achieve their social, political, and military / defense goals.[10] High development theory is a decorative phrase that describes a set of big ideas about how these fit together—how the world economy functions and what countries and firms can do to advance their growth, competitiveness, productivity, and wealth interests within it.[11] This, fundamentally, is what sets up the problem of global organization in the modern era—a world of borders and boundaries needs a high development theory that explains and prescribes what to do, most importantly, about flows that cross those borders and boundaries.

Aspiring global organizations have long had to grapple with the causes and consequences of cross-border flows. This book has focused on the relationship between contemporary technologies, the policies of governments, and the big ideas about firm organization to reach the world that make sense for a particular era. A global organization in the 2020s faces one very important new ingredient in this equation, and that is the shift in crucial flows from container shipping to packet switching. The late twentieth-century globalization story focused on mobility of goods, services, people, and ideas.[12] But the most significant growth in cross-border flows now comes in the form of data, and the stimulus that data provides to a value-creation system that rests heavily on ML. The very notion of a cross-border flow (in this case, of data) embeds a political economy question about the directionality and balance among those flows that has always been at the center of state economic development strategies and firm organization. So let's simply rephrase the same question for the era of data.

It now looks like this: *do data flow imbalances make a difference in national economic trajectories?* If a country exports more data than it imports (or the opposite), should anyone care? To take it one step further: does it matter what lies inside those exports and imports—for example, "raw" unprocessed data as compared to sophisticated high value–add data products?[13]

Consider a thought experiment with two countries (X and Y) and an aspiring global company (Firm A). Country X passes a "data localization" law, requiring that raw data collected from X's citizens be stored in data centers on X's territory (ignore for the moment the various motivations that might lie behind this law). Now, Firm A has to build a data center in Country X in order to do business there. The first-order economic effects are easy to see and pretty small: Country X will probably benefit a bit from construction and maintenance jobs that are connected to the local data center, while Firm A will probably suffer a bit from the loss of economies of scale it would otherwise have been able to enjoy.

But it is the second- and third-order effects that count much more. Imagine that the national statistics authority of Country X develops and publishes a "data current account balance" metric showing that cross-border data flows two years later have declined in relative terms.[14] Now the critical questions of dynamic effects emerge. Is the change in the data flow balance a good or bad thing for Country X? Do companies based inside Country X see benefits or harms? Should Firm A now locate research and development facilities inside Country X? Or maybe it should do the opposite, and consider exiting Country X's market or restricting the sale or use of its products there?

Consider what this suggests for a concrete example like autonomous vehicles. A looming question at the end of the 2010 decade is, will the US government permit autonomous vehicles made by Chinese firms to drive on American roads? Behind this question lies the deeper decision: should the data stream coming off autonomous vehicles be free to cross borders and be stored and used in research and development centers owned by Chinese firms in Beijing?[15] This might be viewed narrowly as a national security concern, since autonomous vehicles are also mobile sensor units that would provide massive and unprecedented intelligence to a strategic adversary (imagine knowing the precise condition of every road and bridge, and having real-time granular information about travel patterns in an adversary's country). But it's equally a critical economic development question, since the firms that win the race to develop and build autonomous vehicles over the next decade will probably be some of the highest value-creating entities of the first half of the century.

These are the types of questions that a high development theory for data will need to address, and the answers will ground what we've been looking for in an economic geography and growth proposition. Country X needs to know how and if cross-border flows of data impact long-term economic growth trajectories and, of course, national security both directly and indirectly. Firm A needs to decide what the geography of its data flows can and will look like, and under what conditions it will be able to use raw data to create, deploy, and sell value-added data products in particular places.

A high development theory for the era of data establishes the contours of both, just as earlier high development theories did in previous eras. The analogies are illuminating, so I'll start with a high-level rendition of two old theories. The core argument of import substitution industrialization (ISI) from the 1950s and 1960s was that decent national growth required having essentially the complete supply chain of an industry located physically within national borders. The underlying mechanisms that would generate self-sustaining growth included "learning by doing," coordination of a large number of interdependent processes, the lumpiness of tacit knowledge, and the like. Either a country had a deep industrial base, or it did not. A country that did not would be stuck in a low productivity box and suffer from detrimental terms of trade that would impede development, possibly indefinitely. The policy question that followed from this was how to actually mobilize and build a complete supply chain within a country. The policy answer was (usually) through a combination of tariffs and other restrictions on imports along with subsidies and other inducements to jump-start domestic import substitution.

The core argument of the Washington Consensus (starting in the early 1980s) was almost 180 degrees reversed. It built on the proposition that reductions in transportation and communications costs made it possible to unbundle (as Richard Baldwin put it) the supply chain.[16] Now the primary mechanism of growth rested on moving parts of the supply chain around the world and beyond national borders, and then putting together the resulting pieces. Global growth became a story about combining high technology with low-cost labor—most likely from a different country—and coordinating the package using contemporary IDT. (Note that in the Washington Consensus, IDT was mainly about organizing a global supply chain of manufacturing processes, not about the value of data in and of itself or discrete data products.) Getting macroeconomic policy "right" was a necessary condition to a country joining these increasingly globalized value chains to access the vast scale economies and cost reductions they made possible. Failing on macroeconomic policy would leave a country isolated from global supply chains and stuck without a ladder on which to climb toward self-sustaining and productivity-enhancing growth. Starkly, it would leave that country poor. Other policy questions addressed the same core logic from different directions: what supply chains are most promising? How do you manage intellectual property (IP) and trade secrets? What's a reasonable trajectory for low-wage labor that starts the growth system rolling and gets your country moving up the ladder? This was the era of the cross-national production network that became the iconic image of 1990s globalization.[17]

These high development theories influenced the shape of the global political economy and set the terms of strategy and organization for firms that aspired to reach the world. They had massive consequences for the viability and competitive advantages of global versus local supply chains, and the importance of scale. They had equal significance for the distribution of wealth and importantly of jobs in a political economy environment where both were (and are) linchpins for political stability.

The same is going to be true of what we come to believe about data flows. So what do we believe?

IS DATA DIFFERENT?

It became fairly common in 2017 for economic commentators to talk about data as the "new oil" or to use similar analogies. This line of thinking immediately connects with the common intuition (and sometimes reflex response) that "data is different" in some crucial respect(s). But how so?

Data *is* different—just as oil was different from manufactured goods, and IP was different from both. To be meaningful, the question needs a more precise formulation and it looks like this: in what ways is data conceptually different from previous growth drivers, that basic analytic categories and variables used in previous generations need to be fundamentally rethought? My answer to that question is that data is not so different at all, once you scratch the surface of the intuitions.

One intuition is that data is different because it is extremely cheap to generate after the basic infrastructure to produce and collect it is in place. That is generally true. But it was equally true of crude oil in the early days, when "black gold" bubbled up out of the Pennsylvania fields and the sand dunes of the eastern provinces of Saudi Arabia.

Another intuition is that raw data is nonrival, because it can be copied an infinite number of times at essentially no cost. But the same is true of much "raw" IP. It's accurate to follow with the argument that most of the time, other inputs—many of which are physical and rival and / or expensive—have to be combined with IP in order to create real value. But precisely the same is true of most data. An autonomous vehicle is certainly a computer, but it is also a car that relies on things like rubber tires and steel body panels.

A third intuition: data is everywhere, and the challenge is simply to collect it and figure out what to do with it. But the same turns out to be nearly true of oil and natural gas.[18] It is fully true of bacteria and viruses that represent raw materials that fuel the pharmaceutical sector.

The point is not to contend that there are no meaningful differences; it is to say that basic variables in growth models are legitimate starting points for an analysis of the data era. More specifically, the point is to contend that a clear point of view on magnitude, directionality, and content of data flows is needed, just as similar points of view were needed in previous eras.

This is an important element to consider regarding a "rising tide lifts all boats" perspective about data flows, which (if correct) would sketch out an economic geography much more amenable to simple and familiar forms of global organization. The proposition behind that perspective is an updated version of what I call a naive globalization mind-set: that data flows "circulate ideas, research, technologies, talent, and best practices around the world."[19] It's an absolute gains story in which data flows generate higher productivity and boost growth, and the more flows you experience, the greater the positive impact on your productivity. From a country perspective, the policy prescription is clearly to position your country as close as possible to the center of the global flow pattern, focusing simply on depth of connectivity rather than directionality or content. From a firm perspective, the prescription is both to maximize openness and scale (the two would be mutually reinforcing) on a global stage and to strive against government policies that would place limits or barriers in the way.

That sounds very much indeed like a naive 1990s globalization narrative. The simple implication is that a greater data flow is better for governments and firms—regardless of directionality, content, or location. The best strategy for growth and development is to increase openness to global flows of data. Putting constraints on data flows for any reason (privacy concerns, for example) might serve other legitimate values, but could come at an economic cost. Imagine an analogy in the world of traded goods, where we count the number of shipping containers that transit a country's borders and a firm's production networks. It would not matter in which direction the containers are moving (in or out) and it would not matter what is inside those containers (raw materials, high value–added products, intermediate products that enter another part of the supply chain in another country, and so on). What matters is the number of containers and the speed with which they move—the level of flows.

Similar arguments about flows of goods and services have been the subject of research and controversy for decades or really for centuries. It is accurate to observe that those controversies are almost never purely theoretical but become politicized; that's why we use the term "political economy of trade." The same is true for data flows. In that context, there is an almost entirely opposite perspective to "a rising tide lifts all boats" that has also emerged, as a package of ideas that I loosely label "data nationalism."

Data nationalism is a reflexive, almost primordial response to the emergence of a new economic resource that appears to be powering a leading-edge sector of modern economies. If no one yet understands precisely how, when, and why this data resource will turn out to be valuable, a hoarding instinct tends to kick in as a default. Barring definitive reasons to believe otherwise, shouldn't countries seek to have their own data value-add companies at home to build their domestic data economies? If data is the fuel that drives those companies, why would a country allow that fuel to travel across borders and power growth elsewhere?

The argument that data is a nonrival fuel may be accurate but is irrelevant within this perspective. It's true that allowing data to cross a border is not like exporting a barrel of oil or even a semiconductor, since the same data can obviously be used inside a country as well as being exported. But the point is that the value of that data depends on its ability to combine with other pieces of data, and that this positive network effect will create benefits *at an increasing rate* in places that are the landing points for broad swathes of data. Put simply, *accumulations* of data become disproportionately more valuable as they grow larger. And this is what enables a virtuous circle of growth in the production and sale of data products.

The more data you have, the better the data products you can develop; and the better the data products you develop and sell, the more data you receive as those products get used more frequently and by larger populations. That view supports a modified mercantilism—not exactly a zero-sum competition for data but rather a competition where it is always better to collect more data at home and deprive rivals of the opportunity to do the same.

A country that sees itself as at risk of falling behind in this dynamic might hoard data in order to subsidize and protect its own companies as "national data champions," in the same way that previous generations of developing economies sometimes provided support for national industrial champions. Hoarding would also deprive other countries' companies of data, which might slow down competitors enough to make catch-up plausible. Leading countries would find themselves in exactly the opposite position, hoarding data in order to press their escalating advantage even further, and to prevent the catch-up dynamic in competitors from taking hold.

If data nationalism is a primordial response of states to a new kind of global competition, it has certainly been reinforced by events like the Edward Snowden revelations that created overlaps with anxieties around espionage and privacy. There are other nationalist drivers. Some countries emphasize consumer protection in advance of demonstrated harms and with more subtle arguments about "digital fairness" than others. Countries exhibit important differences in where lines are drawn between what constitutes legitimate speech or illegitimate and objectionable content. And the centrality of the two biggest national players in this game—the United States and China—has made others wary of their sometimes polarizing policies for the IDT political economy and of their potential acceleration in a power gradient that could exceed the superpower threshold of a previous era.

DATA IMBALANCES, GROWTH, AND THE PLATFORM ADVANTAGE

A current account balance is simply the difference between the value of exports (goods and services, traditionally) and the value of imports that transit a country's borders.[20] When countries argue with each other about an unbalanced current account, it's generally the case that the arguments circle around whether someone—a government that enacts certain policies or firms with particular business practices—is to blame. In fact this has been a consistent theme in international political economy debates in the public realm, most visibly (for Americans at least) in the Japan-US relationship during the 1980s and in the Sino-American relationship in the 2010s. These arguments tend to mount when the magnitude of a current account imbalance becomes, in the estimation of some important actors, too large. But what's too large and how do we know?

In this context let's return to the thought experiment of a current account in data, focusing on the United States for now (we'll take up the

China competition issue later). It was in the late 2010s that countries started to complain about some form of data imbalance and argue whether the dominance of US platform businesses ought somehow to be blamed.[21] Why is this a problem? The modal argument went like this: a small number of very large intermediation platform firms, most of which are based in the United States, increasingly sit astride some of the most important and fast-growing markets around the world. These markets are driven by data products, and the new firms use data products to disrupt existing businesses and relationships without regard to domestic effects that can be economic, social, political, and cultural. The term "intermediation platform" captures the essential nature of the two-sided markets that these firms organize.[22] They collect data from users (on all sides of the two-sided or many-sided market) at every interaction; bring that data home into vast repositories, which are then used to build algorithms that process raw data into valuable data products; and use those data products to create new and yet more valuable products and lines of business.

These products might be algorithms that tell farmers precisely when and where to plant a crop for top efficiency; business-process re-engineering ideas; health-care protocols; annotated maps that power autonomous vehicles; consumer predictive analytics; insights about how a government policy actually affects behavior of firms or individuals, and more—these are just the beginning of what is possible. Because the value-add in these data products is going to be high, so will the prices, at least relative to the price of raw data. And because there is no domestic competition in the raw data–exporting country (Country X again) that can create equivalent products, there's little competition for US data product exports. Because many of these data products are going to be deeply desired by customers in Country X, there's a ready constituency there to lobby against import restrictions or tariffs. And unless there's a compelling path by which Country X can kick-start and / or accelerate the development of its own domestic competitors, there may seem little point to doing anything about this imbalance.

The platform businesses, in this case within the United States, grow more powerful and richer. The users in other countries get to consume the products but are largely shut out of the value-add production side of the data economy. That's a data imbalance of significance in the sense that Country X might see itself as being locked in to the role of raw data supplier and consumer of imported value-added data products; while on the other side, the home country of the platform business imports raw data and adds value to create products that it then exports to its cumulating advantage.

Here's an example of how this might look in practice. Imagine that a large number of Parisians use Uber on a regular basis to find their way around the city. Each passenger pays Uber a fee for her ride, and some of that money goes to the Uber driver in Paris. Uber itself takes a cut, but it's not the money that really matters here. Focus instead on the data flow that Uber receives from all its Parisian customers (including both sides of the two-sided market; that is, Uber drivers and passengers are both customers in this model). Each Uber ride in Paris produces raw data about traffic patterns, and about where people are going at what times of day, which Uber collects. This mass of raw data, over time and across geographies, is an input to and feeds the further development of Uber's algorithms. These in turn are more than just a support for a better Uber business model (though that effect in and of itself matters because it enhances and accelerates Uber's competitive advantage vis-à-vis traditional taxi companies). Other, more ambitious data products will reveal highly valuable insights about transportation, commerce, commercial and social life in the city, and potentially much more (what is possible stretches the imagination).

And here's an obvious public policy consequence: if the mayor of Paris in 2025 decides that she wants to launch a major reconfiguration of public transit in the city to take account of changing travel patterns, who will have the data she'll need to develop a good policy? The answer is Uber, and the price for data products that could immediately help determine the optimal Parisian public-transit investments would be (justifiably) high.

Stories like these could matter greatly for longer-term economic development prospects, particularly if there is a positive feedback loop that creates a tendency toward natural monopolies in data platform businesses. It's easy to see how this could happen, and hard to see precisely why the process would slow down or reverse at any point. The more data the platform firms absorb, the faster the improvement in the algorithms that transform raw materials into value-add data products. The better the data products, the higher the penetration of those products into markets around the world. The more the products are used, the faster they improve. The character of the imbalance would become more severe over time as larger quantities of raw data move from Country X to the United States, and more valuable data products move from the United States back to Country X, in a positive feedback loop.

This simple logic doesn't yet take account of the additional complementary growth effects that would further enable and accelerate the loop. Probably the most important is human capital. If the most sophisticated data products are being built within US firms, then it becomes much easier to attract the best data scientists and ML experts to those companies, where their skills would then accelerate farther ahead of would-be competitors in the rest of the world. Other complements (including basic research, venture capital, and related elements of the technology cluster ecosystem) would follow as well. The algorithm economy is almost the epitome of a "learn by doing" system with spillovers and other cluster economy effects (Figure 6.1).[23] Thus the dominance of a few geographically specific American data science and ML clusters grows.

No positive feedback loop goes on forever. But without a clear argument as to why, when, and how this ML loop would diminish or reverse, there's justification for concern about natural monopolies that concentrate in a small number of places. The potential winners in that game have clear incentives to talk about their business models as if that were *not* the case, and so they emphasize the reasons why their ability to accumulate sustainable market power would be limited (arguments such as multihoming, low barriers to entry, demand for continued innovation, and the recent evidence of platform businesses losing market dominance very quickly when they fail to innovate).[24] But for the potential losers in that game, those counterarguments are mostly abstract and theoretical, while the tendency to natural monopolies seems real, based in evidence, and urgent.

The anxious reflex to intervene somehow would probably be weaker if it were possible to point to compensatory mechanisms outside the business models of the platform firms—"natural" reactions that

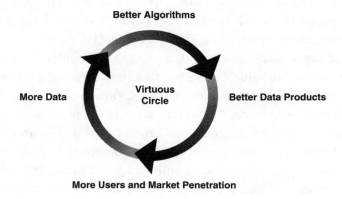

A "Learn by Doing" System That Captures
the Upside of Endogenous Growth

Better Algorithms

More Data

Virtuous Circle

Better Data Products

More Users and Market Penetration

- At the limit, preponderance of data-intensive ML business in a few places
- Increased investments in human capital, higher economic growth rates
- Meta-institutions like IP regimes, data property rights advance quickly
- Spillover into other sectors including advanced military technology

Figure 6.1: Positive Feedback in Machine Learning Economies.

counterbalance the positive feedback loop of an advanced data economy. But the standard compensatory mechanisms that are part and parcel of normal current account imbalances don't translate clearly into the data world. Put differently, there's no natural capital account response that funds the data imbalance per se. And there's no natural currency adjustment mechanism. (In standard current account thinking, a country with significant surplus will see its currency appreciate over time, making imports cheaper and exports more expensive, thus tending to move the overall system at least partially toward a dynamic balance over time.) A data imbalance by itself would have neither of these effects.[25]

It's possible to extrapolate at the limit to a vast preponderance of data-intensive business being concentrated in one or a very few countries. These countries would then own the upside of data-enabled endogenous growth. They would combine investments in human capital, innovation, and data-derived knowledge to create higher rates of economic growth, along with positive spillover effects into other sectors. In Paul Romer's parlance, these countries would be advantaged in both making and using ideas.[26]

And they would almost certainly enjoy a significant advantage in what Romer called "meta-ideas," an awkward phrase to describe ideas about how to support the production and transmission of other ideas. Meta-ideas are answers to these kinds of questions: What is the best means of managing IP like algorithms and software code? What are the most effective labor-market institutions that can support the growth of algorithm-driven labor demand? How do we organize markets for data that function smoothly in price discovery?

It's much easier to make progress on these difficult institutional questions through experiments and learning by doing. Meta-ideas are the innovations that can keep the positive feedback loop going. And they are more likely to emerge in countries and societies that are already ahead in the data economy. In fact, meta-ideas may be the most important ideas of all.

GEOGRAPHIES OF THE DATA ECONOMY

A snapshot of a new economic geography is starting to emerge from this narrative, and it doesn't look a priori auspicious from the perspective of countries and companies outside of the leaders, the United States and China. The early stages of power imbalance were documented in an imperfect but interesting 2016 study by Aurelien Faravelon, Stephane Frenot, and Stephane Grumbach (FFG) who ranked the most visited websites for many countries, coding the country from which the firm that sits behind that website is domiciled.[27] The results aren't generally surprising, but they support the intuition that the largest countries have a substantial "home bias" in data traffic much as they do in trade, in part simply because of their size. Smaller countries (France and Britain, for example) engage at a higher percentage level with external platform businesses—more than 70 percent of intermediation platform visits from both countries land at firms outside France and Britain. One Chinese platform (Baidu) was among the top five in the world, although its influence was limited to a small number of other countries (simply by virtue of China's size, the biggest Chinese platform will rank highly in global measures even if its use is heavily concentrated in China—and in Baidu's case, among a small number of additional countries).

The most notable findings point to an outsized concentration of intermediation platforms in the United States. Only eleven countries hosted in 2016 an influential platform business by FFG's definition. The United States had thirty-two such businesses; China had five; a few other countries had just one. At that time US platforms had a nearly global reach; Chinese platforms were big players in a relatively small number of countries (fewer than ten); Brazilian platforms were big players in an even smaller number of countries (around five); and the numbers go down from there. If this is a proxy measure of power in the data economy and traditional language is warranted, it would be fair to say that in 2016 the United States was the only real superpower with global reach. China was a major regional power, skirting the edge of superpower status. There were other small regional powers like Brazil. And everyone else could be described as weak or dependent.[28]

So what does the data economy look like from that perspective, of the comparatively weak? It starts to sound like a story of persistent development disadvantage with echoes of dependencia theory from the 1970s.[29] It's not hard to imagine using words like "metropole" and "periphery" (which carry ideologies as well as analytic significance) because the implied causal mechanisms are eerily parallel to dependencia arguments: raw data flows from a "data periphery" to a "data metropole"; the metropole becomes wealthier and smarter at the expense of the periphery; the periphery is trapped at the bottom rung of the global division of labor. And to repeat the important point about positive feedback, this dynamic persists over time as the periphery becomes less capable of developing an autonomous process of technological innovation.

For the truly weakest—the third-tier data periphery countries—that sounds like a route to long-term disadvantage. Is there room for a better outcome? One way to think about that possibility is to borrow from the "leapfrog" development arguments that were commonly deployed around an earlier phase of IDT. The question then would be, can very low-income countries simply skip over the 1970s and 1980s development ladder (rooted in low-cost manufacturing) and perhaps even the tradi-tional services sector, to jump right in on the leading edge of the data economy? The leapfrog logic emphasizes Alexander Gerschenkron's view of the advantages of backwardness, in particular being unburdened by the fixed investments and political-economic institutions of an earlier growth paradigm.[30] The banal but still evocative analogy is moving di-rectly to mobile telephones without having to go through a copper-wire landline stage (and it's not just about the technology, but also the mind-sets and institutions of the wired telephone era). In this next-phase hopeful story, the leapfrog would take one more jump beyond the mo-bile phone and the services it offers, to land directly on the data economy where businesses grow out of the data exhaust from the phone as it delivers those services.

But there are big constraints. The service and data sectors are pro-gressively more skill-intensive than most manufacturing. They do not generally have the capacity to employ large numbers of rural-to-urban migrants as did factories making mass production goods for global mar-kets. Even more of a roadblock is the observation that the services made possible by mobile phones are themselves being leapfrogged in value-add by the data economy that sits above them in the stack. Mobile banking is certainly about moving money from person to person, but the future value in that business isn't likely to lie in the small (and di-minishing) transaction fees for payments. It lies in the data about where, when, and why money is moving.

And who is most likely to build high value–add products from the data exhaust coming off of mobile phones and other connected devices in the periphery? If those data exhausts are collected primarily by Amer-ican or Chinese companies, the answer is self-evident. The pushback by the Indian government against Facebook's "free basics" model notwith-standing, it is an entirely rational move for platform businesses to try to structure their relationships with developing countries to support their own growth in exactly this fashion.[31]

None of this looks like good news for third-tier developing countries trying to find routes to growth and economic convergence in the data era. Of course there are compensating factors—for one, the data prod-ucts people get to consume will likely improve the lives of individuals and communities, and certainly could improve efficiency and reduce waste and corruption in public services (this can be true of data products everywhere). It's also possible that there will emerge alternative routes to better economic outcomes that sit aside or are tangential to the highest value–add routes in data.[32] Gerschenkron's core insight about the advantages of backwardness was that the magnitude of the challenge affords the possibility of being able to change the quality of the response: you can do something different that makes you indispensable without trying to climb the primary growth ladder faster than those already on the top.

What those tangential possibilities might be in the data era is not yet clear. And there is another challenge waiting for whatever those Gerschenkron paths may turn out to be. It is that at the limit, the preponderance of value that is created in many other industries could very well migrate to the data overlays that are being added to them. Concretely, who will capture the majority of value from an advanced data-enabled agricultural operation? Or from a data-enabled cobalt mine? How to think about that question and, more importantly, how the global landscape will be shaped over the decade by the fact that firms and countries don't yet know the answer, is an important point of discussion for the next section.

THE DATA SEMI-PERIPHERY

Dependencia theory also had space for a semi-periphery: mid-level countries that were mostly industrialized, capitalist, and moderately prosperous but positioned between the core and the periphery, with economic flows characteristic in parts of both. The data economy's semi-periphery is made up of countries that exhibit similar patterns in data flows. They have parts of the high value–add aspects of the data economy within their borders, but not enough parts to be self-sustaining and competitive with the core countries. They have sufficient wealth to enjoy a high level of data product consumption, but a large proportion of those products will be imports, with the consequent data flow from usage going back mainly to the core to strengthen its future advantage.

Here's a thought experiment that might very well occur to policy leaders in such a country (call it Country F, and for the purposes of the experiment let it sit within the European Union). If Country F decides that its position in the data economy is semi-peripheral and it aspires to more; or if it believes that the risks of a self-reinforcing dependency are such that over time its political economy would drift downward toward a fully peripheral state (a low value–add raw data exporter and high value–add data importer), then what options present themselves? What would a policy maker in the capital of Country F see as plausible means to improve her country's long-term economic growth prospects?

That question is this generation's version of positioning vis-à-vis global value chains, in this case value chains driven by data. There are four high-level options for Country F:

1. Join the predominant global value chain that is led by American platforms, and seek to maximize leverage and growth prospects within it, to enable some degree of catch-up.
2. Join a competing value chain, perhaps grounded in Chinese platform businesses, where catch-up might be easier because (for now) the gap is less wide.
3. Diversify the bets and leverage each for better terms against the other, by combining elements of 1 and 2 above.
4. Insulate or disconnect to a meaningful degree from those value chains, and work to create an independent data value chain within F; or perhaps regionally within the European Union of which F is a part.

The first three options are really just variants on one big decision: does joining existing global data value chains point toward an economic and technologically advantageous future?[33] This depends, as I've argued up to now, on whether data platform intermediation offers a development ladder to countries that start out as raw data providers to the platforms with global reach. The analysis here suggests a healthy dose of skepticism about that prospect for the semi-periphery as well.

If you want to be hopeful that the positive feedback loop that creates increasing advantages for the core could reverse into a dynamic where catch-up and convergence become possible, then you have to sketch out a mechanism by which it becomes increasingly difficult and expensive for the leading players to advance at the horizon of data science and ML leadership, while it becomes cheaper and easier to "fast-follow" and converge for those that are semi-peripheral players in the earlier stages.

Can such an argument be plausibly constructed for Country F? It would in principle depend on F climbing a development ladder that starts with outsourced lower value–add tasks in the data economy, and climbing it at a faster rate than the leading economies climb from their starting (higher) position. More concretely, imagine that the leading edge of the data economy sits in the San Francisco Bay Area where the costs of doing business are extremely high. There are discrete, somewhat standardized, lower-skilled tasks in the data value chain—managing, warehousing, and cleaning of data sets, for example—that could be outsourced to lower-cost locations. Imagine that Firm T in San Francisco contracts with Firm Y in Country F to provide data engineering services that prepare large data sets for use in T's data science models. Firm Y then acts as a draw for human capital as well as training and investment in certain data skills in its home geography (that is, in Country F).

The critical question is whether this represents a rung on a development ladder, or just an outsourced location for relatively low value–add data jobs. Are opportunities present for firms like Y to move up the value chain? Perhaps there will be for small, niche data products that are of local interest. But for larger-scale data products that address global markets, the case is much harder to see. Firm Y will be at a huge disadvantage as it lacks access to all the data raw materials that would enable that kind of product development. That is because Firm T back in San Francisco is likely to distribute the outsourced work across multiple geographies, simply to get better terms on the work in the short term and prevent single-supplier hold-up. If Firm T is thinking long-term, it could distribute the work in a strategic way, to intentionally limit the ability of any firms like Y in the semi-periphery to attain a critical mass of data that would facilitate catch-up competitors entering T's potential markets.

The government of F might try to push back by passing a law that requires more high value–add data processing to take place in-country (inside F). Firm T in San Francisco would most likely respond by moving its outsourced data operations elsewhere, outside of Country F. This is an easier move in the data economy than it ever was in the industrial economy, simply because investments in fixed capital for T's outsourcing operations in F are likely minimal. Maybe a few buildings, maybe some local server capacity, maybe some high-bandwidth connectivity and security systems . . . and that's probably it when it comes to fixed capital that would be stranded. Because there are no expensive factories and assembly lines, T can move its work outside of F quickly and at low cost.

Of course (assuming rational expectations), if this is accurate and known to both parties, F's government is recursively stopped from changing the rules in the first place since it knows how the game will end. Another option for T to cut off F would be for T to invest in automation and "re-shore" the work in the form of automated systems, which most likely would be located back in the Bay Area. It turns out that host government F and Firm Y have very little leverage in this game.

The best fitting analogy here is not to industrial catch-up that took place in "Factory Asia" during the 1970s. It is instead to something like call centers for customer service that are located in developing economies to serve the low-value activities of firms in the core. Consider a software helpline call center as an example. There's very little skill spillover or ladder climbing between a call center and a globally competitive software firm. And call center functions can be relocated at low cost and in very short periods of time if the terms of trade change.

The burden of proof has to be on those who believe that these kinds of outsourcing arrangements can create plausible catch-up development paths, rather than simply to perpetuate and extend the advantage of the leading economies and companies that make up the core. And if they can't meet that burden of proof, then the government of Country F needs a different strategy.

That conundrum sets the stage for the missing element of strategy going forward. It will be, I believe, a return to vertical integration tied to a new form of ISI for the data world (minus, of course, the industrial part).

THE LOGIC OF VERTICAL INTEGRATION

Counterintuitive as vertical integration might seem in the modern era, it's worth noting that the notion of a "full-stack" company came back into vogue in conversations about corporate strategy during the second half of the 2010s.[34] There are potentially many reasons for this revival of vertical integration thinking. Data flow and the externalities that accompany it are the most important.

One way to see clearly the logic behind this, is to engage in a final thought experiment: deconstructing the value chain that leads from a dirty shirt to a clean shirt, with two critical nodes—the laundry detergent and the washing machine.[35] In 2015 or before, the conventional view of this value chain would label the washing machine as a "white good," an undifferentiated product where price is the main basis of competition. (A trip to Best Buy or any other home appliance outlet in the United States confirms that intuition: GE, Samsung, LG, and a few other manufacturers offer washing machines that are essentially alike, at nearly identical prices.) The differentiating part of the value chain was the laundry detergent. The chemistry of cleaning a delicate fabric is a complicated one, and so the IP that goes into the formulations of a laundry detergent (which now needs to be environmentally acceptable, effective in cold water, and the like) was the important asset.

Now update this clean-shirt value chain to the present, focusing on the data flow that is embedded within it. The detergent doesn't produce much data by itself. Its IP is important but *static* in the sense that it doesn't learn from or respond to its interaction with shirts in the wild. The interesting element of the value chain from a data perspective is now taking place inside the washing machine—where the detergent, the shirt, the water, agitation, and so forth meet in the act of cleaning, and the IP is placed into motion. And that is where the most relevant and valuable data is created. Now it is the sensors in the washing machine collecting that data; the sensors become the key node in the value chain. And the data flowing off those sensors becomes the most important asset if a firm seeks to create new value (a more effective detergent, a better washing machine, a warning about zippers that are about to fail, almost any other set of value-add services that go beyond simply a one-time clean shirt).

This thought experiment suggests a migration of critical value from detergent to washing machine, tracking the migration from conventional IP (detergent chemistry) to data flows that come out of the machine. The logic of competition is now going to be mixed, with value-add happening in both domains. Recognizing that, a firm might choose to own both nodes so that its bet is robust.

But even more substantial value would be created in a vertical re-integration that takes full advantage of externalities linking the domains together. In practical terms, what that means is extensive data from washing machines in the wild will inform the chemical development process for the next detergent formulation and vice versa. For example, Samsung (a washing machine manufacturer) might merge with a laundry detergent manufacturer to internalize, accelerate, and make bidirectional the information flow between the two. Or Procter & Gamble (the detergent manufacturer) might buy a washing machine company. Regardless of who leads in strategic vertical re-integration, the logic is the same. If the promise of internalizing the data economy within one firm exceeds the costs of placing these two rather different functions underneath a single firm's administrative structures (and out of "the market"), then the move to data also implies a move back to vertical integration.[36]

That's the language of transaction-cost economics theory. In the language of real-world practice, vertical re-integration will probably also reflect the consequence of some continuing uncertainty about the value of data and precisely where the greatest profits and defensible advantages can be found. If you don't quite know where that locus will be, one rational response is to hedge your bets by owning as much of the value chain as you can plausibly assemble.

How might this scale up from a firm's strategy to a national development strategy? Obviously, one way to scale is simply through a concatenation of the strategies of many individual firms. An earlier version of another mechanism, which relies on a new kind of ideas dynamic, is best explained by Romer.[37] In that prior generation of argument, there is consensus on the view that governments should subsidize education in order to improve human capital, because human capital is the key ingredient for the creation and use of ideas.

In the data economy though, the most important ideas depend on not just smart people but also "smart" algorithms. The ideas that are embedded in algorithms sometimes are formalizations of ideas in the smart peoples' heads. But increasingly, the ideas in the algorithm are the outcomes of ML processes that depend on access to data sets.

In that context, the case for governments to support the creation of those algorithms is logically equivalent to and just as compelling as the case for government to support education. And that means governments might want to support and subsidize the creation and retention of data, for use at home, in exactly the same way that governments seek to train and retain smart people.[38]

Data science and ML can be thought of in this context as a quicker, more systematic, and highly efficient means of distinguishing useful or productive ideas from non-useful nonproductive ideas. I emphasized in Chapter 1 the critical importance of this function to modern economic growth. The simplest development bet then is to wager that you are most likely to achieve smart algorithms that can distinguish good from bad ideas, through a combination of smart people *and* lots of data. Why wouldn't a government then act to support the creation and retention of both at home? In this way, vertical re-integration and a nationalist-leaning data development strategy become mutually reinforcing aspects of the new landscape.

HEADING TOWARD A NEW REGIONAL GEOGRAPHY

There is a core tenet in Buddhist thought about the impermanence of what are called compound phenomena, or in plain language, things in the world that humans engage with. Your new car will get scratches and dents. The framing of your house will suffer dry rot and termite damage. The human body gets old and frail. Over the course of time the arrow only points in one direction; entropy is built into the universe as we know it. I sometimes call it "the recalcitrance of the physical world" as a way of softening some of the inevitable frustrations that accompany this reality, no matter how thoughtful and aware one becomes about its nature.[39]

Parts of the digital world defy that ancient wisdom. Data products in principle will get better the more they are used. Not always, and not forever. After all, data products often meet the world through software code, and code has bugs. Data products often meet the world also through physical interfaces—a Tesla has tires that will wear out, even while the autonomous driving system improves with use. But the substantial reversal of the entropy arrow in the data world is a crucial change that reshapes political economy and geography. It changes calculations that firms make around IP, around scale, around organizing a value chain, and around competition. A 2017 report on Chinese data platforms put it this way: "a very good scientist with a ton of data will beat a super scientist with a small amount of data."[40] That won't be true in every particular instance, but from a large-scale national economic growth perspective it's a good bet.

Amazon's "Fulfillment by Amazon" program is another contemporary example (this is where independent businesses ship their products, which they still own, to Amazon's warehouses and let Amazon do everything else—like picking, packing, shipping, and customer service). It certainly is a way of keeping Amazon's discipline high and thus guarding against internal processes getting lazy and inefficient, the organizational scourges of vertical integration. It also utilizes excess capacity in warehouses, enhances leverage with shippers, and, of course, earns commissions for Amazon on sales that take place through the program. But it is most importantly a massive channel through which valuable data flows—data about pricing, data about demand, data about the performance of Amazon's own systems. Amazon does everything it can to expose its systems to external competition for exactly this reason. The data flow is much more valuable than the 12 or 15 percent fees (a rough estimate) that Amazon earns on a sale. And I believe that data flow will prove to be more valuable than the competitive discipline it imposes on internal processes, because it has the potential to do much more than guard against competitive corrosion, the large business equivalent of the impermanence of compound things.

This narrative also changes how governments view their role in the game of political economy. Being a stand-aside umpire with a laissez-faire light touch isn't as attractive as it once was believed to be. Simply getting the macroeconomics right won't do as much good as was once believed. Positive feedback loops can be tremendous blessings if you are inside of them, and deeply problematic if you are on the outside looking in. The boundary between inside and outside was at least in part a function of physical geography for most of human history, again because of the recalcitrance of the physical world. But it doesn't have to be a feature of the physical world, not in the digital data era. This means government policies have new power to shape those de facto boundaries and, by extension, geography. Jobs, taxes and public finances, technological and military leadership, and just possibly ideological and cognitive leadership are at stake. Many governments are not going to want to sit back and let it just happen to them.

ORGANIZATION AND OUTCOMES

THE ECONOMIC GEOGRAPHY OF the 2020s will have to get four key issues right that concern data flows. The first is how to manage the pressures around inequality and the concentration of wealth that threaten the stability of political regimes and the social license to operate, which big firms rely on. The second is how to sustain credibility of commitments and contracts in an era of cyber-insecurity. The third is how to manage friction between the economic growth imperatives in developed and developing markets. And the fourth is how to finesse the line between productivity-enhancing competition and the hypercompetitive world that nobody really wants to live in.

All of these issues embed within them a frame of human values. Economic growth isn't an end in and of itself; it's a means of enabling lives that people want to live. The ability to have confidence in the accuracy of data matters only if the data describes or affects something that human beings care about. Not all political regimes are worth stabilizing and not all firms deserve a social license to operate. It's important to keep in mind that economic geography, as important as I've tried to make it in this book, is really just an intermediate plot line in a bigger story about humanity and progress. The proposition I've tried to defend is simply that it is a major plot line, because it drives how we create organizations that extend our reach toward the world.

With that caveat, what is the appropriate scale at which these issues become most manageable for the modern era of data? This book has built toward the argument that reaching for the endpoints of the scale continuum is no longer viable. Small is *not* beautiful anymore, regardless of the nostalgic romance for artisanal local production that some rich country elites can indulge.[1] Global is not beautiful anymore, despite the compelling vision that might have been the globally integrated enterprise (GIE), done right. The argument here is that a landscape organized into several regions is more likely to emerge because it has a better chance of hitting the sweet spot on the key issues around data flows, and it will deal better with the main challenges and frictions that this world presents.

The notion of a regional economic geography is obviously not a new one. But the emerging regional geography won't look at all like what the trading companies and multinationals of Chapter 2 experienced. Two differences are most important. The new regions will be quite densely connected internally and quite loosely linked to each other—more like scale-free in a topology of networks. That will matter quite a lot to how firms organize and operate. The new regions will also have borders that are not mainly defined by physical contiguity, the features we represent on maps as mountain ranges and oceans and other "natural" boundaries. Instead, regions will be the product of government policies that manifest in technology rules and standards, including competition policies aimed at the political economy of data and machine learning (ML). Obviously that will also matter quite a lot to how firms organize.

The job of this chapter is to propose a new organizational template that makes sense on this landscape, and to make it seem real and tangible enough to escape the world of abstract theory. The second part of that task is harder than it sounds, because new ways of organizing to reach the world almost always seem counterintuitive, radical, or outlandish when they are first proposed. Think back to the audaciousness of the British East India Company's early ambitions as it would have looked to contemporaries who didn't see technology and the state the way the Company did. Or the extreme boldness of IBM's GIE vision at the time it was put forward.

The challenge this time is multiplied by the cognitive lock-in that human decision makers have when it comes to maps and the way they represent physical geography. There is no network diagram I know of that is nearly as intuitive for people in the way that the Mercator projection is. We all grew up with maps like that for good reason: physical geography has played a dominant role in organization for most of human history. Physical space still matters (as I said, everybody still has to be somewhere) but not so much as we imagine when it comes to organization.

From here on in when I use the word "region," it is essential to keep in mind that I mean something *logical, not physical:* a space that is defined not by physical boundaries and geographic contiguity, but by densely connected data flows.

The rest of this chapter describes what this really looks like from the perspective of firms and governments. I won't offer a precise to-do list, but if the argument is convincing, getting from here to there isn't all that hard. There's a fine line between explicating the driving forces behind the shape of a new economic geography, and making point predictions about where the boundaries will fall and what different actors (government and firm) will do about it at any given moment. I will try to stay on the safe side of the line and avoid those kinds of point predictions, not because I believe they are impossible to make in some cases but because I think they can be a distraction to the main argument. When I use examples to illustrate the argument, they should be thought of as examples of the *kinds of things* we are going to see more of and less of, not precise predictions that this particular example will come to pass.[2]

The final pages offer some additional propositions that reflect economic geography back upward to the dimensions of human values and experience that matter most. It's a fair question to ask, is the world I describe here going to be a better world for people to live in? The answer is that it will be better in some respects (more diverse, wealthier, and innovative) while worse in some respects (more dangerous and potentially more ridden with violent conflict). The point of these propositions is not to be a deterministic purveyor of hope or doom. It is to explain why those vectors are pointing in the directions they are, so that people can do things that modify their directionality and magnitude just enough to accentuate the good and decelerate the bad. Every argument about economic geography through time has had room for human agency to make the most of what is possible, and the era of data will have that room as well.

WHY REGIONAL IS RIGHT-SIZED

Probably the most important proximate force behind the emerging regional geography is the newly prominent presence of governments in the game. Of course governments never really left the game in the 2000s (or, for that matter, either before or after), but the *relative* pullback was real, as was its reversal during the global financial crisis (GFC) and the decade that followed.

Governments in most parts of the world found themselves after 2008 playing newly important roles in economic coordination as economies struggled with the unfamiliar dynamics of deflation or even the threat of deflation. Even more so than inflation, deflationary pressures confound and muddle the role that price plays as a coordinating mechanism in modern economies. Deflation is worse because the generations in power in Europe and the United States in particular have had almost no experience of deflation and are still operating with an inflation-phobic mind-set honed during the 1970s and 1980s.[3] For at least a decade and probably substantially longer after the GFC shock, governments have had to play increasingly active roles in driving capital investment (among other things), not least through unconventional monetary policies that would have been unimaginable minus the crisis. Their role is not set to diminish greatly in the United States, Europe, and China, because all three major growth centers still have to contend with secular deflationary pressures and the mass economic psychology that accompanies it.

At the same time there are a number of additional things that governments have found they need to be back in the game in a much more active way in order to get done. Since I've named inequality and labor-market displacements as one of the four key issues around which geography will organize, let's consider just a subset that relates to labor. Governments are going to have to answer the question of "education for what and in what, exactly" when anyone (or just about everyone) proclaims that education is a central part of the answer to how human labor can compete with ML and robots. Governments then are going to place bets on how to increase the productivity of unskilled workers and at the same time retrain some of those unskilled workers into skilled workers, based on a theory about what skills are distinctively more efficient to engage with in human beings than in machines. Governments will be responsible to provide income support to people who can't earn enough in the ML economy (and there may be many of them).[4] Governments will have to contribute to reducing friction in labor markets, extending to seemingly mundane policies, such as making it easier for people to move to where jobs are locating. And governments will likely be promoting policies that facilitate new entrepreneurship, ranging from access to capital and markets to even cheaper access to compute power than commercial cloud services will provide.[5]

How many of today's roughly 195 sovereign states have governments capable of carrying out an agenda like this?[6] Actually, only a few. And even the most capable governments can't really count on the assistance or support of the largest firms as they were able to do in past generations. The largest "American" companies today aren't nearly as closely tied to government elites and the state per se as were the largest American companies of previous generations; they see themselves as autonomous from government in a way that the industrial-era giants did not. A poignant comparative illustration of that from the interwar years is the 1921 founding of the Council on Foreign Relations, which was set up by banks and other major corporate interests in New York as a place where elites from the government and corporate sectors could together develop a set of world order propositions that would benefit both (to start, combating US isolationism). You simply can't imagine Google, Apple, and Facebook engaging with Washington, DC, or any other government at that level of intimate alignment today. The business-government cleavage in China is somewhat less, but headed in the same direction as the major Chinese platform firms look to expand their reach and influence beyond their (admittedly very large) domestic market. In the data economy, 1.8 billion is a very large number, but it is still not large enough for optimal progress in the medium term.

Governments are now going to have to do much of this foundation-building work on their own, at times in opposition to the strategies of the biggest firms on the planet. Autarky isn't an option in that game. Governments too will need the advantages of scale. This is one important way that the logic of regional blocs comes to the fore. What governments need are blocs big enough for scale and scope, but small enough for a major geopolitical power that has the needed capacity for "logical regulation" through technology rules and standards to steer.

There are a number of advantages for governments to thinking about a global economic geography configured around several regions. One big and obvious advantage is that it offers a manageable response to the hypercompetition dynamic that I explored in Chapter 4. Hypercompetition on a global playing field is simply too relentless for most societies to sustain. There is not now and never has been grounds for a Polanyi double-move or an embedded liberalism compromise at the global level that would make the harsh consequences of hypercompetition politically bearable.[7] The problem is that data-enabled markets are so extraordinarily good (and will become still much better) at producing desirable products and efficiencies, that they will if left to themselves override other considerations, to the point of bludgeoning them.[8]

But the option of returning to a national basis for these types of bargains is essentially ruled out by the positive feedback dynamics of the ML economy that I explained in Chapter 6. Only a very small number of countries (perhaps only two) are in a position to internalize those dynamics to their advantage—and that would leave the rest of the global political economy in a dependencia-like relationship.

The middle ground of scale is regional and is a kind of sweet spot in this context. At the very least it creates a space big enough to move jobs around and diversify some of the pressures of inequality that will continue to undermine political stability. And, of course, it offers larger pools of data that power the ML feedback loop of Chapter 6. In the broadest terms, the regional scale strikes a balance between that data appetite and the differentiation among strategies for dealing with the four key issues around data that I named in the beginning of this chapter. More broadly, for diversity in views about many of the other values connected to data that politics will have to manage, consider two of the most important.

The most visible of those values, at least in some parts of the world, are generally lumped together under the label "security and privacy." It's an awkward and intellectually lazy label, because security and privacy are quite different things.[9] But the overall sentiment behind the lazy label and the observations it points to is important. There is a great deal of diversity in the values that people bring, and that societies and countries try to aggregate, when it comes to the data economy. This is visible in the so-called politicization of business that became particularly evident in the United States during and after the 2016 election.[10] Their libertarian roots and continued rhetoric notwithstanding, the big information and data technology (IDT) firms have some of the largest and most expensive lobbying operations in Washington, DC, and are similarly ramping up in other national capitals as well as at the European Union in Brussels.[11] What a decisive reversal of the GIE belief, which (as I described in Chapters 3 and 4) had imagined IDT to be generally a technocratically neutral sector that could focus on productivity and in doing so avoid contentious politics.

It is also visible in the different ways that societies grapple with the speech-democratizing features that digital networks have made possible. Not inevitable, to be certain, but possible—which is why governments have found space to differentiate among policies that bear on speech. Bluntly, the United States has been particularly hypocritical on this score—the "free and open" access agenda as foreign policy, which is both rhetoric and policy (including the funding of technologies aimed at circumventing controls in other sovereign states), blithely ignores the fact that for some regimes, free and open communication is a major security challenge (sometimes the primary security challenge). I don't mean to imply that US policy is wrong (or right, for that matter); what I mean is simply that for anyone to talk about the policy as an implementation of a universal political value is demonstrably false. What better illustration of that than the failure of the United States and other Western liberal countries to define consistently the fine line between control of institutions that are used to manipulate elections, and what is just smart and ruthless political maneuvering. That failure presents arbitrage opportunities that Russia (and perhaps others) took advantage of in the 2016 US presidential election, and that's likely to be just the beginning.

Whereas in China, the absence of a clear definition of acceptable speech limits the impact of US policies by allowing limited pluralism, a source of strength for the government in part because it is so flexible to circumstances. China's Great Firewall can be tuned for purpose, such as allowing for the expression of discontent (and thus providing useful feedback to government institutions) so long as that expression does not promote mass mobilization or political organization.[12] A secular, technocratic, modernizing middle class with internationally oriented elements does not in this context necessarily mean a class that demands democracy or uninhibited speech on the internet; it is more "attentive" than it is "mobilized" in the traditional political meaning of that term.[13] What's actually mobilized is not its politics but its data-generating potential, in particular via mobile devices that start with and increasingly go beyond smartphones.

In the 1970s, political economists coined the acronym BAIRS to describe bureaucratic authoritarian industrializing regimes (such as South Korea prior to partial democratization, and including China under Deng's reform program after 1978).[14] The new descriptor for the next decade is what I call BADGRS, or "bureaucratic accelerating data growth regimes," where the aspiration is to jump-start and accelerate the data-development-growth feedback loop that I described in Chapter 6.

The value-tradeoff for BADGRS would naturally prioritize data access over almost everything else and certainly over abstract definitions of privacy, along the lines of what currently is happening with social credit systems run both by Chinese government agencies and some of the largest Chinese platform firms. Security is crucial to this system, but privacy most definitely is not. Scale is a major benefit, but only to the extent that regulations enable the use of data to drive ML and—equally— enable the use of the resulting algorithms in transactions, relationships, and other interactions.

It may be a bit too simplistic to imagine the world dividing up cleanly into regions that are delimited from each other by rules and standards that oversee the use of data to drive algorithmic decision making, algorithmic transparency, and requirements for humans-in-the-decision-making-loop. But it's not that oversimplified. My hypothesis and expectation is that if you had to draw a map of the world in 2025 with regional boundaries on the basis of a single variable only, these rules and standards around algorithms would come much closer to defining the economic landscape than would any set of physical features, geographic contiguities, or "old" gritty standards around physical manufacturing.

Like a river exploring the top of its banks at flood stage, data flows will occasionally spill out of these logical channels. But for most purposes and most of the time, data flows will encounter the least resistance and create the most additional value at the margins when they move freely within the channels. Those channels will be what we call regions in 2025.

Here's one more way to visualize the same causal dynamic, by contrasting the micro-foundations of connectivity between individuals with the macro-environment of aggregate political economy. In simpler terms, the new geography can be characterized by the tensions between *vastly increased connectivity* among people and *diminishing relative connectivity* between institutions like firms, governments, and even organized markets.

It turns out that the internet idealists have been proven largely right about digital connections between people, which continue to multiply in breadth and depth. The trend is intact toward peer-to-peer and social connectivity in—make your own list—expertise, lending, raising capital, education, news and media, consumer behavior, and so on. The boundaries between people are breaking down, with a mix of technology enablers (just wait until we have really good machine translation, which is not far off) and mind-set shifts that together drive this forward. This trajectory has been in place for some time but was accelerated by the delegitimization and trust crisis consequent to the highly visible, enormously consequential, amazingly expensive, and morally stunning institutional failures of the last decade. But at the macro-level and in contrast, connections between firms, between governments, and between organized markets are being re-architected and reinforced with new boundaries and borders in a flurry of protective insularity, in part a response to the same legitimacy crisis.

The contrast couldn't be starker. Many people in 2018 came to loathe the company Facebook, while they cherish the connectivity with other people that Facebook provides to them. And so we should expect more rules that segment and divide rather than join together institutions, while tolerating leakage for individuals to exploit and enjoy. To repeat the point, the rules don't and won't take the form of physical borders like the Berlin Wall; they are and will be legal and logical, software and technical standards. But they are just as or more effective in raising new boundaries and demarcating the new regional order.

ORGANIZING FOR THE NEW REGIONAL LANDSCAPE

The vision of globalization in the late 1990s to early 2000s is not coming back any time soon. That's nearly conventional wisdom at the start of the 2020s, but the implications are more serious than just acknowledging that the world isn't flat and isn't going to be.[15] Taking this recognition to heart means that organizations cannot build scale and competitiveness on the foundation of a flattening world, because the world isn't heading in that direction. Even more important is an admonition for the largest and most powerful organizations, which might try to create or at least tilt conditions toward a flattening world. Politics will push those efforts back; if lucky that will just end up a waste of energy and if less lucky it will end up considerably more damaging than that. This warning is equally true for digital as it is for physical enterprises, perhaps even more so for digital because of its greater visibility and political salience right now in many parts of the world.

The new goal for an organization seeking to reach the world should now be this: organize to achieve as many of the upside benefits of the old globalization as you can, on the new regional playing field, with particular attention to the political economy of data. That's simple at a conceptual level and more complicated in practice, as always. The precise and granular ingredients of an implementation strategy will be different depending on the type of organization in question, the sector(s) of the economy at play, the risk appetite of leaders, and, of course, the history of the organization and its people.

Neither human nor organizational psychologies can ever really start from a blank slate. What I prescribe here are directional moves, which you can think of as an arrow that points from where you are at present to where you need to be a few years hence. There are four big moves to follow.

Point 1: Functional Decomposition of Production

Whether you think of value-creation systems as chains or networks, they still have nodes—places where particular functions cluster. This remains a compelling economic proposition and when people are involved, a human proposition as well. App designers will want to be near other app designers in the SOMA neighborhood of San Francisco. Office furniture designers will want to be near other office furniture designers in northern Michigan. Manufacturing facilities, even those predominantly staffed by robots, will want to be near other manufacturing facilities in Shenzhen.

Economies of scale are a powerful force behind this. So are what I call economies of resiliency, which describes the ability to substitute and slot in seamlessly a production factor (it might be a person or a robot) when an existing factor goes down. Geographic proximity is still a basic relevant fact for both. People are embodied physical beings and so are (hardware) robots, so moving them from place to place isn't trivial. When it comes to people, Richard Baldwin points out the importance of nonstop airplane flights.[16] When it comes to robots, the organizing principle is going to be different (robots don't mind long layovers in airports, unlike most people) but—even in an imaginary world where all factories were built to a common standard, allowing robots to slot in and out seamlessly—geographic distance still matters. When robots require modification and customization to particular settings and uses, distance matters quite a lot, in part because it comes back (at least for now) to people who will do that customization work.

It's a commonplace but still powerful truth that tacit knowledge transfer between people is more effective with physical proximity. Learning-by-doing depends on physical proximity. Knowledge network effects fall off significantly with distance. It's possible that advanced video-conferencing and augmented or virtual reality applications will change that equation, but they haven't done so yet, and every prediction that they will do so "in a few years" has been pushed back repeatedly not only by the limits of the technology but also by the magnetism of sociability that human beings seek with each other. App makers want to be around other app makers in order to swap stories about how they solve problems, but also because people like to be around people whose lives they sort of recognize and understand.

For these reasons the functional decomposition of production into concentrated nodes is going to be a continuing feature of modern economic geography. So is the fact that the outputs of these nodes (whether widgets or software modules) will need to be brought together into products or services for the market. The GIE vision, remember, was that this could be done on a global basis, which would maximize the economies of scale and resiliency as well as promote human sociability. That's not going to happen very much on a global basis, which leads us to points 2–4 below.

Point 2: Vertical Integration to Capture Data

Firms and governments alike have been saying for at least two decades that it is important to be "close to the customer." In fast-evolving markets where technology enables lots of new shortcuts to that closeness, the further mantra is about "owning the relationship to the customer."[17]

Why is this so important? The common wisdom from the GIE era was that closeness conferred the ability to design and provide customized products, to respond quickly to changes in demand, to receive granular feedback about how products are used in the wild, and to learn in an interactive or co-creative manner with customers about the real nature of demand. Owning the relationship to the customer was important because that relationship was the place where brands had meaning and where loyalty or at least trust could be secured in an otherwise hyper-competitive value circle where everyone was competing for everything. These drivers aren't wrong or obsolete, but how they work has changed shape.

The most important change in this new setting is *enabling the firm to capture and control data from the customer.* That has become the essential meaning of closeness: do you have continuing access to the data exhaust that customers produce, and do you have the social license to use that data to feed the ML loop?

The meanings of "capture" and "control" matter a lot here. Because data is nonrival in a purely economic sense, to capture and control it is not something you can do in a traditional physical sense. Control happens through standards, regulations, and other logical constraints, as well as through the brand loyalty that helps secure social license. Data is nonrival in its purest form, but you can still deny data access to other firms in ways that seek to slow down their ML loops and render them more or less commodity suppliers to yours. For governments, the analogy is keeping data out of the hands of other political jurisdictions—to avoid oversight and regulatory arbitrage, but also to empower national development strategies that seek to benefit and subsidize IDT firms on home territory.

An obvious example is the data from autonomous vehicles. Does that data stream empower the ML loop for Delphi or for General Motors? Uber or Tesla? Might it or should it be a public utility that is made available to all firms equally, or should it be required to be licensed in a "reasonable and non-discriminatory" fashion?[18] And what about data flow through export markets—will autonomous vehicles made by Chinese firms that send their data to the firms' servers in China be permitted on the New Jersey Turnpike?[19] I raised that question earlier and said that it pretty much answers itself from a national security perspective. But even if national security considerations were not so obvious, the competitive dynamics would still point in the same, data-protectionist direction. It's hard to see a national security issue behind YouTube's desire to own the relationship to the customer that now belongs to Comcast or even NBC, but there is certainly a competitive reason behind that strategy, and it is just as strong in effect.

What this leads to is selective vertical re-integration. I hinted at why and how this would happen with the clean-shirt value-chain example in Chapter 6. Firms will want to control the data collection point, wherever in the value chain or value circle that might come to lie. And the motion part of that story could be strategic and intentional: a firm may want to shuffle data collection points around to different parts of the chain or circle in order to keep competitors off-balance and maintain that control, or to keep up with technology developments that enable new data streams. Governments may want to do exactly the same with their data efforts.

To put this in another simple everyday example, consider the supermarket checkout counter as a natural data collection point. That barcode scanner is right now the nexus for data about what groceries I buy, in a granular and very valuable way (so much so that Safeway will give me a meaningful discount for using a loyalty card that associates the purchases with me). The suppliers to the supermarket and the makers of the products that land on the shelves only get highly aggregate demand data, for example when they restock inventory, and that's far less valuable. But that data architecture is not a fact of nature. Supermarket shelves can now assess what is happening in front of them as customers browse. It wouldn't take a massive engineering breakthrough to have the cellophane bag that holds my favorite sourdough pretzels become a data collection point and report my precise pretzel consumption, as well as variables that surround it, to Snyders. But since I usually am drinking my favorite beer with those pretzels, Sierra Nevada Brewery wants to do exactly the same thing. Vertical integration is a robust response to all that, and it is surely part of the logic behind Amazon's 2017 acquisition of Whole Foods and the 2018 opening of Amazon Go.[20] Of course there are things the vertically integrated supermarket firm can do with that data in the United States that it can't do in Germany. And that leads to point 3.

Point 3: Regionalization of Cross-National Production Networks

Production networks have never really wanted to respect the constraints of national borders. When physical constraints that coincided with those borders became much less important as a consequence of cheaper transport, the mismatch became an even greater source of friction. Modern economies are not capable of reconfiguring themselves on a national basis, even if there were serious arguments in favor of doing that (and it is hard to find those arguments being expressed in a compelling way). Even the largest national economies like the United States and China aren't really that large when it comes to the scale at which data wants to operate. And they are demonstrably insufficient at diversification to get an adequate degree of protection against exogenous and endogenous shocks (the GFC certainly revealed that).

Organizations need more space to reach the world. But they can't aspire to do that on a global basis for reasons that I've enumerated at length. Add that recognition to the two points above—the drive for functional decomposition of production, and selective vertical integration to capture data—and what emerges is a logic of regionalism.

What that means in practice is logically straightforward even if it seems unfamiliar. The modal scheme for a global organization would have *multiple copies of functionally decomposed production systems around the world, each anchored in a major geopolitical power.* Because it will take a major geopolitical power to establish and hold together the technical standards and regulations that make up the logical borders between regions, that means likely three or four regional copies. And because logical borders are at least as constraining as physical borders (and when it comes to data flows probably quite a lot more so), we should expect these regional production networks to be quite deeply integrated within themselves, and relatively sparsely connected to each other.

This point bears repeating: the regions that define the boundaries of these production networks do not need to be geographically contiguous. At the same time, some recognizable geographic contours will remain, that reflect a kind of hysteresis from the previous era(s) where geography really did matter. It's also true that the kind of political-economic power that enables what we still call a geopolitical great power to establish and maintain standards and regulations does have some foundations in physical geography.

The upshot is that new regions won't be entirely free of familiar geographic patterns; it's more that those familiar patterns of contiguity are no longer the determining feature. Regions will be delineated instead by rule sets and standards. The most important rule sets and standards will be those that establish property rights around data and govern how data flows.

And one more point bears repeating: these rule sets and standards are not in any way a function of nature, nor are they technical at their root. In other words, the fact that digital data can be replicated infinitely at zero cost is largely irrelevant except insofar as rules and standards can now shape what is possible in almost any way. It is misleading or worse to idealize the technical affordances of digital as so powerful that the system will always want to lean toward the open end of the continuum—which is my much less eloquent but more accurate rendition of the implicit meaning behind the aphorism "information wants to be free." Information and data don't "want" to be anything, and how freely or not they are priced or flow does not reflect transcendent technical properties. These critical factors are political creations, the product of human imagination and institutional action.

It's crucial to recognize this irony, that as technology has advanced it is actually human agency that has become ever more important. Adam Smith's pin factory had far fewer affordances than does Google's machine learning factory. And it is precisely the greater affordances of the latter that make human agency more capable of shaping it. Iron, steel, coal, and oil have physical properties that humans can only do so much with. What information and data actually want to be, is almost anything human beings decide to shape them as. Which brings us to the fourth and final point: about what that agency is pointing to now and in the near future.

Point 4: Reprioritization of Employment

Traditionally, corporate leaders in capitalist systems have not had to obsess about job creation as a primary component of their strategy.[21] The deep assumption was that if business focused on its principal objective of creating value, then jobs would be created along the way as a natural part of the equation making up the inputs to that process.[22] When and where that equation faltered and enough new jobs failed to materialize, it was the responsibility of governments first to address the imbalance. Sometimes that took the form of policies incentivizing more employment by firms and employment in particular locations, but if those policies didn't deliver (or didn't deliver in a cost-efficient way, which was more frequently the complaint) it was the government making the ineffective policy that was held to be mainly accountable.

The IDT and ML economy is slowly but surely destroying that deep assumption. The most successful firms in this economy employ a very small number of workers relative to value creation and market capitalization. In 2014, for example, the top three American IDT firms had a combined market capitalization of over $1 trillion and just 137,000 employees. In June 2018 Apple alone had a market capitalization of over $900 billion and just about 123,000 employees while Alphabet (Google's parent company) was about $800 billion and about 80,000 employees. The contrast is stark: in 1990 the top three Detroit automakers had a market capitalization of $36 billion and 1.2 million employees. That's an even more fundamental mismatch than is the substitution of robots for manual labor in factories.

In all the literature that seeks to assess the future of labor markets against automation, robotics, and AI, one common theme stands out: that routine work, at almost any level of skill and regardless of its cognitive or manual character, is going to decline as something that human workers are employed to do.[23] There have been a number of methodologically innovative efforts to put an estimate on the percentage of jobs that this dynamic places at risk. One of the most widely cited papers (by Frey and Osborne) puts this number at 47 percent of US employment.[24] I doubt the accuracy of the model that yields this number, as do many others; to their credit, the authors of the paper made clear that their model should be taken as a very rough cut. But the number was sufficiently shocking that it became a kind of social fact as it was repeated endlessly in talks, media, and other research papers.

This isn't the place to engage in a detailed analysis of the Frey and Osborne model, because the implications don't depend on it being even approximately right. Let's just stipulate for the sake of discussion that their estimate is double the size of the real effect. Then consider the impact on modern societies of something like a 20 percent loss in employment, perhaps over a decade. Now consider that these lost jobs are certain to exhibit geographic clustering—in a place like the United States, it's obvious on casual observation that there will be places where routine work makes up considerably more than one out of five jobs, and places where it makes up less. (The same, of course, was true of vulnerability to competition from Chinese manufactures.)[25]

Optimists in this debate point out, rightly, that new jobs will emerge as the economy changes shape (to believe the opposite is known as the "lump of labor" fallacy and it is clearly wrong, from both a theoretical and historical perspective). But the issue here is not simply one of labor-market evolution, it is one of political economy, and the wild card in the equation is timing. If the rate of job destruction is rapid and the rate at which new jobs emerge is gradual and delayed, as seems likely, then the long-run vector toward some new equilibrium hardly matters. The period of disequilibrium in which job destruction overwhelms job creation could last for a decade or more, which is de facto forever in political terms.

What this means immediately is that employment will be one of the most important scarce factors to be distributed across the new economic geography. Put differently, I believe that in both developed and developing countries it will be the case that firms, governments, and national systems of economic growth and innovation will be judged on the basis of how many and what types of jobs they create, as much as (and sometimes more than) on the basis of how much value or wealth they create.

That sentence contains within it more change and disruption than it might seem at first glance. Consider these implications. If firms are held to account for creating employment *in particular physical locations aligned with political authority* as much or more than creating value, how would global markets assess their competitive credentials? In the United States at the end of the 2010s, firms stand to win points for every *domestic* job created or even, possibly, maintained; and these direct rewards may pale alongside the intangible goodwill a firm can win by visibly stepping up to the challenge of job creation *at home*. After all, employment—and particularly the quality of jobs, not just the number of jobs—is calibrated, measured, and evaluated by political institutions like governments and their associated statistical agencies, more so than by markets. And there is a mounting awareness around the world of just how crucial jobs are to individual psychological well-being and aggregate social order, which are issues much more central to national political authorities than to anything global.[26]

A simple way to sum this up is to say that the prioritization of employment reinforces the new politicization of economic geography. At a minimum, subsidies of all different sorts from governments aimed at sustaining and creating jobs will become a more significant determinant of location decisions by firms, as well as the mix of capital expenditures for automation and robotics versus labor. Large and wealthy governments can surely beat out smaller and less wealthy governments in this game—but they can't easily beat out each other, and particularly in cases where firms are ruthlessly strategic in trying to play governments off against each other. The natural place for this game to end up is, again, in regional configurations where a major geopolitical power sets the principal terms of employment distribution domestically and, to a lesser but still meaningful extent, within its region. The public opinion elements of firms' social license to operate coincide with these terms and the statistics and metrics that governments use to assess them—not because any of those are perfect but because there really is no alternative, and certainly nothing at a global level that could even come close.

REACHING THE WORLD

So what does this look like from the perspective of an organization trying to reach the world in the next decade? In Chapter 1, I suggested that the words "global" and "integration" will mean very different things than they did in the 2000s. I said that to be a global organization on this new playing field will mean developing three or possibly four copies that operate to a considerable degree on their own. The new global organization will be less centralized in a formal sense, while cultural fit and government relations within regions will matter more than it has for decades.

Think of this as a semifractal pattern where each region has a largely self-contained organization with its own independent set of functions, customized for the political economy of the geopolitical center that anchors the region. I used the example of a hypothetical Apple in 2025 to make this more concrete.

Look backward first. In a rough approximation of the GIE model, Apple during the 2000s and 2010s mostly designed its products in California, built them in China, and shipped them around the globe.

Now look forward. The argument is that Apple 2025 will be different. It will have at least three such systems, each of which will be relatively self-contained—with design, production, and distribution connected internally for each region. Most important, the data that flows from Apple devices and products will largely be stored and used internally to each region. And that will reinforce the boundaries between them going forward.

An iconic indicator of these developments came in the form of Apple's 2018 actions to comply with China's 2017 cybersecurity law which, among other relevant provisions, requires foreign companies to store data generated from China inside China.[27] As Apple put it in an email notification to iCloud users in China, "With effect from 28 February 2018, iCloud services associated with your Apple ID will be operated by GCBD." GCBD (Guizhou-Cloud Big Data) is a domestic Chinese data-management firm originally set up by the local Guizhou Province government, which opened a data center in partnership with Apple for this purpose in 2017.[28] Apple went out of its way to remind its Chinese customers of the firm's strong commitment to data privacy. But the new terms of service state explicitly that "Apple and GCBD have the right to access your data stored on its servers. This includes permission sharing, exchange, and disclosure of all user data (including content) according to the application of the law."[29] And that means Chinese law, of course. Amazon Web Services (AWS) has a parallel arrangement with its own local infrastructure providers, and it specifies in its terms of service that "data or objects stored in AWS China (Beijing) Region and AWS China (Ningxia) Region remain exclusively in the Regions unless moved to other locations by the customer."[30]

What then will link these fractal units together into something that would be recognizable as a global organization? Branding, to start. It's wrong to think that branding is a trivial matter or minor source of value. Brand matters quite a lot in markets for what are increasingly intangible products; in Apple's case, it is an ecosystem of products, some of which are intangible and some of which are differentiated by design and hardware-software integration. For a customer deciding whether or not to enter that ecosystem, the long-term benefits are almost impossible to assess in advance in any concrete way, which is why brand is such an important asset. Yet it will be natural for the Apple brand to differentiate a bit over time by region as the regional units evolve somewhat differently. Managing that brand evolution and maintaining balance between its global characteristics and its regional specificities will be a crucial organization function at the center of the firm. For organizations where brand is tightly connected to internal corporate culture—or at least what customers and outsiders perceive to be internal corporate culture—this balancing act will be particularly challenging.

Another global glue will most likely be financial linkages, having to do with the allocation and re-allocation of capital among regional networks. The firms that do this on a global basis can achieve a degree of diversification that begins to approach that of "pure" financial firms, at least insofar as capital can be redeployed quickly and with low transaction costs. The more the firm's products and services rely on data, the more that condition holds. What is much less likely to work are the financial tricks that involve moving profits around for tax arbitrage. Governments have been losing patience with profit-shifting and protected domiciles and tax inversions for some time, and the greater concentration of economic activity within regions (with its inverse, relatively less activity between them) will empower governments to act more decisively and more effectively on taxes.

The global firm will also be held together by some data flows that will continue to move between regions, though much less so than in the late 2010s and much, much less so than the firm's data scientists and ML researchers and product designers would prefer. The same is true of human assets and talented people. It was previously the case that a rising star within a global firm would have looked to gain experience and run business units in several geographies around the world (and the leadership of the firm would have wanted her to do that). In the emerging regional geography, this will be less common, because that particular kind of experience will be less valuable. The rising star will have more to gain by developing deeper expertise and relationships in the region in which she is operating—which also suggests that first postings will be particularly important to people's career paths in global organizations.

Digital security will have to be reconfigured as well. Because regions will be experimenting with divergent security standards and protocols (as well as different regimes of property rights around personal data, or privacy), centralizing tendencies for security technologies and practices will seem increasingly clunky and dysfunctional. There's a simple analogy to how airports manage physical security that illustrates this.[31] At an airport in a U.S. city like San Francisco, there are three central TSA checkpoints that are essentially alike, where all travelers are subject to personal and baggage screening. You go through one of these and you're ready to board your plane. If you are in an airport like at Frankfurt and traveling to the United States, you have to go through a two-layer security check—first, the general security screening and, second, an additional security screen at the gate for your US-bound flight, where further checks are made to satisfy unique US requirements. But the new economic geography for digital security will feel more like Changi Airport in Singapore. Changi's security system is fully distributed, with machines and systems set up *at each gate* so that processes can be reconfigured independently for planes traveling to different parts of the world, or if requirements change for flights to particular places. It's not the most cost-efficient or scalable way to manage security in an abstract sense, but it may very well be the most adaptable model if you believe that requirements and protocols are going to be changing, divergent, and in some cases intentionally aimed at making it harder to move from one region to another.

The new regional geography will not be particularly amenable to global flows of tacit knowledge and probably not of algorithmic knowledge either. Let's be clear about the baseline: large organizations have continuously struggled to circulate tacit knowledge effectively because of its human-embedded nature. Digital technologies haven't done that much to change the fact that tacit knowledge flows best when people are physically close. Less circulation of people in a regional configuration means fewer tacit knowledge flows outside of those boundaries. Some kinds of tacit knowledge encoded in algorithms can flow more freely in principle. But to the extent that algorithms will be governed by regional standards and regulations, the ability of the global organization to move them around and deploy them effectively could be surprisingly limited.

The closer you look at this new regional model, the more it suggests a set of self-reinforcing tendencies that would, once it got started, grow and evolve in the direction of a scale-free network configuration. Put differently, a regional economic geography of the type I've described would tend to sustain itself through positive feedback loops that increase the connectivity within regions and reduce connectivity between them. There is doubtless a limit to that and at some point the process would hit an asymptote. And, of course, as I've recounted in this book, the history of organizations trying to reach the world is a sure reminder that today's and tomorrow's critical driving forces will not be the driving forces ten or twenty years from now. Technology and the state will change and create new ways to reach the world, which is simply a way

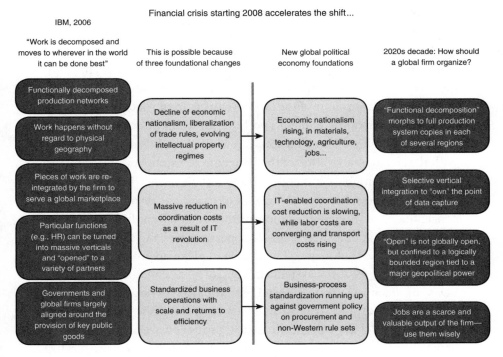

Figure 7.1: Old to New: Economic Geography and Global Reach.

of saying that no economic geography landscape lasts forever or anywhere close to it. But the emerging regional landscape, just getting started in the late 2010s, has a long way to go (see Figure 7.1).

It may seem peculiar to this point that I've avoided naming explicitly the geopolitical power centers that anchor regions and that I've hedged the question of whether there will likely be three or four. There are no big surprises here. As I argued earlier, the regulatory, political, and market capacities needed to structure a regional economic geography around data flows represent a significant hurdle for governments. At the intersection of regulatory capacity, market scale, and political coherence, there are clearly two power centers that dominated the late 2010s: the United States and China. The European Union is a third power center that also has the capacity and scale to structure a region, though it does not have (yet) the same level of IDT and platform businesses in place. If the European Union holds together as a political and regulatory unit, it will likely create a center of gravity that will anchor a third region; the major uncertainty here is whether in fact it will hold together.[32]

The largest uncertainty (and the reason I hedged on numbers) is whether a fourth region can plausibly get over the threshold. I'm confident there will be demand for at least a fourth autonomous region that will originate from some of the late developers in the data economy that are otherwise wealthy enough and have sufficient political capacity to make a leadership claim plausible. The United Arab Emirates, possibly with the close collaboration of the Kingdom of Saudi Arabia (for wealth and scale), would be a contender. There may be others, including India (which, of course, has the advantages of market scale and a history of conceptualizing "non-aligned movements" in global configurations). But it's also possible that these late developers are coming to the competition too late and that they will be unable to make up ground in the context of positive feedback systems in data, or seize enough of the advantages of backwardness to establish themselves as leaders.[33] The consequences of that struggle will be a big part of the global political economy story that I will sketch next, as part of answering the question of what life in this new economic geography will really look and feel like from the perspective of human values.

ORGANIZATION AND ALIGNMENT

Imagine for a moment that you are the CEO of a rising professional services firm—an aspiring global consultancy that aims to compete with the big three of McKinsey, BCG, and Bain—and you are just now setting up your structure and geographic footprint. How might you organize for effective global reach in the next decade? You'd need to place a bet, based on how many functionally decomposed production system regions you think will emerge and where you think each geopolitical anchor point will be. Then, you'd want to open an office in the capital of each geopolitical anchor state. And you'd staff each of these offices with representatives of each functional part of your business. That's the important move—to create what would essentially be several mini-copies of your firm, with the full range of capabilities in each location. Each of these fractal units would do most of its client work independently of the others and would function almost as a separate business most of the time. It's obviously a different and more limited scale equation than you might have sought a decade earlier. What you get in return for giving up global scale is the ability to align with the regional topography, and the success of your bet will be determined by how well you align yourself with government policies that structure data flows in that region.

I said earlier that government relations will matter for firms in this regional order more than it has for a very long time and this is a large part of what that means. Any assumptions about a natural or even latent alignment of interests between firms and governments left over from the GIE model should be dropped at this point. The language that people use around public-private partnerships sounds attractive, but I also think it is best left behind because it assumes too much.

Alignment is going to be much more demanding on firms, and it will need to be constructed in a proactive way and nourished with political and cultural sensitivities in clear focus. Issues around privacy and personal data will continue to capture headlines and get the attention of individuals and so those can't be ignored. But deeper and more fundamental areas of business-government alignment will have to be sought and nurtured around how data flows shape geopolitical positioning, national competitiveness, competition policies that are relevant to both, and, of course, as I emphasized earlier, jobs and employment at the aggregate societal level.

When people talk about trust in these settings, what I take that to mean is a shared belief between parties that their interests are basically compatible. The implication is that if trust is going to be a regional glue of any relevance, it will have to be based in alignment between states and firms around government priorities, with public opinion squarely in the background. That's an intriguing twist for Chinese firms as they develop their strategies to reach the world in this new era and with fewer legacy mind-sets, in particular relative to American firms. China's IDT firms are, after all, emerging out of a state-led economy and entering a world where "state determination" is becoming more important than is "self-determination" or individual political rights. About a decade ago, Naazneen Barma, Ely Ratner, and I described this "world without the

West" logic as sovereign states empowered to set the terms of relation-ships inside their borders between the government and the governed; and to deal with each other externally in a starkly market-oriented set-ting that recognizes no real rights or obligations other than to fulfill agreed contracts.[34]

Updating these same governance concepts to the modern era of data flows arguably will be easier for many Chinese firms, since their existing practices and mind-sets around data are already closely in line with this way of thinking. It isn't as much of a leap for TenCent or Baidu to see and move in the world this way as it would be for Google or Facebook. The kinds of intimate relationships that many oil companies maintained with governments in the mid-twentieth century are a better model for the future than are the Silicon Valley narratives of independence, open-ness, and liberal globalist sentiment powered by digital technologies. Those may sound like harshly judgmental words, but I do want to stress the distance between where many American IDT firms believe they are right now and where they will need to be a few years hence.

The Chinese IDT firms have another starting advantage in their gov-ernment relations—familiarity with state-directed allocation of capital in digital technology industry investment. A BADGR, as I described it earlier, is one manifestation of this relationship. Another is simply a rec-ognition of the contemporary IDT reality, which is the demonstrated *success of a non-democratic, state-led, innovation-robust economy at the digital technology frontier, at very large scale.*

Remember, Western political economy and competitiveness theory of the last several decades said it wasn't possible—China and Chinese firms would at best be fast-followers and more likely would run up against an innovation and competition threshold where the presence of the state would hold them back. That theory was wrong. As important, competing firms and governments outside China don't really believe it anymore. If they did, why worry about Chinese state-led technology ini-tiatives like the "New Generation Artificial Intelligence Plan"? If the theory about state-led investment as a handicap were accurate, competi-tors outside China should positively welcome these government schemes as more likely to weaken Chinese firms than to strengthen them, and they are decidedly not welcoming or sanguine about it. It's an uncomfortable realization to come to, but state intervention in the data economy—from a regulatory *and* investment perspective—can be done well. And Chinese political economy institutions are more practiced and more ideologically comfortable with using state-led tools to accelerate the data economy feedback loops that are the source of advantage.

As the new consensus about growth and development in the data economy emerges with a much more central role for governments, liberal economies will probably call it something like "smart capital allocation" to give it a more positive valence. But developmental economic nationalism is still developmental economic nationalism no matter what you call it, and when applied to the data economy, right now the Chinese system is out in front.

How will competition policy contribute to this regional differentiation? Governments need to experiment as they seek to balance the growth imperative against risks associated with positive feedback loops. The issues surrounding size, concentration, market power, and new business formation that I discussed in Chapter 6 aren't abstractions; they have risen to the forefront of debate in many parts of the world during the second half of the 2010s. The economics of data and ML do change the nature of competition in ways that competition policy authorities are just starting to grapple with. A very simple rendition of some of the core issues would include these:

- The US competition model has stressed consumer welfare via pricing effects and the opportunity costs associated with a lack of new entrants that might have otherwise appeared. But this is very hard to assess when two-sided markets support many services that are free in traditional price terms. And the type of fine-grained price discrimination that machine learning enables may very well be efficient for the economy as a whole even if it results in a higher price that some consumers pay than they would have otherwise paid in a less efficient price discovery system.
- Increasing concentration could reduce incentives to invest and innovate. But the counterfactual is hard to define and defend, and it is tricky on the face of it to argue that present-day IDT firms are less innovative than some alternative market structure might enable,

given the stunning things they have achieved. "What might have been" with regard to new entrants can be a theological debate, and even more controversial when the biggest companies are themselves still quite new in historical terms.

- The question of market definition and the boundaries of "adjacent" markets are complicated by the natural tendency of data platforms to violate those boundaries. It is after all at the core of data science to discover patterns that emerge *across* distinct or disparate activities. A related question is whether it makes sense to talk of algorithms that "collude" and whether that is a matter of intent, consequence, or something else.

- User lock-in through network effects and the improvement in data products the more they are used, is something that some societies and governments might abhor on principle even if the aggregate economic benefits are real and substantial. Conversely some societies and governments might value these effects or want to own them themselves (for surveillance or security purposes, for example). The notion of making data sets fully portable and interoperable or open as an essential utility or a public infrastructure will be attractive to some governments (just as the same notion was in other industries) and less so to others (preferences for stability over innovation or the other way around will come into play here, for example, in countries with very large banks whose customer data is an essential ingredient for small fintech startups).

- The discourse around "technology addiction" is imprecise and emotional, but likely to stay on the agenda as data products continue to improve. One interpretation would be that IDT companies create products that people love to the point of obsession, and another is that the products are damaging people either intentionally or unintentionally by taking away their free will and self-control (though it's unclear that this is a competition policy question rather than some other regulatory issue—why would a new entrant offer a product less addictive?). The important point is that societies will have very different views on what constitutes de facto addiction.

- Ultimately even the basic question of super-profits or massive economic rents is not definitive. The accompanying shift of income from labor to capital is perceived as a major problem in some countries, and a natural part of an economic development program in others (where it might simply be called capital accumulation). And regardless of whether the notion that consumers might develop class consciousness as data workers is realistic or ridiculous, some governments would really not want that to happen for reasons that have little to do with economic growth and everything to do with security and social control.[35]

It should be obvious from these bullet points that competition policy for the ML economy can be complicated and technical, bordering on arcane. And I want to be clear that the challenges I've named to defining a coherent competition policy agenda is not by implication an argument for taking no action at all. Uncertainty about the "right" policy is not the same thing as endorsing IDT firm laissez-faire. What it is, is an explicit recognition that these are first and foremost political choices. More precisely, competition policies will be political decisions informed in part by economic theory and not the opposite. It's another reason why (and a means by which) governments can and will on a regional basis define the economic geography for data flows in the coming decade.

THE WORLD IT MAKES

Is this new data-led regional landscape going to be a better place for people to live? I've argued through the course of this book that the answer is bivalent—in some respects yes and in some respects no. Let's start with a yes. There is lots of good news for people and societies that care about innovation.

I defined innovation as "the use of ideas, both new and recombinant, in the creation of value."[36] Because in practice there are many more recombinant ideas than there are new ones, having multiple systems in which those recombinations can happen simultaneously is going to be a relatively good thing. Machines are excellent at recombinant "thinking" and may become even better at testing the viability of those recombinant solutions in silico before anyone implements them in higher-stakes settings. Having multiple systems that do this under different standards and rule sets should expand the overall space for and rate of experimentation. That's valuable, because after decades of debate around the geography of innovation in multiple dimensions, we still don't really have a solid theory that explains precisely when innovation prospers in small versus large companies, or public versus private sector, or closed versus open intellectual property settings.

What we have gained is a deep awareness of the distinctive role that governments play in shaping innovation systems by constructing the public sphere and the commons and by designing and implementing property rights, among other enablers. It's reasonable to hope and expect that with a small number of regions competing to do this better, we will upgrade our collective understandings of what works at a more rapid rate. What's almost certain is a higher rate of innovation around innovation—by which I mean experimentation with Paul Romer's meta-ideas and institutions (from Chapter 6), the rules and processes that set the playing field for innovation overall. Regions will differ in how they organize these playing fields and—if history is any guide—they will learn from each other to some extent. In the twentieth century one meta-institutional means of learning was the idea of "special economic zones" in places like southern China and the Gulf States, places where alternative rule sets could be implemented and observed for effect. I would expect to see within the next decade new regions called "special data zones" where parallel experimentation takes place. And all of this should be positive for the rate of innovation overall because ultimately it is the meta-institutions that matter most.

There is a less-good news side to this same story, which concerns relationships between the great powers (and their regions) on this emerging landscape. International relations scholars have long argued about whether economic interdependence between political actors is associated with greater or lesser risk of conflict. A theory called commercial liberalism proposes that interdependence should reduce the risk of conflict because conflict disrupts economic exchange, and the more value there is in those exchanges the greater the reluctance to suffer the costs of disruption (by governments directly and, of course, by firms that presumably influence governments). This was the logic behind Norman

Angell's poorly timed 1913 book *The Great Illusion*—high levels of economic interdependence were supposed to constrain conflict between great powers at the beginning of the twentieth century. World War I (which started soon after the publication of *The Great Illusion*) was taken as evidence that Angell's argument was wrong, or more accurately that other driving forces like nationalism, rigid alliance structures, and failed crisis management had overwhelmed commercial liberal causal forces.[37] Partly in reaction, another theory called structural realism emerged during the Cold War and made the opposite argument, pointing to low levels of interdependence between the United States and the USSR as a cause of peace.[38] The two superpowers were largely disconnected from each other and thus reliant on successful management of their own domestic systems and spheres of influence to maintain a balance of power between them, and the low level of economic interdependence in particular meant there was little to argue about in that sphere.

Which of these dynamics around interdependence is likely to be more prominent going forward? I've painted here a landscape where several regions evolve in a manner more *independent* of each other with regard to data flows, reducing in relative terms the *interdependence* of what were more highly globalized value chains during the late twentieth and early twenty-first centuries. Less interdependence means less to argue about; higher levels of competition mean greater experimentation and innovation (as above). I would place a bet that the driving forces of the structural realist argument will be stronger going forward, and that less interdependence between regions will tend to reduce friction among them. A major reason is that the driving forces behind commercial liberalism that should reduce conflict through interdependence don't operate as strongly when it is relatively easy and cheap to relocate production nodes, as it will be when those nodes are more about data than about factories and physical supply chains.

Societies have a lot to figure out about how to deal with intimate values around the data economy, starting with issues like property rights around personal information (privacy) and distribution of wealth; the regional landscape provides greater degrees of freedom to work through these issues at smaller scale. But keep in mind that these new regions—defined by rules and standards—are overlaid on what is still a conventional map of physical space, a geographic plane where states maintain many traditional interests like physical borders and natural resources in the ground and the like. I foreshadowed in Chapter 1 that there would be places where these two realities grind gears, where the plane of physical geography and the plane of data geography collide—and these are where the greatest risks of conflict are likely to arise. The Baltic States along with Japan and Australia are obvious candidates. There may be less obvious cases, such as Great Britain should it find itself in a US-dominated data economy with a geographic and legacy institutional layer still tying it to the European continent.

At the global level, international politics could be surprisingly thin in many respects, organized loosely around a logic of coexistence and minimum viable cooperation. What will these several regions identify as common ground that truly necessitates cooperation on the global account?

Many issues that have been thought of as "global public goods" in the last several decades aren't really global in a profound sense—even climate change is in practice dominated by the carbon emissions of a small number of very large countries. Treating issues like climate change as a global public good, conceptually and politically, hasn't achieved great results. And so reducing global institutional overhead isn't likely to make things worse. It might end up focusing more of the biggest players' attention on each other, which could very well be positive overall for efficient bargaining among them. That is not a new argument, but while it is one that makes global governance scholars and practitioners uncomfortable, there is a case to be made for greater diversity of effort and innovation in testing new approaches made possible by the IDT revolution, in another example of "parallel processing" among several regions trying different things. When thinking about supposedly global public goods that are obviously and directly subject to new approaches through the creative use of data—such as pandemic disease surveillance and intervention—the case for parallel regional experimentation becomes even more compelling.

The template for cooperation between regions will, I believe, more closely resemble the logic of the Concert of Europe, a mid-1800s arrangement where great powers found common interests in collaboration to reduce the risks that their status would be challenged by lesser powers or, more profoundly, by unconventional ideologies and transnational movements seeking to upset the established order. The contemporary challenges that would inspire analogous collaboration include transnational violence, of course, but more interestingly also the potential for ideological movements that would place the fundamentals of the IDT economy at risk. In other words, the IDT leaders share a common interest in forestalling the development of transnational movements that would constrain regions' freedom to structure data flows. A strong transnational ideology around personal privacy would be constraining to all (even if not equally so). What seemed in 2019 like quixotic ideas around inspiring a global class consciousness for modern labor (all of us who produce data as a critical input to the IDT economy, which will mean essentially everyone on the planet) might not seem so outlandish in a few years.[39] The political powers that anchor data-led regions have a common interest in preventing any such development, just as the industrial capitalist political powers had a common interest in diverting nascent class consciousness for factory labor.

Another bivalent consequence of this new regional order will emerge from the more rapid growth of illicit markets for trade in drugs, human organs, stolen artwork, rare animals, and the like that make up "deviant globalization." These are illicit transactions that produce, move, and consume goods and services that violate localized normative restrictions. Twentieth-century deviant globalization made life worse for many people and societies that were targets of exploitation, but it also made life better for illicit entrepreneurs, their employees, their customers, and to some extent societies for whom deviant globalization was in practice "actually existing economic development." This remains true even though the particular forms of economic activity and growth were and are morally repugnant to some.[40]

Moral arbitrage (the animating force of deviant globalization) is just like other kinds of arbitrage in that it releases economic value by connecting supply and demand through semipermeable membranes that licit entrepreneurs won't transgress. The digital economy has been and will continue to be full of these kinds of opportunities, in part because the technology is moving so quickly and because it touches on such intimate aspects of human life. For example, it's long been true that pornography often pushes the boundaries of publishing and now experiential technologies (such as virtual reality) faster and farther than more mainstream or legitimate business applications, because the deviant entrepreneurs who drive that process are fearless of regulation, ruthlessly competitive, and not much concerned about broad social license to operate. They appeal to (prey on, if you prefer the morally loaded valence of that term, but the economic consequences are the same) base instincts of human beings and revel in the fact that legal and ethical strictures protect them from normal forms of licit competition. Their businesses are protected by a moral moat of sorts, and they make an enormous amount of money because of it.

The emerging regional geography is likely to super-charge deviant globalization in the digital realm because the moral gradients between regions will almost certainly increase as regions become more autonomous and chart their own regulatory paths. Here's a concrete and very real example, as disturbing as it may be: in some parts of the world, it will be illegal to create fake virtual pornography with computer-animated images of people, regardless of age or gender or for that matter consent, while in other parts of the world it will be protected speech or artistic expression. And right there is the moral gradient that makes moving things across boundaries to satisfy demand an extremely profitable arbitrage play.

Opportunities like these attract some of the sharpest minds and ruthless competitors around the world, particularly in places where legitimate and legal employment and business opportunities are harder to find. The cybersecurity challenge—that is, the fact that data moves through channels that are extremely hard or impossible to make secure—is for deviant entrepreneurs a major feature of the digital economy. This is another way in which the new economic geography will foster higher rates of growth and innovation, but also greater friction and possibilities for violent conflict. Because one important thing that deviant globalizers don't have is recourse to institutionalized nonviolent means of contract adjudication and enforcement of agreements. Deviant globalization works with the shadow of violence just barely in the background, and the more widespread and profitable it becomes, the more likely (at least in the short term) that the violence will break through to the surface.[41]

Ideological overlays matter a lot in human affairs. The good news is that data science is massively improving our ability to see and measure how ideologies are expressed in writing and thinking, and perhaps even predict when and where they manifest in thought. But it's still a very long road to a world where data science vanquishes ideology as a source of surprise and discontinuity. The digital revolution has over the last fifty years given birth to some important new ideological threads, or at the least invigorated ideological tendencies that had been on the margins in the past. Consider the open-source movement, or John Perry Barlow's digital libertarianism, or some of the other strands of techno-idealism and pessimism that I described earlier. It's impossible to say what new ideological movements might emerge as the data revolution progresses. For example, I offered in Chapter 6 the observation that data products have the capacity to overcome and even reverse the recalcitrance of the physical world and the corroding of compound things that have burdened the physical universe and the humans that interact with it, because data products can get smarter, better, and more resilient the more they are used. Might this single observation become the fount of a new antimaterialist ideology, or, more interestingly, an "a-materialist" ideology, one that simply downgrades the desirability of and eschews the physical and material world whenever possible?

Who knows? Speculating about future ideologies is still a fool's errand. But what is possible to hypothesize with some confidence is that a regional landscape creates more space for experimentation and growth of new ideologies than we have come to expect. Put it in opposite terms: can anyone imagine another "end of history" argument being put forward and taken seriously in the next decade or two? I can't. What I can imagine much more readily is a further loss of innocence, a still deeper and more widespread recognition that data and its associated technologies represent the most profound challenge to human values that human beings have yet created. The debates around privacy and related issues that took up so much airtime in the late 2010s, important as they are, barely scratch the surface. It is still the case in 2019 that research projects and educational curricula generally start with technology and then bolt on a segment that reflects ELSI (ethical, legal, and social implications). It's as if those elements could be an afterthought or a harmonic accompaniment to what is the melody of technology.

I find it difficult to believe that this model will continue, and particularly as the ELSI components diverge more freely and fully in a regional economic geography. Bio-ethicists have for at least three decades now talked about how the manipulation of human genomes would be subject to different ELSI overlays in different societies—for example, in Western Europe versus China. Privacy scholars have made similar claims and comparisons about the United States versus Europe versus Asia. The intensity of these differences is set to increase in a regional economic geography, which means those sometimes theoretical differences are likely to become quite real and visible. But as with meta-institutions in the case of property rights and innovation and the like that I discussed above, I think that here too the increased range for diversity and experimentation is a better outcome than the alternative. History shows time and again that it is very hard or impossible for people to decide what they truly value and care about when it comes to trade-offs that are abstract, scientifically complex, and located in future time. What's needed more than an elusive (imaginary?) ELSI solution is a set of meta-institutions that can manage discussion, debate, and deliberation around the ELSI components of digital technologies, and do that sooner, not later as a reactive afterthought. If several regional systems find themselves in a competition to design and deploy potential ways of doing this, that is going to be a good thing overall.

There is one final bivalent subject to consider—an issue that is both extremely important and highly uncertain—and it lies in the area of political risk, in particular regarding the two biggest data powers, the United States and China. Organizations that try to reach the world have throughout history been subject to political risk, even if the terminology is modern. For much of that history, of the two major determinants of strategy (technology and the state), it has generally been the state and political risk connected to it that has been the more important of the two.

The late twentieth and early twenty-first centuries were mild exceptions to that rule. Mind-sets and beliefs around globalization and the overwhelming force of digital technologies made political risk seem even less prominent than it actually was. John Perry Barlow was skirting the edge of reality, but his 1996 manifesto was taken seriously at that moment, as a directional signal at least. The IBM leadership's argument that information and data technologies could be thought of as largely outside conventional politics for the GIE looks a bit naive in retrospect, but it was taken in a similar way. What remained in terms of political risk was going to be concentrated in what were relabeled as "frontier markets," a code-word for countries and places even less stable than "emerging markets." And even there, political risk was becoming sufficiently predictable and diversified that one could price a hedge against it in many cases.

Those hopeful thoughts about the secular decline of political risk were dashed in the decade after the GFC. Most importantly, they have been dashed in developed markets, and in the two largest data powers. In the late 1990s and early 2000s, the United States and China were both in their own manner predictable and auspicious environments for global organizations to operate within. That's no longer true of either. And it is increasingly clear that the shift is systemic in nature, not an idiosyncratic moment associated with a particular leader such as Trump or Xi.[42] Nor is it true of Britain after the Brexit referendum or other rich European industrial democracies that have seen their political spectrum expand dramatically to the right and the left at once.

Political risk is now everywhere, and managing it is a much higher priority for an aspiring global enterprise. I argued earlier that for organizations seeking to reach the world, government relations is more important than it has been for decades; job creation has become a metric for firms' license to operate; data nationalism and techno-nationalism more generally is on a self-reinforcing and accelerating upswing. Firms will need to harness serious political power to have a chance of bargaining effectively with governments around these issues, and that is another driving force behind regional organization. Countervailing political power is plausible on a regional basis. Here too global is too big and national too small to be efficient. It's also another reason why we should expect both firms and governments to be economical or even stingy with investments in global governance—there's just not that much that can be done effectively at global scale right now.

Look for this effect of broad and deep political risk in three related areas at least. First, the design of domestic political institutions for the data era will have to be inclusive enough to be sustainable. The industrial era required high levels of capital accumulation, and in the minds of many political economists that requirement drove the development of inclusive political institutions. Peter Evans's work on intellectual property suggests that data accumulation (the "capital" equivalent growth driver going forward) will demand even greater levels of inclusiveness— simply because to collect a lot of intimate data about people will require a state-society-business trust pact that is much deeper, with broader participatory ties than we have been accustomed to.[43] I think that is a hopeful perspective in some respects, but not an empirically defensible one at present. Around the world, people have been willing to hand over all sorts of data in exchange for better commercial products and performance. Might they not do the same for government performance? In the United States we assume not, because Americans are historically fearful of government access to personal data. But this hasn't been tested for the data era, really, because the profound improvements in government performance that are possible haven't arrived yet. And those improvements will probably come first in places like Singapore and, of course, China, where the default assumption is that people have somewhat greater tolerance for government access to data. To put this in stark relief, consider this question as something that Americans may have to confront in the 2020s: what if the Chinese social credit system works to improve government performance and enhance economic and social interactions in a way that Chinese society and citizens generally accept or even enjoy?

The second phenomenon to look for is the broad articulation of meaning and value in what Mimi Ito has called "off-market labor," the everyday phenomenon of work that people engage in and societies depend on but that are not structured within conventional labor markets and bargained and compensated that way.[44] Governments and firms through regulations and labor practices can help societies parse what is meaningful in those activities, but it is people and cultures that ultimately have to define it. And job displacement from automation and robotics is accelerating dramatically the rate and depth at which that process has to happen. Not everyone will write poetry and philosophy. And societies will continue to have different attitudes toward stay-at-home parents who tutor their kids and the like. The rise of human-on-human, mixed cognitive-emotional labor in off-market settings is at one level a very local and personal thing, but at the aggregate social level it will require some significant new thought about how to distribute resources outside labor markets to the people who do it. The late 2010s discussion of "universal basic income" merely scratches the surface of how governments will have to negotiate this issue with both societies and firms, and it's another example of how parallel experimentation in several regional settings at good-enough scale is likely a positive thing.

The third phenomenon concerns the nature of truth, or at least truth as it gets deployed in social settings. Part of the uptick in political risk lies in what media commentators called the "post-truth" world after 2016, but that is too simple and cynical a concept. A better way to think about it, is to recognize that in practice truth is now just a tool that people and organizations use to seek their objectives. More precisely, epistemology is the most powerful tool—epistemology as the set of standards by which people assess confidence about an assertion. Any single truth-claim on its own isn't worth all that much. The rules for how we determine what is true enough to matter are worth a great deal. (It's like giving a person a fish versus teaching a person how to fish.) So the question of political risk becomes in part a matter of who can articulate a practical epistemology in a manner compelling enough that others care? Until and unless this can be done by disembodied algorithms (and I don't believe that time is anywhere close), that's a very human phenomenon, rooted as much or more in emotions than in cognition.

Emotional appeal as a key ingredient of political risk? It sounds very conventional, traditional, almost instinctual. That's because it is exactly those things. Digital technology and data science make it possible to A/B test at large scale what works and doesn't work, at least in some settings. It makes it possible to organize around ideas on a regional basis. But testing and organizing are not the same as creating. Political leadership still lies in the act of creation, even more so now that other elements can be partially automated. Creation is human, human creativity creates risk, and thus political risk is everywhere. The good news for aspiring global organizations is that there remains competitive advantage to be had in deep understanding of those things. There are scale advantages to be captured, but human agency and ingenuity don't scale in the same way. I am confident that in 2030 we will still be saying that it is far too early to give up on the genius of human insight.

A final synthetic prescription for thriving in the next phase of global economic geography, then, boils down to these five elements. The best strategic positioning for an aspiring global organization will be to do these things:

- keep your robots close to home (the central power anchoring a region);
- keep your data close to your chest (vertical integration along the value chain);
- keep your capital expenditure under control (to ride out volatility);
- keep your job creation in the spotlight (to manage political risk);
- and keep your fingers crossed for minimum viable global security cooperation among political powers (and don't expect or rely on much more than that).

It may not add up to the best of all possible worlds for global organizations that an idealist could imagine. But there's plenty of room to make the new regional order a better world for those organizations, and for people, than most people on this planet have ever experienced.

NOTES

1. TO REACH THE WORLD

1. E. Brynjolfsson and L. Hitt, "Beyond Computation: Information Technology, Organisational Transformation and Business Performance," *Journal of Economic Perspectives* (Fall 2000).

2. Eric S. Raymond, *The Cathedral and the Bazaar: Musings on Linux and Open Source by an Accidental Revolutionary* (Cambridge, MA: O'Reilly Media, 1999).

3. Edgar Schein, *Organizational Culture and Leadership* (San Francisco: Jossey-Bass, 1992), 10.

4. Stewart Brand, *How Buildings Learn: What Happens after They're Built* (New York: Viking, 1994).

5. Gregory A. Petsko, "The Blue Marble," *Genome Biology* 12, no. 4 (2011): 112.

6. Ernst Friedrich Schumacher, *Small Is Beautiful: A Study of Economics as If People Mattered* (New York: Blond and Briggs, 1973).

7. John Gilmore, quoted in Philip Elmer-Dewitt, "First Nation in Cyberspace," *Time Magazine* no. 49, December 6, 1993.

8. Cisco, "Internet of Everything FAQ," http://ioeassessment.cisco.com/learn/ioe-faq.

9. One of Facebook's corporate mission statements is to "make the world more open and connected." I'll discuss the more complicated and ambiguous logic around "open" in later chapters.

10. Ronald Coase, "The Problem of Social Cost," *Journal of Law and Economics* 3 (1960): 1–44.

11. Clay Shirky, *Here Comes Everybody: The Power of Organizing without Organizations* (New York: Penguin, 2008).

12. McKinsey Global Institute, "Digital Globalization: The New Era of Global Flows," March 2016.

13. Gillian B. White, "How Many Robots Does It Take to Replace a Human Job?," *Atlantic*, March 2017, https://www.theatlantic.com/business/archive/2017/03/work -automation/521364/.

14. "A Leaked Draft of the Pentagon's Nuclear Review Shows a Desire for New Kinds of Weapons," *Washington Post,* January 13, 2018, p. 4.

15. Amanda Wills, Sergio Hernandez, and Marlena Baldacci, "762 Murders. 12 Months. 1 American City," CNN, January 2017, https://www.cnn.com/2017/01/02/us /chicago-murder-rate-2016-visual-guide/index.html. In 2017 there was a slight decline to about 650 murders.

16. Joseph Schumpeter, *Capitalism, Socialism, and Democracy* (New York: Harper and Brothers, 1942).

17. Andrew Flowers, "Big Business Is Getting Bigger," FiveThirtyEight, May 2015, https://fivethirtyeight.com/features/big-business-is-getting-bigger/.

18. That is precisely what the Chan Zuckerberg initiative, funded by Facebook founder Mark Zuckerberg, put forward as its goal in 2016 with a $3 billion pledge.

19. I'll unpack some of those explanations for digital platform companies in Chapters 5 and 6.

20. Benjamin M. Friedman, *The Moral Consequences of Economic Growth* (New York: Vintage, 2005).

21. United Nations Development Programme, "Sustaining Human Progress: Reducing Vulnerabilities and Building Resilience," *Human Development Report* (2014), 19; World Bank Group, *Taking on Inequality* (Washington, DC: International Bank for Reconstruction and Development, 2016).

22. Steven Weber, "The End of the Business Cycle?," *Foreign Affairs* 76 (1997): 65–82.

23. "GDP Growth (Annual %)," World Bank (2017), https://data.worldbank.org /indicator/NY.GDP.MKTP.KD.ZG/.

24. This evocative image is from Martin Sandbu, "Global Economic Growth: What Could Possibly Go Wrong?," *Financial Times,* February 7, 2017.

25. Tyler Atkinson, David Luttrell, and Harvey Rosenblum, "How Bad Was It? The Costs and Consequences of the 2007–9 Financial Crisis," Dallas Federal Reserve Bank Staff Papers 20 (July 2013).

26. Naazneen Barma, Ely Ratner, and Steven Weber, "The Mythical Liberal Order," *National Interest* 124 (March / April 2013).

2. THE LOGIC OF GLOBALIZATION FOR GLOBAL ENTERPRISE

1. John F. Richards, *The Finances of the East India Company in India, c. 1766–1859,* Working Paper No. 153 / 11, London School of Economics (August 2011); Marguerite E.

Wilbur, *The East India Company and the British Empire in the Far East* (Stanford, CA: Stanford University Press, 1950).

2. Stephen R. Bown, *Merchant Kings: When Companies Ruled the World, 1600–1900* (New York: Thomas Dunne Books, 2010); Nick Robins, *The Corporation That Changed the World: How the East India Company Shaped the Modern Multinational,* 2nd ed. (London: Pluto Press, 2012).

3. Anthony Sampson, *The Sovereign State: The Secret History of ITT* (London: Hodder and Stoughton, 1972); Rosanna Ledbetter, "ITT: A Multinational Corporation in Latin America during World War II," *Historian* 47 (1985): 524–537.

4. Nils Gilman and Steven Weber, "Megaphilanthropies and the New Globalization," 2009, available from the author.

5. See, for example, Jonathan Taplin, *Move Fast and Break Things: How Facebook, Google, and Amazon Cornered Culture and Undermined Democracy* (New York: Little, Brown and Company, 2017).

6. Wilbur, *East India Company and the British Empire in the Far East,* 15; Robert Brenner, *Merchants and Revolution: Commercial Change, Political Conflict, and London's Overseas Traders 1550–1653* (Princeton, NJ: Princeton University Press, 1993).

7. John Keay, *The Honourable Company: A History of the English East India Company* (New York: Macmillan, 1991): 10 (spelling modernized).

8. Keay, *Honourable Company,* 25.

9. Keay, *Honourable Company,* 222.

10. H. V. Bowen, *The Business of Empire: The East India Company and Imperial Britain, 1756–1833* (Cambridge: Cambridge University Press, 2008), chapter 2; Richards, *Finances of the East India Company in India.*

11. L. S. Sutherland, "The East India Company in Eighteenth-Century Politics," *Economic History Review* 17 (1947): 15–26.

12. Keay, *Honourable Company,* 331.

13. A fascinating history is Roy Ruffin, "David Ricardo's Discovery of Comparative Advantage," *History of Political Economy* 34 (2002): 727–748.

14. Karl Polanyi, *The Great Transformation: The Political and Economic Origins of Our Time,* 2nd ed. (Boston: Beacon Press, 2001). The first edition was 1944.

15. See, for example, Tim Buthe, "Private Regulation in the Global Economy: A Preview," Special Issue of *Business and Politics* 12 (2010): 1–38.

16. Dani Rodrik, *The Globalization Paradox: Why Global Markets, States, and Democracy Can't Coexist* (Oxford: Oxford University Press, 2011).

17. See, for example, S. Prakash Sethi, "The Influence of 'Country of Origin' on Multinational Corporation Global Strategy," *Journal of International Management* 5 (1999): 285–298; Sarah S. Snoup, *Borders among Activists: International NGOs in the United States, Britain, and France* (Ithaca, NY: Cornell University Press, 2012);

Niels G. Noordrhaven and Anne-Dil Harzing, "The Country of Origin Effect in Multinational Corporations: Sources, Mechanisms, and Moderating Conditions," *Management International Review* 42 (2003): 47–66.

18. Raymond Vernon, "Where Are Multinationals Headed?," in *Foreign Direct Investment,* ed. Kenneth A. Froot (Chicago: University of Chicago Press, 1993), 57–84.

19. Paul J. DiMaggio and Walter W. Powell, "The Iron Cage Revisited: Institutional Isomorphism and Collective Rationality in Organizational Fields," *American Sociological Review* 48 (1983): 147–160.

20. James P. Womack, Daniel T. Jones, and Daniel Roos, *The Machine That Changed the World* (New York: Scribner, 1990).

21. See, for example, Stephen S. Cohen and John Zysman, *Manufacturing Matters: The Myth of the Post-Industrial Economy* (New York: Basic Books, 1987).

22. Francis Fukuyama, "The End of History," *National Interest* 16 (1989): 3–18.

23. "InfoWorld," (34), August 21, 1995, cited in a Wikipedia entry, https://en .wikipedia.org/wiki/Mosaic_(web_browser)#cite_ref-32.

24. This metaphor was widely used (and misused) at the time and still is, now applied to other technologies and startups. See, for example, "A Cambrian Moment," *Economist,* January 17, 2014.

25. The phrase was created by the Victorian-era philosopher Herbert Spencer; it was adopted and popularized by Thatcher in the mid-1980s.

26. Steven Weber, "Origins of the European Bank for Reconstruction and Development," *International Organization* 48 (1994): 1–38.

27. P. A. David, "The Dynamo and the Computer: A Historical Perspective on the Modern Productivity Paradox," *American Economic Review,* Papers and Proceedings 80 (1990): 355–361.

28. Alex Winter, "The Short History of Napster," *Wired,* April 16, 2013.

29. Though it sometimes felt that way—and was expressed in similar terms—by musicians and artists, as well as some software companies.

30. The phrase "castles in the air" describes a fanciful shared narrative about corporate valuations that boosts share prices. See Burton G. Malkiel, *A Random Walk Down Wall Street,* 4th ed. (New York: W. W. Norton, 2011).

3. THE ERA OF THE GLOBALLY INTEGRATED ENTERPRISE

1. Samuel P. Huntington, *The Clash of Civilizations and the Remaking of World Order* (New York: Simon and Schuster, 1996).

2. Samuel J. Palmisano, "The Globally Integrated Enterprise," *Foreign Affairs* 85 (2006): 127–136.

3. Huntington, *Clash of Civilizations and the Remaking of World Order.*

4. Carlota Perez, *Technological Revolutions and Financial Capital: The Dynamics of Bubbles and Golden Ages* (Northampton, MA: Edward Elgar, 2003).

5. Perez, *Technological Revolutions and Financial Capital*. Quotes are from p. xvii; the model is diagrammed on p. 74.

6. Interview on NBC-TV, transcript, February 19, 1998, United States Information Agency, Washington File, "Archived copy," archived from the original on March 8, 2016.

7. Joseph Nye, *Bound to Lead: The Changing Nature of American Power* (New York: Basic Books, 1990); Matthew Kroenig, Melissa McAdam, and Steven Weber, "Taking Soft Power Seriously," *Comparative Strategy* 29 (2010): 412–431.

8. Bernard Lewis, *What Went Wrong? Western Impact and Middle Eastern Response* (Oxford: Oxford University Press, 2002).

9. Speech on September 21, 2001, https://www.voanews.com/a/a-13-a-2001-09-21-14-bush-66411197/549664.html. See also Steven Weber and Bruce W. Jentleson, *The End of Arrogance: America in the Global Competition of Ideas* (Cambridge, MA: Harvard University Press, 2010).

10. I am enormously grateful to Daniel McGrath and Irving Wladawsky-Berger for giving me this once-in-a-lifetime opportunity.

11. Thomas L. Friedman, *The World Is Flat: A Brief History of the Twenty-First Century* (New York: Farrar, Straus and Giroux, 2005).

12. United Nations Conference on Trade and Development (UNCTAD), *World Investment Report* (2006), https://unctad.org/en/pages/PublicationArchive.aspx?publicationid=709.

13. The IBM System 360 is the iconic example. S / 360 was launched in 1964 and delivered to customers through 1978. See http://www-03.ibm.com/ibm/history/exhibits/mainframe/mainframe_FS360.html.

14. Adding to its mystique, this advertisement was broadcast nationally only once, during the third quarter of the 1984 Super Bowl on January 22, 1984, in a game between the Washington Redskins and the Los Angeles Raiders (the Raiders won). One of the great ironies of the time was that Apple during the 1990s built its personal computer business on a proprietary operating system called System 7, which it licensed only for a very short period of time to a few selected alternative hardware companies. Meanwhile, the IBM PC evolved into a more open standard, giving birth to an entire global industry of what were known at the time as "PC clones" (not exactly what the 1984 commercial portrayed). System 7 later was given up by Steve Jobs in favor of OS X, which was based on an open-source BSD UNIX kernel.

15. Steven Weber, *The Success of Open Source* (Cambridge, MA: Harvard University Press, 2005), chapter 4.

16. Richard Baldwin, *The Great Convergence—Information Technology and the New Globalization* (Cambridge, MA: Belknap Press of Harvard University Press, 2016).

17. Samuel J. Palmisano, "Competing in the Global Era," slide deck at www.thecge.net/?s=competing+in+the+global+era. Emphasis added.

18. See Michael Porter, *On Competition: Updated and Expanded Edition* (Cambridge, MA: Harvard Business Review Press, 2008).

19. Steven Weber and Eammon Kelly, "A Co-creation Discipline," Monitor Group 2012, available from the author.

20. Navi Radjou, "India Leads IBM's New Global Business Model" (2007), Forrester Report, https://www.forrester.com/report/India+Leads+IBMs+New+Global+Business+Model/-/E-RES41750.

21. Interview with Christopher Caine, July 2017.

22. P&G annual reports, 1999–2007.

23. Most industry analyses put the total export of cement at less than 10 percent of global consumption.

24. Donald R. Lessard and Cate Reavis, "CEMEX: Globalization the CEMEX Way," MIT Sloan School of Management Case Study 09-039, November 16, 2016. I was also an occasional consultant to the CEMEX global strategy team during this period, though far less than involved than I was with IBM.

25. Marc Austin, "Global Integration the CEMEX Way," *Corporate Dealmaker,* February 2004.

26. Joel Whitaker and Rob Catalano, "Growth across Borders," *Corporate Strategy Board,* October 2001.

27. Peter Evans, *Embedded Autonomy, States and Industrial Transformation* (Princeton, NJ: Princeton University Press, 1995). See also Atul Kohli, *State-Directed Development: Political Power and the Industrialization in the Global Periphery* (Cambridge: Cambridge University Press, 2004).

28. See Paul Romer, "The Origins of Endogenous Growth," *Journal of Economic Perspectives* 8 (1994): 3–22. An excellent review is David Warsh, *Knowledge and the Wealth of Nations: A Story of Economic Discovery* (New York: W. W. Norton, 2006).

29. This is not precisely true in all cases. It's possible to imagine technologies that would themselves enforce IP arrangements, and many such technologies have been tried—for example, software licenses that can't be used on multiple machines. But ingenious people have generally found ways to reverse-engineer these kinds of technologies, unless they are prevented from doing so, at least legally, by governments.

4. WHAT WENT WRONG?

1. We called this memo the "Doha Scenarios Wrap," February 21, 2007, available from the authors.

2. Samuel J. Palmisano, "The Global Enterprise: Where to Now?," *Foreign Affairs,* October 14, 2016, https://www.foreignaffairs.com/articles/2016-10-14/global-enterprise.

3. Shawn Donnan, "Trade Talks Lead to 'Death of Doha and Birth of New WTO,'" *Financial Times,* December 20, 2015.

4. Palmisano, "Global Enterprise: Where to Now?," 4.

5. Adam Przeworski, *Democracy and the Market: Political and Economic Reforms in Eastern Europe and Latin America* (Cambridge: Cambridge University Press, 1991).

6. Aaron Belkin and Philip E. Tetlock, eds., *Counterfactual Thought Experiments in World Politics: Logical, Methodological, and Psychological Perspectives* (Princeton, NJ: Princeton University Press, 1996).

7. Richard Baldwin, "Trade and Industrialisation after Globalisation's 2nd Unbundling: How Building and Joining a Supply Chain Are Different and Why It Matters," National Bureau of Economic Research Working Paper 17716, December 2011, http:// siteresources.worldbank.org/INTRANETTRADE/Resources/Baldwin_NBER _Working_Paper_17716.pdf; Richard Baldwin, *The Great Convergence: Information Technology and the New Globalization* (Cambridge, MA: Belknap Press of Harvard University Press, 2016).

8. Steven Weber, ed., *Globalization and the European Political Economy* (New York: Columbia University Press, 2001).

9. Baldwin, *Great Convergence.*

10. Baldwin, *Great Convergence,* 11.

11. John Rawls, *A Theory of Justice* (Cambridge, MA: Belknap Press of Harvard University Press, 1971).

12. Hypercompetition was in many respects the equivalent in the first decade of the 2000s to what the phrase "disruptive innovation" would become in the second decade of the 2000s.

13. Richard D'Aveni, "Waking Up to the New Era of Hypercompetition," *Washington Quarterly* 21 (1997): 183–195.

14. As compared to the fluid, complex, and more variegated security environment of the 1990s, typified by the wars in the former Yugoslavia. It's hard to imagine in retrospect any serious international politics scholar or practitioner pining for the "good old days" of the Cuban Missile Crisis and the Vietnam War, but this was the mood of the time.

15. Joseph Schumpeter, *Capitalism, Socialism and Democracy* (New York: Harper-Collins, 1942).

16. Jason Furman and Peter Orszag, "A Firm Level Perspective on the Role of Rents in the Rise in Inequality," a presentation at "A Just Society" Centennial Event in Honor of Joseph Stiglitz, Columbia University, October 16, 2015. This paper is focused on a different subject (inequality), but the data on firm concentration is relevant. See also Tim Koller, Marc Goedhart, and David Wessels, *Valuation: Measuring and Managing the Value of Companies,* 6th ed. (New York: Wiley Finance, 2015).

17. Furman and Orszag, "Firm Level Perspective," 9. They exclude "goodwill" as an intangible asset.

18. See, for example, Federico Diez, Daniel Leigh, and Suchanan Tambunlertchai, "Global Market Power and Its Macroeconomic Implications," IMF Working Paper,

2018, https://blogs.imf.org/2018/06/06/chart-of-the-week-the-rise-of-corporate-giants/?utm_medium=email&utm_source=govdelivery.

19. "An Open and Shut Case," *Economist,* October 1, 2016, p. 13. See also "Too Much of a Good Thing," *Economist,* March 26, 2016.

20. Steven J. Davis and John Haltiwanger, "Labor Market Fluidity and Economic Performance," NBER Working Paper No. 20479, December 2014, http://www.nber.org/papers/w20479.pdf; J. D. Harrison, "The Decline of American Entrepreneurship—in Five Charts," *Washington Post,* February 12, 2015. The Kauffman Foundation has been a major source and supporter of research on these trends; their 2017 report shows and explains a moderate revival of startup activity, which still remains in significant deficit following the Great Recession. Ewing Marion Kauffman Foundation, *State of Entrepreneurship 2017,* https://www.kauffman.org/what-we-do/resources/state-of-entrepreneurship-addresses/2017-state-of-entrepreneurship-address Data set at https://www.kauffman.org/kauffman-index.

21. A related argument that connects IP and other intangible assets to concentration is Nicolas Crouzet and Janice Eberly, "Understanding Weak Capital Investment: The Role of Market Concentration and Intangibles," paper prepared for the Jackson Hole Economic Policy Symposium, Federal Reserve Bank of Kansas City, August 23–25, 2018.

22. The core arguments of this section are detailed in Steven Weber, *The Success of Open Source* (Cambridge, MA: Harvard University Press, 2005).

23. Albert O. Hirschman, *Exit, Voice, and Loyalty: Responses to Decline in Firms, Organizations, and States* (Cambridge, MA: Harvard University Press, 1970).

24. *The Pharmaceutical Sector: A Long-Term Value Outlook,* Report of PharmaFutures study group, Phase 1, 2004, http://pharmafutures.org/pharmafutures-1/a-long-term-value-outlook/.

25. See, for example, Charles Cooper, "Dead and Buried: Microsoft's Holy War on Open-Source Software," CNET.com, June 1, 2014, https://www.cnet.com/news/dead-and-buried-microsofts-holy-war-on-open-source-software/.

26. Thanks to Kevin Rivette, a former IBM senior executive, who used this evocative phrase in a conference at Chalmers University, Gothenberg, Sweden, in 2007.

27. Fred J. Hellinger, "Cost and Financing of Care for Persons with HIV Disease: An Overview," *Health Care Financing Review* 19, no. 3 (1998): 1–14.

28. Donald G. McNeil Jr., "Indian Company Offers to Supply AIDS Drugs at Low Cost in Africa," *New York Times,* February 7, 2001, http://www.nytimes.com/2001/02/07/world/indian-company-offers-to-supply-aids-drugs-at-low-cost-in-africa.html.

29. William W. Fisher and Cyrill P. Rigamonti, "The South Africa AIDS Controversy: A Case Study in Patent Law and Policy," *Law and Business of Patents* (2005): 3, https://cyber.harvard.edu/people/tfisher/South%20Africa.pdf.

30. "The Price of Africa's Cheap Drugs," *Economist,* April 18, 2001, http://www.economist.com/node/578817.

31. McNeil Jr., "Indian Company Offers to Supply AIDS Drugs."

32. "12-Year-Old Settles Music Swap Lawsuit," *CNN*, February 18, 2004, http://www.cnn.com/2003/TECH/internet/09/09/music.swap.settlement/.

33. David Silverman, "Why the Recording Industry Really Stopped Suing Its Customers," *Harvard Business Review*, December 22, 2008, https://hbr.org/2008/12/why-the-riaa-stopped-suing.

34. See Lawrence Lessig, *The Future of Ideas: The Fate of the Commons in a Connected World* (New York: Random House, 2001).

35. An example of the former would be a government acting against a pharmaceutical patent in the context of a public health crisis; an example of the latter would be a firm engaging in the manufacture of counterfeit luxury goods or pirated DVDs.

36. Arthur Okun, "Upward Mobility in a High-Pressure Economy," *Brookings Papers on Economic Activity* 1 (1973): 207–261.

37. Office of the United States Trade Representative, *United States Files WTO Cases against China over Deficiencies in China's Intellectual Property Rights Laws and Market Access Barriers to Copyright-Based Industries* (Washington, DC: Office of the United States Trade Representative, 2007), https://ustr.gov/about-us/policy-offices/press-office/press-releases/archives/2007/april/united-states-files-wto-cases-against-china.

38. Nils Gilman, *Mandarins of the Future: Modernization Theory in Cold War America* (Baltimore, MD: Johns Hopkins University Press, 2003).

39. Charles Duhigg and Keith Bradsher, "How the U.S. Lost Out on iPhone Work," *New York Times*, January 21, 2012, http://www.nytimes.com/2012/01/22/business/apple-america-and-a-squeezed-middle-class.html.

40. A good review is Zidong An et al., "Does Growth Create Jobs? Evidence for Advanced and Developing Economies," *IMF Research Bulletin* 17 (2016). See also Erica L. Groshen and Simon Potter, "Has Structural Change Contributed to a Jobless Recovery?," *Current Issues in Economics and Finance* 9, no. 8 (2003).

41. Rebecca J. Rosen, "The Mental-Health Consequences of Unemployment," *Atlantic*, June 9, 2014, https://www.theatlantic.com/business/archive/2014/06/the-mental-health-consequences-of-unemployment/372449/.

42. International Labour Organization, *Global Employment Trends for Youth 2017: Paths to a Better Working Future* (Geneva: International Labour Office, 2017), http://www.ilo.org/wcmsp5/groups/public/---dgreports/---dcomm/---publ/documents/publication/wcms_598669.pdf.

43. "Youth Unemployment in the Arab World Is a Major Cause for Rebellion," International Labour Organization, April 5, 2011, http://www.ilo.org/global/about-the-ilo/newsroom/features/WCMS_154078/lang--en/index.htm.

44. Dani Rodrik, "Premature Deindustrialization," *Journal of Economic Growth* 21 (2016): 1–33.

45. Martin Neil Baily and Barry P. Bosworth, "US Manufacturing: Understanding Its Past and Its Potential Future," *Journal of Economic Perspectives* 28 (2014): 3–25.

46. See, for example, Kiminori Matsuyama, "Structural Change in an Interdependent World: A Global View of Manufacturing Decline," *Journal of the European Economic Association* 7 (2009): 478–486.

47. David Blumenthal and Shanoor Seervai, "To Combat the Opioid Epidemic, We Must Be Honest about All Its Causes," *Harvard Business Review,* October 26, 2017, https://hbr.org/2017/10/to-combat-the-opioid-epidemic-we-must-be-honest-about-all -its-causes.

48. Sutki Dasgupta and Ajit Singh, "Manufacturing, Services and Premature Deindustrialization in Developing Countries: A Koldrian Analysis" UNU-WIDER Working Paper No. 49, May 2006, https://www.wider.unu.edu/sites/default/files /rp2006-49.pdf.

49. Rodrick, "Premature Deindustrialization."

5. INGREDIENTS FOR A NEW ECONOMIC GEOGRAPHY

1. IMF World Economic Outlook Database, available at https://www.imf.org /external/pubs/ft/weo/2018/01/weodata/download.aspx.

2. Estimates vary slightly according to source. These are from the World Bank global data set at https://data.worldbank.org/indicator/NY.GDP.MKTP.KD.ZG.

3. Josh Zumbrun, "IMF Lowers Global Growth Forecasts for 2018 and 2019," *Wall Street Journal,* October 8, 2018; Josh Zumbrun, "IMF Lowers 2019 Global Growth Forecast," *Wall Street Journal*, January 21, 2019.

4. Data from US Bureau of Economic Analysis, Department of Commerce, https://www.bea.gov/national/index.htm#gdp.

5. Data from St. Louis Federal Reserve Bank, https://fred.stlouisfed.org/series /MEHOINUSA672N.

6. Daniel Kahneman, Jack L. Knetsch, and Richard H. Thaler, "The Endowment Effect, Loss Aversion, and Status Quo Bias," *Journal of Economic Perspectives* 5 (1991): 193–206.

7. Paul Krugman (a columnist at the *New York Times*) and Martin Sandbu (a columnist at the *Financial Times*) have been two of the most thoughtful and eloquent voices taking this position.

8. Galen Panger, "Emotion in Social Media" (Ph.D. diss., University of California, Berkeley, 2017), available at http://people.ischool.berkeley.edu/~gpanger/dissertation /emotion_in_social_media.pdf.

9. David Autor at MIT has been the leading researcher in this area. See, for example, David H. Autor, David Dorn, and Gordon H. Hanson, "Untangling Trade and Technology: Evidence from Local Labour Markets," *Economic Journal* 125 (2015): 625–646.

10. See, for example, Robert J. Gordon, "Is US Economic Growth Over? Faltering Innovation Confronts the Six Headwinds," National Bureau of Economic Research Working Paper 18315, 2012, http://www.nber.org/papers/w18315.pdf.

11. The oft-heard quote "everything that can be invented has been invented" is often misattributed to Charles Holland Duell, commissioner of the United States Patent Office from 1898 to 1901. There is no record of Duell having made this precise comment. The sentiment precedes his tenure in office and has been traced back to an 1843 report to Congress by an earlier Patent Office commissioner.

12. Coen Tuelings and Richard Baldwin, eds., *Secular Stagnation: Facts, Causes, and Cures* (Brussels: Center for Economic Policy Research, 2014). This e-book is available at https://voxeu.org/content/secular-stagnation-facts-causes-and-cures.

13. This is commonly known as the "Solow productivity paradox." Robert Solow originally wrote it in a 1987 review of *Manufacturing Matters* with the title "We'd Better Watch Out," *New York Times Book Review,* July 12, 1987, p. 36.

14. An early articulation is Jonathan Hankins, "What Does 'Responsible Innovation' Mean?," *IEEE Spectrum,* June 24, 2015, https://spectrum.ieee.org/tech-talk/at-work/innovation/what-does-responsible-innovation-mean.

15. See, for example, J. R. Bell, "Underdiagnosis of Depression in Primary Care: By Accident or Design?," *Journal of the American Medical Association* 18 (1997): 1433.

16. A good summary history is Andrew Jordan and Timothy O'Riordan, "The Precautionary Principle: A Legal and Policy History," in *The Precautionary Principle: Protecting Public Health, the Environment and the Future of Our Children,* ed. Marco Martuzzi and Joel A. Tickner (Geneva: World Health Organization, 2004), chapter 3.

17. The original paper is available from David Isenberg's website, www.isen.com.

18. The "5 9's" was a phrase used by the telephone networks to describe 99.999 percent reliability.

19. Clayton M. Christensen, *The Innovator's Dilemma: When New Technologies Cause Great Firms to Fail* (Cambridge, MA: Harvard Business School Press, 1997). Christensen introduced the theory of disruptive innovation in an earlier article with Joseph Bower, "Disruptive Technologies: Catching the Wave," *Harvard Business Review* (January–February 1995): 43–54. A trenchant critique is Jill Lepore, "The Disruption Machine: What the Gospel of Innovation Gets Wrong," *New Yorker,* June 23, 2014.

20. Christensen, *Innovator's Dilemma,* 15.

21. Lockheed Martin provides a short but wonderful history of its skunk works facility at https://www.lockheedmartin.com/en-us/who-we-are/business-areas/aeronautics/skunkworks/skunk-works-origin-story.html.

22. An excellent review is Robert C. Tucker, "The Theory of Charismatic Leadership," *Daedalus* 97 (1968): 731–756.

23. Marc Andreessen, "Why Software Is Eating the World," *Wall Street Journal,* August 20, 2011. This phrase later became the tagline for Andreessen's venture capital firm, Andreessen Horowitz (also known as "a16z").

24. The Apple and Android app stores are different in this respect: Apple is more restrictive and Android less so.

25. The DARPA "Grand Challenge" to build autonomous vehicles, the first long-distance competition, was originally launched in 2004. That year, none of the robot vehicle entrants were able to complete the 150-mile route in the Mojave Desert.

26. Mikhail Chester, Andrew Fraser, Juan Matute, Carolyn Flower, and Ram Pendyala, "Parking Infrastructure: A Constraint on or Opportunity for Urban Redevelopment? A Study of Los Angeles County Parking Supply and Growth," *Journal of the American Planning Association* 81 (2015): 268–286.

27. See, for example, Brian Fung, "Uber Settles with FTC over 'God View' and Some Other Privacy Issues," *Los Angeles Times,* August 15, 2017.

28. This provision was known as OCILLA, or Online Copyright Infringement Liability Limitation Act. The European Union adopted a parallel exemption in its Electronic Commerce Directive of 2000.

29. "YouTube Serves Up 100 Million Videos a Day Online," *USA Today,* July 16, 2006. By 2017 YouTube was adding about 400 hours of content *per minute.*

30. The complete text of the Digital Millennium Copyright Act of 1998 is at https://www.gpo.gov/fdsys/pkg/CRPT-105hrpt551/pdf/CRPT-105hrpt551-pt2.pdf.

31. It was a strategic business decision, of course. In some cases, copyright owners would demand payment for the use of their content. In other cases, they would file takedown notices. In still other cases, they might choose to simply ignore the infringement, such as when they believed that the primary result of the YouTube video was to serve as a form of unintentional marketing for the licensed content.

32. Many Europeans—citizens and governments—had fallen out of love much sooner, or never really were enthralled in the same manner.

33. See, for example, Timothy B. Lee, "Here's Everything We Know about PRISM to Date," *Washington Post,* June 12 2013.

34. Farhad Manjoo, "Tech Giants Seem Invincible. That Worries Lawmakers," *New York Times,* January 4, 2017. Emphasis added. Later that year, FANG would become, in the common parlance, FAANG, with the inclusion of Amazon.

35. Manjoo, "Tech Giants Seem Invincible."

36. A good summary of the arguments is in Harold Abelson et al., *Keys under Doormats: Mandating Insecurity by Requiring Government Access to All Data and Communications,* MIT-CSAIL-TR-2015-026, July 6, 2015.

37. See https://www.people-press.org/2016/02/22/more-support-for-justice-depart ment-than-for-apple-in-dispute-over-unlocking-iphone/?utm_source=viz&utm

_medium=viz.referral&utm_campaign=viz.ref&utm_viz_id=jjvOqTxYGDX&utm
_pubreferrer=www.forbes.com%2Fsites%2Fnelsongranados%2F2016%2F02%2F20%2
Fapple-can-should-and-will-help-fbi-unlock-shooters-iphone%2F. Fifty-one percent
said Apple should unlock the phone; 38 percent said Apple should not; and 11 percent
said "don't know." Interestingly, there were no significant differences on party affiliation for Democrat versus Republican.

38. Lawrence Lessig, *Code and Other Laws of Cyberspace* (New York: Basic Books,
1999).

39. Steven Weber and Bruce W. Jentleson, *The End of Arrogance: America in the
Global Competition of Ideas* (Cambridge, MA: Harvard University Press, 2010).

40. Mark W. Zacher, "The Decaying Pillars of the Westphalian Temple: Implications
for International Order and Governance," in *Governance without Government: Order
and Change in World Politics,* ed. James N. Rosenau and Ernst-Otto Czempiel (Cambridge: Cambridge University Press), 58–101.

41. Nils Gilman, Jesse Goldhammer, and Steven Weber, "Can You Secure an Iron
Cage," *Limn* 8 (2017).

42. Soroush Vosoughi, Deb Roy, and Sinan Aral, "The Spread of True and False
News Online," *Science* 359 (March 9, 2018): 1146–1151.

6. HOW TO ORGANIZE

1. Steven Weber, "Counterfactuals, Past and Future," in *Counterfactual Thought
Experiments in World Politics: Logical, Methodological, and Psychological Perspectives,*
ed. Aaron Belkin and Philip Tetlock (Princeton, NJ: Princeton University Press, 1996),
268–291.

2. AnnaLee Saxenian, *Regional Advantage: Culture and Competition in Silicon
Valley and Route 128* (Cambridge, MA: Harvard University Press, 1996).

3. *China Embraces AI: A Close Look and a Long View,* Sinovation Ventures and Eur-
asia Group White Paper, December 2017, p. 7. Data on mobile subscriptions can be
found at https://www.statista.com/statistics/278204/china-mobile-users-by-month/.

4. Alyssa Abkowitz, "The Cashless Society Has Arrived—Only It's in China," *Wall
Street Journal,* January 3, 2018.

5. For example, see Li Yuan, "Google and Intel Beware: China Is Gunning for Dominance in AI Chips," *Wall Street Journal,* January 4, 2018; Abkowitz, "Cashless Society
Has Arrived."

6. Qi Lu, a prominent AI researcher formerly at Microsoft, was appointed as COO
of Baidu in January 2017. See Louise Lucas, "China Seeks Dominance of Global AI
Industry," *Financial Times,* October 15, 2017.

7. Shazeda L. Ahmed and Steven Weber, "China's Long Game in Techno-
Nationalism," *First Monday* 23 (May 7, 2018), http://firstmonday.org/ojs/index.php/fm/
article/view/8085/7209.

8. Paul Mozur, "Beijing Wants AI to Be Made in China by 2030," *New York Times*, July 20, 2017.

9. The Japanese case is described and explained in Daniel Okimoto, *Between MITI and the Market: Japanese Industrial Policy for High Technology* (Stanford, CA: Stanford University Press, 1990).

10. Other goals are also affected. See, for example, Benjamin M. Friedman, *The Moral Consequences of Economic Growth* (New York: Random House, 2010).

11. Paul Krugman used the phrase "high development theory" in "Toward a Counter Counter-Revolution in Development Theory," *World Bank Economic Review* 6, suppl. 1 (1992): 15–38.

12. Steven Weber, ed., *Globalization and the European Political Economy* (New York: Columbia University Press, 2001).

13. The arguments in the following pages are drawn from my earlier paper, Steven Weber, "Data, Development, and Growth," *Business and Politics* 3 (2017): 397–423.

14. At the time of writing and as far as I know, there is no country that has developed such a metric. I expect that this will change very soon, if it has not already by the time this book reaches print.

15. See, for example, Jamie Manley, "Could Data Privacy Concerns Spoil China's Autonomous Vehicle Ambitions?," *Technode*, January 2018, https://technode.com/2018/01/19/autonomous-vehicle-privacy/.

16. Richard Baldwin, "Trade and Industrialization after Globalization's Second Unbundling: How Building and Joining a Supply Chain Are Different and Why It Matters," National Bureau of Economic Research Working Paper 17716, 2011, http://www.nber.org/papers/w17716.

17. For the "cross-national production network," see John Zysman, Eileen Doherty, and Andrew Schwartz, "Tales from the 'Global' Economy: Cross National Production Networks and the Re-organization of the European Economy," Berkeley Roundtable on the International Economy Working Paper 83, June 1996.

18. We have discovered this in the last fifteen years with shale oil, tight oil, and other unconventional sources.

19. See, for example, James Manyika et al., *Digital Globalization: The New Era of Global Flows*, McKinsey Global Institute, March 2016, p. 98, https://www.mckinsey.com/~/media/McKinsey/Business%20Functions/McKinsey%20Digital/Our%20Insights/Digital%20globalization%20The%20new%20era%20of%20global%20flows/MGI-Digital-globalization-Full-report.ashx.

20. It can also be expressed as an accounting identity, the difference between national savings and national investment.

21. See, for example, Tom Fairless, "Europe Looks to Tame Web's Economic Risks," *Wall Street Journal*, April 23, 2015; Tom Fairless, "EU Digital Chief Urges Regulation to Nurture European Internet Platforms," *Wall Street Journal*, April 14, 2015.

22. The classic paper on two-sided markets is Jean-Charles Rochet and Jean Tirole, "Platform Competition in Two-Sided Markets," *Journal of the European Economic Association* 1 (June 2003): 990–1029.

23. Michael E. Porter, *On Competition* (Cambridge, MA: Harvard Business Review Publishing, 1985).

24. A short but clear articulation of these arguments is in Robert D. Atkinson, "Why Internet Platforms Don't Need Special Regulation," Information Technology and Innovation Foundation Working Paper 5, January 2016, https://itif.org/publications /2016/01/05/why-internet-platforms-dont-need-special-regulation.

25. Except insofar as the data imbalance causes a traditional current account imbalance, which would then drive a capital account and currency adjustment response in financial flows, not in data flows per se.

26. Paul M. Romer, "Two Strategies for Economic Development: Using Ideas and Producing Ideas," *Proceedings of the World Bank Annual Conference on Development Economics* (1992), published in a supplement to the *World Bank Economic Review* (March 1993): 63–91.

27. Aurelien Faravelon, Stephane Frenot, and Stephane Grumbach, "Chasing Data in the Intermediation Era: Economy and Security at Stake," *IEEE Security and Privacy Magazine* 14, no. 3 (May–June 2016): 22–31.

Their principal data source, alexa.com, is widely used, but it is important to recognize that it is limited and may be subject to nonrandom bias. Jeanie Oh and I used data from SimilarWeb in 2017, a company that measures web traffic in different ways and thus should be subject to different biases, to replicate the basic imbalance findings of Faravelon, Frenot, and Grumbach. An alternative metric, also imperfect but interesting, is to count the share of profits of the fifty biggest listed platforms by country. US firms have more than 80 percent while European firms have only about 5 percent. See "Taming the Beasts," *Economist,* May 28, 2016, p. 57. None of these metrics is anywhere near perfect, but all point in the same direction and comport with observation.

28. A large-scale survey, also in 2016, by Peter C. Evans and Annabelle Gawer examined platform companies with a valuation (publicly or privately held) above $1 billion and came to generally similar conclusions about geography. They make an additional interesting observation about headquarters and cities: a quarter of the platforms in their survey (forty-four) have headquarters in the San Francisco Bay Area; the second largest concentration is in Beijing (thirty) and the third largest in Shanghai (fifteen). Peter C. Evans and Annabelle Gawer, *The Rise of the Platform Enterprise: A Global Survey,* Center for Global Enterprise, January 2016.

29. See Fernando H. Cardoso and Enzo Faletto, *Dependency and Development in Latin America* (Berkeley: University of California Press, 1979). Dependencia theory also carried with it a set of claims about distorted politics and economy on the periphery that were the result of this process; an assessment of these dynamics for the

era of data is beyond the scope of this chapter but is an intriguing subject for future work.

30. Alexander Gerschenkron, *Economic Backwardness in Historical Perspective* (Cambridge, MA: Belknap Press of Harvard University Press, 1962).

31. See Ravati Prasad, "Ascendent India, Digital India: How Net Neutrality Advocates Defeated Facebook's Free Basics," *Media, Culture, and Society* 40 (October 2017): 415–431.

32. Naazneen Barma and Elliot Posner independently made this argument to me, noting that countries like Canada and Australia and Norway did exactly this with "lower-tier" industries like agriculture and commodities in the last quarter of the twentieth century and the first decade of the twenty-first.

33. To repeat once more the limitations of this argument, it by intention here does not take real account of other concerns and objectives that the data economy raises with regard to privacy, surveillance, and the like.

34. See "The Full Stack Startup," Andreesen Horowitz blog, http://a16z.com/2015/01/22/the-full-stack-startup/; Ryan Craig, "The Full Stack Education Company," *Forbes*, May 26, 2015, http://www.forbes.com/sites/ryancraig/2015/05/26/the-full-stack-higher-education-company/#24a13126459d; and "Keeping It under Your Hat," *Economist*, April 13, 2016, http://www.economist.com/news/business-and-finance/21696911-tech-fashion-old-management-idea-back-vogue-vertical-integration-gets-new.

35. There are two nodes for now. There could and likely will be more discrete steps, as automation makes it possible to reduce the human labor still engaged in the clean-shirt value chain. I would welcome a robot that put the shirt in the laundry, removed it from the dryer, folded it, and hung it in my closet. Many of the same arguments above about data flow through that part of the value chain would still apply.

36. This is basic transaction-cost economics reasoning along the lines developed by Oliver Williamson. See, for example, Oliver E. Williamson, "The Economics of Organization: The Transaction Cost Approach," *American Journal of Sociology* 87 (1981): 548–577.

37. Romer, "Two Strategies for Economic Development."

38. Governments have within their existing policy toolboxes ways to do this, including but not limited to data localization regulations, tariffs and nontariff barriers to imported data products, public procurement rules, and so on. If some of these policy moves were to be defended publicly for other reasons (such as privacy), that makes them no less important as development strategies. Using other rationales would be nothing new: governments have long justified protectionism on other grounds when it suits them to do so.

39. I am grateful to Gil Fronsdal and Michael Singer for teaching me about this profound truth.

40. *China Embraces AI*, p. 7.

7. ORGANIZATION AND OUTCOMES

1. Pickles in Brooklyn, gin in Alameda, salami in Oakland, and whiskey in Wyoming are my personal favorite examples.

2. This is an intentional contrast with the perspective of Philip Tetlock; for example, see Philip E. Tetlock, *Expert Political Judgment: How Good Is It? How Can We Know?* (Princeton, NJ: Princeton University Press, 2005).

3. Japan is the obvious exception to "no experience" with deflation and it is the exception that proves the rule, given the prominent presence of the Japanese government in economic coordination.

4. The late 2010s debate about universal basic income proposals in some rich countries is an example of this; see, for example, Amy Downes and Stewart Lansley, *It's Basic Income: The Global Debate* (Chicago: Policy Press, 2018).

5. The proposition here is that subsidizing compute capabilities would be one way for governments to give startups a competitive leg up against much larger incumbents who can buy compute power, like any commodity, at a much greater scale and thus likely at lower prices.

6. This total of 195 should be considered a rough number, even at the moment of writing (February 2018), because of all the obvious political controversies that surround the formal status of a number of these "states."

7. Karl Polanyi, *The Great Transformation: The Political and Economic Origins of Our Time* (New York: Farrar and Rinehart, 1944); John Gerard Ruggie, "International Regimes, Transactions, and Change: Embedded Liberalism in the Postwar Economic Order," *International Organization* 36 (1982): 379–415.

8. See the parallel analysis of Polanyi's critique in Steven Klein, "How (Not) to Criticize Karl Polanyi," *Democracy,* June 2017, https://democracyjournal.org/alcove/how-not-to-criticize-karl-polanyi/.

9. It is easy to imagine a highly secure system that has very little privacy—consider Google's email service Gmail as an obvious example. And not all security breaches have a negative impact on what people consider to be privacy. In fact it could go the other way—consider the hypothetical of a security breach that compromises data integrity in a set of electronic medical records, which might have the peculiar effect of enhancing privacy by corrupting what would have otherwise been personally identifiable information. Conceptually this represents a deviant form of differential privacy, a technique that can introduce statistical noise into a large data set in ways that makes it harder to de-anonymize particular records without meaningfully reducing the value of the aggregate data.

10. "America Inc. Gets Woke," *Economist,* December 2, 2017.

11. See, for example, Mark Sullivan, "Big Tech Lobbying Spree: Here's How Much Apple, Amazon, and Others Gave D.C. in 2017," *Fast Company,* January 23, 2018,

https://www.fastcompany.com/40520529/big-tech-lobbying-spree-heres-how-much
-apple-amazon-and-others-gave-d-c-in-2017.

12. Gary King, Jennifer Pan, and Margaret E. Roberts, "How Censorship in China Allows Government Criticism but Silences Collective Expression," *American Political Science Review* 107 (2013): 1–18.

13. Naazneen Barma, Ely Ratner, and Steven Weber, "A World without the West," *National Interest* 90 (2007): 23–30.

14. See, for example, David Collier, ed., *The New Authoritarianism in Latin America* (Princeton, NJ: Princeton University Press, 1979).

15. Thomas L. Friedman, *The World Is Flat: A Brief History of the Twenty-First Century* (New York: Farrar, Straus, and Giroux, 2005).

16. Richard Baldwin, *The Great Convergence: Information Technology and the New Globalization* (Cambridge, MA: Belknap Press of Harvard University Press, 2016).

17. Jonathan Sallet and I referred to this in previous work as a "value-circle" logic where many of the competitors in a market array themselves in a schematic circle around the customer, and then compete to organize the circumference while controlling the relationship to the customer at the center. Sallet developed these ideas further in Jonathan Sallet, "The Creation of Value: The Broadband Value Circle and Evolving Market Structures" (April 4, 2011), https://ssrn.com/abstract=1821267.

18. The rich complexities of this concept and its implementation in technology markets are explored in Bowman J. Heiden, "The Battle to Define the Meaning of FRAND—The Changing Role of Intellectual Property in the Knowledge Economy," doctoral dissertation, Chalmers University of Technology, 2017.

19. Jamie Manley, "Could Data Privacy Concerns Spoil China's Autonomous Vehicle Ambitions?," Technode, January 2018, https://technode.com/2018/01/19/autonomous -vehicle-privacy/.

20. Amazon Go is a grocery store operated by Amazon that has no checkout lines but instead uses advanced sensors to track customers' progress through the store, what they take from a shelf and / or put back, and more.

21. This statement is powerfully true of the more "laissez-faire" capitalist systems, like those in the United States and the United Kingdom. It is somewhat weaker in managed or social welfare capitalist systems, like those in Germany or Sweden.

22. An Apple executive responding to a *New York Times* reporter's questions about job creation captured this perfectly when he said "our only obligation is making the best product possible." Charles Duhigg and Keith Bradsher, "How the U.S. Lost Out on iPhone Work," *New York Times,* January 21, 2012.

23. David Autor of MIT is in my view the leading thinker on this issue. See, for example, David Autor, "Polanyi's Paradox and the Shape of Employment Growth," National Bureau of Economic Research, Working Paper 20485, 2014, http://www.nber.org/papers/w20485.

24. Benedikt Frey and Michael A. Osborne, "The Future of Employment: How Susceptible Are Jobs to Computerization," Oxford Martin School, September 17, 2013, https://www.oxfordmartin.ox.ac.uk/downloads/academic/The_Future_of_Employment.pdf.

25. See, for example, David H. Autor, David Dorn, and Gordon H. Hanson, "The China Shock: Learning from Labor-Market Adjustment to Large Changes in Trade," *Annual Review of Economics* 8 (2016): 205–240.

26. See, for example, R. H. Price, D. S. Friedland, and A. D. Vinokur, "Job Loss: Hard Times and Eroded Identity," in *Perspectives on Loss: A Sourcebook,* ed. J. H. Harvey (Philadelphia: Taylor and Francis, 1998), 303–316; Paul Taylor et al., "The Impact of Long-term Unemployment, Lost Income, Lost Friends—and Loss of Self-respect," Pew Research Center, July 2010, http://www.pewsocialtrends.org/files/2010/11/760-recession.pdf.

27. Shazeda L. Ahmed and Steven Weber, "China's Long Game in Techno-Nationalism," *First Monday,* no. 23 (May 7, 2018), http://firstmonday.org/ojs/index.php/fm/article/view/8085/7209. The law, like other Chinese techno-nationalist initiatives in digital over the last twenty years, has many vague provisions open to interpretation, which in the past have largely been used to restrict foreign companies and support domestic competitors.

28. In practice, Apple has stored most Chinese customer iCloud data in China for several years; the change here reflects the new government requirement that domestic companies own the infrastructure on which the data is stored. Apple says that it will retain encryption keys, but it is unclear precisely who will have access to the data under what conditions. It is also notable that this GCBD deal represents the first time Apple has co-branded its iCloud product.

29. See https://www.apple.com/legal/internet-services/icloud/cn_si/gcbd-terms.html. See also Alyssa Abkowitz and Eva Dou, "Apple to Build China Data Center to Meet New Cybersecurity Law," *Wall Street Journal,* July 12, 2017.

30. See https://www.amazonaws.cn/en/about-aws/china/. AWS's arrangements are with two Chinese firms, NWCD and Sinnet. AWS describes it this way: "AWS China (Beijing) Region operated by Sinnet and AWS China (Ningxia) Region operated by NWCD offer a technology service platform that is similar to other AWS Regions around the world. Developers can easily and efficiently deploy cloud-based applications inside of China with the same APIs, protocols, and de-facto operating standards used by AWS customers around the world."

31. Thanks to Alan Cohn for suggesting this elegant analogy.

32. Nils Gilman and Steven Weber, "Back in the USSR: Is the European Union Heading for a Soviet-Style Collapse?," *American Interest* 12, no. 3 (2016).

33. Alexander Gerschenkron, *Economic Backwardness in Historical Perspective* (Cambridge, MA: Belknap Press of Harvard University Press, 1962).

34. Barma, Ratner, and Weber, "World without the West," 5.

35. Imanol Arrieta Ibarra et al., "Should We Treat Data as Labor? Moving beyond Free," *Papers and Proceedings of the American Economic Association* 1 (2018): 1–5.

36. Steven Weber and Eamonn Kelly, "A Co-Creation Discipline," unpublished manuscript from Monitor Group, 2014, available from the author.

37. Norman Angell, *The Great Illusion: A Study of the Relation of Military Power to National Advantage* (New York: G. P. Putnam's Sons, 1913). The book was actually first published in the United Kingdom in 1909 under a different name, but it achieved public prominence in 2013.

38. Kenneth N. Waltz, *Theory of International Politics* (New York: McGraw-Hill, 1979); Steven Weber, "Cooperation and Interdependence," *Daedalus* 120 (1991): 183–201.

39. Ibarra et al., "Should We Treat Data as Labor?"

40. Nils Gilman, Jesse Goldhammer, and Steven Weber, eds., *Deviant Globalization: Black Market Economy in the 21st Century* (New York: Continuum Press, 2011).

41. That may not be true in the medium and longer term. Deviant entrepreneurs understand perfectly well (like licit entrepreneurs) that violence is largely a deadweight loss for most of their businesses. And so they will likely be in the forefront as well of using technology to find ways to manage contracts (for example, blockchain applications). Gilman, Goldhammer, and Weber, *Deviant Globalization,* chapter 1.

42. It is worth pointing out here that Standard & Poor's downgraded US sovereign debt for the first time in 2011, five years before Donald Trump won the presidential election.

43. Peter B. Evans, "In Search of the 21st Century Developmental State," Center for Global Political Economy at the University of Sussex, Working Paper No. 4, December 2008, https://www.scribd.com/document/172429664/Evans-2008-In-Search-of-the-21st-Century-Developmental-State-1. His argument is actually about intellectual property and the trust of people who create and control it, at least in a primitive sense; but it can readily be extended from IP to data, where the same logic ought to apply.

44. Mimi Ito credits this term to her colleague Juliet Schor; their notion of "nonmarket work" is discussed in Mizuko Ito et al., *Hanging Out, Messing Around, and Geeking Out* (Cambridge, MA: MIT Press, 2010), chapter 7.

INDEX

Barma, Naazneen, 80–82, 201
Benefits, accelerating, 60
Berkeley Roundtable on the
International Economy, 41
Berners-Lee, Tim, 43, 44
Bin, Eric, 44
Biotechnology, 124
Bipolarity, 45. *See also* Cold War
Bitcoin, 15
Blockchain, 15
Borderless-world narrative, 54
Boundaries: physical, 5; politically
determined, 5; production
networks and, 190–192; in
regionalism, 149, 178, 185,
191
Brand, Stewart, 8
Branding, 196
Brexit, 13, 144
British East India Company, 26,
30–34, 143, 178. *See also* Firms,
multinational
Buildings, 8
Bureaucracies, 144
Bureaucratic accelerating data
growth regimes (BADGRS), 184,
202
Bureaucratic authoritarian industri-
alizing regimes (BAIRS), 75, 184
Bush, George W., 59, 106
Businesses, new, 93, 94, 95
Business-government alignment,
201–205. *See also* Government
Business operations: in GIE
arguments, 64–66; of modern
multinational, 38; policies / rules
and, 118, 147; standardized, 118,
146
Business-to-business (B2B) web,
62–63

Capital, invested, 93
Capture, 188
Car ownership, 134–135
CEMEX, 72
CERN, 43
Change, 3–4
Chicago, 16
China, 89; acceptable speech limits
in, 183–184; AI Development Plan,
152; data localization in, 195;
economic reform program in, 61;
IDT firms in, 201–202; IP and, 96,
103–107; markets in, 42; ML in,
150–153; platform firms in,
165–166; as power center in
regionalism, 199; regulatory
environment in, 151; rule sets in,
152
Christensen, Clayton, 130–131, 135
Cipla, 99
Cisco, 12
Civil society, developmental state
and, 74
Clash of civilizations, 55
Climate change, 208
Clinton, Hillary, 13. *See also*
Election (US presidential, 2016)
Closeness, 188–189
Cloud services model, 133
Cluster model, 68
Coase, Ronald, 12
Coase theorem, 12, 44, 46, 47, 52
Code, 97. *See also* Intellectual
property (IP); Open-source
software
Cold War, 27, 207; distribution
of power and, 45 (*see also*
Bipolarity; Sole superpower
thinking; Unipolarity); end of,
42–43, 121 (*see also* Emerging